ROUTLEDGE LIBR

WOMEN'S F

THE MAGD╌╌╌NES

THE MAGDALENES

Prostitution in the nineteenth century

LINDA MAHOOD

Volume 25

Routledge
Taylor & Francis Group

LONDON AND NEW YORK

First published in 1990

This edition first published in 2013
by Routledge
2 Park Square, Milton Park, Abingdon, Oxfordshire OX14 4RN

Simultaneously published in the USA and Canada
by Routledge
711 Third Avenue, New York, NY 10017

First issued in paperback 2014

Routledge is an imprint of the Taylor and Francis Group, an informa company

British Library Cataloguing in Publication Data
A catalogue record for this book is available from the British Library

ISBN: 978-0-415- 62353-7 (Volume 25)
ISBN: 978-0-415-75257-2 (pbk)

Publisher's Note
The publisher has gone to great lengths to ensure the quality of this reprint but
points out that some imperfections in the original copies may be apparent.

Disclaimer
The publisher has made every effort to trace copyright holders and would
welcome correspondence from those they have been unable to trace.

The Magdalenes

Prostitution in the nineteenth century

Linda Mahood

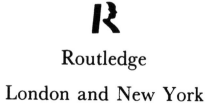

Routledge

London and New York

First published 1990
by Routledge
11 New Fetter Lane, London EC4P 4EE

Simultaneously published in the USA and Canada
by Routledge
a division of Routledge, Chapman and Hall, Inc.
29 West 35th Street, New York, NY 10001

Phototypeset by Input Typesetting Ltd, London
Printed in Great Britain by
T. J. Press Ltd, Padstow, Cornwall

British Library Cataloguing in Publication Data
Mahood, Linda
The magdalenes : prostitution in the nineteenth
century.
1. Great Britain. Women. Prostitution. History
I. Title
306.7'42'0941

ISBN 0–415–00166–8

Library of Congress Cataloging in Publication Data
Mahood, Linda
The Magdalenes: prostitution in the nineteenth century / Linda Mahood.
p. cm.
Bibliography: p.
Includes index.
ISBN 0–415–00166–8
1. Prostitution—Scotland—History—19th century. 2. Sexually
transmitted diseases—Law and legislation—Scotland—History—19th century. 3. Prostitutes—Rehabilitation—Scotland—History—19th
century. 4. Working class women—Scotland—Sexual behavior—
History—19th
century. 5. Law enforcement—Scotland—History—19th
century. I. Title.
HQ187.A5M34 1989
306.74'2'0941109034—dc20   89–6323

For my Grandparents
Bill and Verna Hoy

Contents

Acknowledgements

The contributions of many people have made it a pleasure to work on this project. I would like to thank Mary Murray for first suggesting it to me and Eleanor Gordon for providing me with criticism, advice, and an ear for my ideas, Barbara Littlewood, J.H. Treble and Dave Frisby for supporting it as a dissertation, the members of the Glasgow University Research Unit on Migration and Racism, the West of Scotland Women's Research Group, and the contributors to the Scottish Women's Bibliography for their friendship, moral support, and interest in my work throughout my stay in Glasgow. Anne Dunlop and Joanne Trantor have read and commented on parts one and two of the manuscript. For assistance of a different kind, I wish to acknowledge the 'emergency' financial aid that I have received from the University of Glasgow Sociology Department and the British Sociological Association's 'Hardship' fund: without it this project would certainly have suffered.

The labour of librarians and archivists throughout Scotland and England has contributed to this research. I wish to express my thanks to the librarians at the Universities of Aberdeen, Edinburgh, Glasgow, and St Andrews. The archivists at the Mitchell Library, the Strathclyde Regional Archives, the Edinburgh Public Library, the Scottish National Archives, Mr Pierce at the Royal Faculty of Procurators Library, and, finally, the staff at the British Museum and Fawcett Library for their interest in my progress. The material in chapters four and five appears in an abridged form in David McCrone, Stephen Kendrick, and Patricia Straw (eds) (1989) *The Making of Scotland: Nation, Culture and Social Change*, Edinburgh University Press; E. Breitenbach and E. Gordon (eds), *The World is Ill Divided: Women and Work in Scotland, 1830–1940* volume 1, Edinburgh University Press (forthcoming, 1990); and Women's Studies International Forum, *Special Issue: British Feminist Histories* (forthcoming, 1990). I thank the publishers for permission to re-use the material.

Finally, I am grateful to B. Singh Bolaria, Professor and Head of the Department of Sociology at the University of Saskatchewan, Canada, for his valuable assistance. To Vic Satzewich, who has read and discussed the entire manuscript with me, I would like to say thank you for making it so easy for me to do my research and, among other things, for Lucy. Above all, I would like to thank Barbara Littlewood, who has contributed greatly to the writing of this book and gone beyond a supervisor's 'call of duty' so many times.

Linda Mahood

1988

Introduction

The deployment of 'dangerous' female sexualities

In 1986 an eminent Scottish historian wrote: 'The history of the family, and of child upbringing and the place of women within and without the home, is so neglected in Scotland as to verge on becoming a historiographic disgrace.'[1] At first glance a book which aspires to address this silence by focusing on prostitution must appear curious, to say the least. Today prostitution conjures up images of family breakdown, pornography, drugs, and most recently AIDS. But the relationship between prostitution and the social class and female gender roles which emerged within the mid-nineteenth-century social structure provides a particularly good opportunity to study some aspects of the experience of women in male-dominated society. This book examines four empirical and theoretical issues concerning prostitution in Scotland in the nineteenth century.

Beginning with the Scottish perspective and experience, this research arose initially out of an interest in the Contagious Diseases (C.D.) Acts which were enforced in parts of England and Ireland between 1864 and 1884. In her study of the impact of the Acts on Plymouth and Southampton, Judith Walkowitz argues that these 'technologies of power'[2] transformed the structure of prostitution in regulated towns. Her hypothesis raises interesting questions concerning prostitution in port and garrison towns and large industrial cities, such as those in Scotland, where the Acts were not enforced. Frances Finnegan's study of 'prostitutes' in York, during roughly the same period, for example, implies that the lives of York's 'prostitutes' were largely unaffected by the Acts; other evidence suggests that attacks on prostitution by moral reformers, evangelical philanthropists, and rescue workers before and after the introduction of the Acts was not without impact. Moral reformers[3] claimed success in suppressing street soliciting and brothels throughout Britain in areas where the Acts were not enforced. The question arises, then, what happened in Scotland? Did the women labelled as 'prostitutes' remain relatively unharassed and unstigmatized? In pursuit of answers to these questions, it became clear that technologies of power, technologies not unlike the C.D. Acts themselves, were already in place in Scotland. Some, like the lock hospitals and magdalene asylums, existed long before the C.D. Acts were passed. Others, like the system of police repression which I call the 'Glasgow system', were developed as a reaction to the Acts. The historical interest of the Glasgow system is that it was not confined to Scotland, but was adopted as a model for similar systems of police repression in English cities, most notably in Manchester and Leeds as well as in Edinburgh and other Scottish towns.

As this research progressed, it became clear that the Glasgow system could not be studied as an isolated historical entity, and this brings us to the second issue examined in this book. The public discourse on prostitution in Scotland did not commence with the implementation of the C.D. Acts in England. Tracts and essays on the state of Scottish morals had been published with increasing regularity throughout the century. Similarly, Scottish lock wards and magdalene asylums, which were among the first in the United Kingdom, began to open around the turn of the century. A great deal of discursive terrain had been covered by the time the Glasgow system was developed in the 1870s. This book, therefore, traces the public discourse on prostitution as it emerged throughout the century.

The third issue is the technologies of power themselves. In this case these are apparatuses and institutions for the regulation, surveillance, and control of female sexuality. In particular, special emphasis is placed on magdalene homes in Glasgow and Edinburgh and a case study of the operation of the Glasgow system, which was composed of the Lock Hospital, Magdalene Institution and the Police Act (1866). As Jessica Evans points out, in most cases more is known about the clients, patients, and inmates of institutions than the interested institutions and discourses that are authorized to categorize them.[4]

In the nineteenth century interest groups in industrial cities throughout the United Kingdom were increasingly dissatisfied with the role of the police, prisons, and poorhouses in controlling young female misdemeanants, paupers, and orphans. Moral reformers were critical of the state institutions and the penal system for the part they played in 'hardening' young female offenders, particularly those charged with sexual misconduct. They argued that the traditional practice of bringing women charged with sexual offences before the court and subjecting them to prison sentences aided their corruption. Reformers did not object, however, to detaining 'fallen' women provided that they were not incarcerated with 'criminals'. Their solution was to establish non-statutory female penitentiaries, to entice these women into direct care early in their careers and to personally supervise their moral reformation. This involved persuading a woman to commit herself to long periods of voluntary incarceration in a magdalene home, where she would be subjected to moral education and industrial training, and expected to conform to middle-class standards of femininity. The moral reform activities in Scotland in the nineteenth century provide a unique opportunity to examine the process whereby local state representatives and philanthropists working on behalf of the state established, or gained control of, existing apparatuses designed for the social control and moral reform of women who defied middle-class standards of sexual and vocational propriety.

The final issue examined is the social construction of one 'dangerous' female sexuality. This is not an empirical study of 'prostitutes' and prostitution *per se*, but raises the more general question of the moral regulation of working-class female sexuality. In relation to class, it is argued that working-class women were overwhelmingly the targets of legislation designed to clean up street disorders, which the bourgeoisie perceived as plaguing their cities' streets. Following recent contributions to the literature on the history of sexuality, it is suggested that working-class sexuality was increasingly the object of middle-class scrutiny and attempts at colonization.[5] The contemporary discourses and apparatuses did not address the working class directly, however, but appeared to divide the population up on other grounds, by singling out specific objectionable sexual characters and certain behaviours. What are apparently non-class-based characters emerge. However, on closer examination we find that these characters were mobilized in class- and gender-specific ways. It is significant that it was, by and large, working-class women whose behaviours were scrutinized and stigmatized. For a brief period efforts were made in Glasgow to reach a 'better' class of girl, who the directors of the Magdalene Institution believed existed to cater to upper-class men. After a notable lack of success this was abandoned and the institution concluded that no such women existed in the city. Furthermore, there was no suggestion that 'prostitutes' might ever be male. Discussions of the sexual behaviour of male clients remained marginal to the public discourse. Basically then, public attention and initiative was overwhelmingly directed at one section of the urban population: specifically, working-class women.

Studies of the sexual behaviour of the Victorians have become considerably more sophisticated since the 1970s.[6] It has been accepted that contemporary sexual practices fell short of the ideal moral code to which the Scottish establishment paid lip-service.[7] Recent studies of pornography, illegitimacy, drunkenness, incest, homosexuality, lesbianism, and prostitution have successfully challenged the assumption of a unitary Victorian culture and a single repressive standard of sexual behaviour.[8] Of these, studies which address the question of prostitution directly can be loosely divided into three paradigms: the double standard model, the oppression model, and the problematization model.

Beginning with the double standard model; the belief that unchastity – in the form of premarital or extramarital sex – is pardonable for a man, but a matter of grave importance for a woman, is generally known as the double standard. At its most basic, the ideology of the double standard suggests that the high standard of premarital chastity placed on middle-class couples in the nineteenth century meant that men were forced to resort to 'prostitutes' in order to preserve the virtue of women of their own class. After marriage, 'model' wives were expected to turn a blind eye to their husband's extramarital liaisons. This is an essentialist view of human sexuality, which argues that while sexual desire was virtually absent in middle-class women, it was rampant in men. 'Respectable' women were instructed to regard the act of procreation as a necessary, shameful, and repulsive duty; men, on the other hand, were encouraged to regard sex as the part of marriage which existed entirely for their pleasure.[9] The central problem for Victorian males was how to combine sexual freedom for men with chastity for their women. The solution lay in prostitution, where working-class girls and non-virtuous or 'fallen' women were sacrificed so that the wives and daughters of the upper classes could remain chaste and pure-minded.[10]

In an attempt to establish a causal relationship between the double standard and prostitution, historians who use this model provide it with a plausible biological and psychological basis by using Freud's dissociation theory. Freud argued that the universal characteristic of 'civilized' men was their inability to feel love and sensuality for the same person; in this case, married men were incapable of obtaining sexual satisfaction from their wives, for whom they felt only tenderness, affection, and esteem. Sexual satisfaction could only be experienced with women of a 'lower social order'. In contrast, the sexual elements of affection and sensuality were aroused simultaneously in 'healthy' women. In cases where dissociation did occur, it was usually expressed in the form of frigidity or occasionally produced 'Lady-Chatterley-like' situations. It follows then that a woman's infidelity would be considered far more serious than a man's. The chief problem with this approach lies in its explanation of the origin of the double standard as being rooted in biology or psychology. The concept of the double standard itself can be useful and its existence cannot be denied, but it must be seen as an historical and social construct.[11]

Finnegan's study of prostitution in York typifies the oppression model. She argues that studies of prostitution frequently concentrate on the institutional aspects of Victorian prostitution rather than on the 'prostitutes' themselves and the biting poverty which drove them to prostitution. She demonstrates that prostitution did not fit the double standard model of middle-class demand and working-class supply. Her empirical data indicate that 73 per cent of the men reported as associating with 'prostitutes' belonged to the working class.[12] Her analysis of court and poor-law records, local newspapers, and hospital and penitentiary reports suggests that the main characteristic of prostitution was not simply the exploitation of one class by another, but the sexual exploitation of indigent women by all classes of men. She concludes that 'prostitutes' were generally working-class women who were forced into prostitution by destitution, poor wages, and lack of employment opportunities; conditions which were the consequences of exploitative class relations.

The pitfall of the oppression model involves the question of agency. By defining women as passive victims of male oppression, Finnegan fails to recognize women as full historical agents capable of making their own history. This is most evident when compared to Walkowitz's study of prostitution in Plymouth and Southampton, which has taken up similar sources yet reached significantly different conclusions. Walkowitz opposes the portrayal of 'prostitutes' as silent victims of social injustice and male oppression.[13] Instead, she portrays them as important historical actors, as women trying to survive in towns that offered them only poor wages and unsteady employment. Their move into prostitution was neither pathological nor deviant but a rational choice given their limited opportunities.[14]

In contrast to the double standard model, which focuses on the relationship between male sexuality and the demand for 'prostitutes', and the oppression model, which emphasizes the sexual exploitation of working-class women, the problematization model[15] locates prostitution within the larger social, economic, and institutional structures of the nineteenth century. By conceptualizing prostitution at this level it is possible to perceive contradictions which shaped the market economy of prostitution (poor wages, unemployment, and class prejudices), while at the same time to examine how changing cultural processes, like the double standard, influenced the problematization of prostitution in the nineteenth century.

Unlike the first two models, problematization theorists do not regard labels such as 'prostitution' or 'prostitute' as valid observational categories. They argue that prostitution, like other forms of sexual behaviour, acquired a new meaning in the nineteenth century. Foucault, for example, argues that sexuality is an historical construct. He claims that the nineteenth century was characterized by the 'deployment of sexualities': the attempt to identify and classify diverse forms of human sexuality,[16] notably the 'hysterical' woman, the masturbating child, the Malthusian couple, and the homosexual. His argument can be applied to the 'prostitute', which he does not directly examine.

Other theorists working within the problematization paradigm argue that the image of the 'prostitute' possessed a wide cultural currency and occupied a symbolic place in the class and gender hierarchy of the nineteenth century. Walkowitz argues that the 'prostitute' was 'simultaneously an object of class guilt as well as fear, a powerful symbol of economic exploitation under industrial capitalism'.[17] Shifting the emphasis, Erna Hellerstein, Leslie Parker, and Karen Offen claim that the symbol of the 'prostitute' was used as a threat to women of all social classes who challenged established gender roles.[18] For Linda Gordon and Ellen Dubois, 'prostitutes' were living symbols of women's economic and sexual vulnerability and prostitution was perceived as the end result of the artificial constraints placed on their social and economic status.[19] Finally, Lynn Nead argues that the Victorians defined 'prostitutes' as victims rather than oppressors in order to disarm them of their power. She interprets the image of the 'prostitute' as a 'wretched outcast' ravaged by feelings of 'remorse and shame' as part of an attempt to deflect the power and threat of working-class women.[20]

This study of the policing and control of 'prostitutes' attempts to build on the problematization model. It deconstructs the category 'prostitute' and examines the discursive field in which it emerged in the nineteenth century. The central objective of the book, then, is an examination of discourses on prostitution and the deployment of social-control apparatuses designed for its surveillance and control. This work is informed by three main bodies of literature. The first is Foucault's contribution to the history of sexuality and the development of discourse theory. The second is the literature on social control and criminology. Finally, the extensive body of feminist historiography is used to supplement and illuminate these sources, which are used critically in so far as, with few exceptions, they fail to recognize that the construction of sexualities and the resulting technologies of power is a gendered process.

Before proceeding, it is appropriate to make a few remarks concerning the relevance of Foucault's work in this study of prostitution. To write about the histories of punishment and social control and, I would add, sexuality without acknowledging Foucault's contribution is, as one sociologist recently pointed out, like studying the unconscious without making reference to Freud.[21] Foucault's work is controversial and it is not my intention to enter into a debate,[22] but simply to state that Foucault's ideas have been invaluable tools for enabling me to make sense of the data available on nineteenth-century prostitution. The problem with using official records such as annual reports, crime statistics, government hearings, as well as private documents, records, and minute books are well known to the social scientist. The methodological drawbacks are resolved, however, when one recognizes that one cannot enter into these records without also entering into the subjective world of the discursant. In this research Foucault is used as a methodological guide and for the questions he raises, and not for an all-encompassing theoretical perspective.

In *The History of Sexuality* Foucault challenges conventional studies of sexuality. He criticizes what he calls their 'repressive hypothesis'. Conventional studies consist of histories which portray sexual behaviour as more and more subject to 'repression' until the enlightenment of our own times. These studies create the impression that Victorians procreated by remote control[23] and that sex was a secretive deed, confined to the marriage bed, and then only for the purposes of procreation. As Jeffery Weeks argues, following Foucault, these studies are misleading because they provide too narrow an interpretation of the family, mystify class differences, and are based on a misinterpretation of power.[24] Foucault argues instead that the nineteenth century was not a period of sexual repression, but a period of 'incitement'. He claims that historians have failed to acknowledge that since the eighteenth century, sexuality has been continually and volubly 'put into discourse'. The last three centuries have witnessed 'a veritable discursive explosion'[25] around the subject of sex. Foucault explains that these discourses arose in all branches of the medical profession, churches, laws, schools, and organized philanthropy, and through them these institutions actually created 'sexualities' for their clientele.

Foucault uses the term 'discourse' to refer to the set of concepts, values, and practices that define, inform, and justify a set of social relations. This 'language', however, is neither descriptive nor objective. As stated above, a discourse creates its object. Through the process of identification and classification each discursive field constructs specific 'sexualities' for its subjects. The concept of a discursive field is used by Foucault as a guide to understanding the relationship between 'language, social institutions, subjectivity and power'.[26] Social institutions and processes such as the law, the family, the church, and the education system are organized through institutions, each of which is located in and structured by a particular discursive field. Discursive fields can be distinguished from each other by their different perceptions of the world and on the basis of their ideas about the way society should be organized. Sexualities, therefore, have no reality outside a particular discourse,[27] and so the history of sexuality is the history of what certain discourses have said about sex.[28]

For Foucault, the study of sexuality is guided by the aim of analysing not an essential sexuality, but what various discourses said about sexuality, why they emerged when they did, and some of the consequences of their pronouncements.[29] In order to make this point clearer, it is necessary to consider the case of the 'homosexual' who, according to Foucault and Weeks, was a creation of the nineteenth century. They argue that the nineteenth century witnessed a new taxonomic and labelling zeal which attempted to classify the characteristics and increasingly the aetiologies of the forms of sexual variety 'scientifically', and in so doing established them as objects of study.[30] For example, Foucault argues that there were no 'homosexuals', in the modern sense, in the eighteenth century. There were simply individuals who committed acts of sodomy. A man convicted of sodomy was simply guilty of a crime. The guilt did not transform him into a particular kind of person, other than a law-breaking one. In the nineteenth century individuals who committed felonies such as sodomy, which were still recognized as crimes, suddenly became 'characters' as well. The 'homosexual' became a 'personage, a past, a case history, and a childhood, in addition to being a type of life'.[31]

The Foucauldian analysis of the process of identification, classification, and subsequent persecution of peripheral sexualities, can also be extended to the female 'prostitute' in the nineteenth century. This is not to suggest that the century marked some sort of break in the historical process. On the contrary, the changing symbolic role of sexuality was a product of long and complex social changes in Scotland. It has been attributed to a backlash against the relative 'moral' laxity of the preceding centuries which clashed with nineteenth-century evangelicalism,[32] as well as the consequence of social changes associated with industrialization.[33] Accompanying the changes were also strong elements of continuity, especially with regard to the influence of Christianity, which had always structured beliefs and formed the basis of custom and law, if not behaviour.[34] Similarly, in Scotland the Kirk Session had always considered prostitution, adultery, and fornication as punishable offences; but their perpetrators were regarded as nothing more than the juridical subject of them. Yet, between the seventeenth and nineteenth centuries, the climate of continuity and change around the subject of sex produced a discursive explosion.[35] 'Rather than massive censorship . . . what was involved was a regulated and polymorphous incitement to discourse'.[36] Everybody was talking about sex.

one had to speak publicly and in a manner that was not determined by the division between licit and illicit . . . one had to
speak of it as of a thing to be not simply condemned or tolerated
but managed, inserted into systems of utility, regulated for the
greater good of all, made to function according to an optimum.
Sex was not something one simply judged; it was a thing one
administered. It was in the nature of a public potential; it called
for management procedures, it had to be taken charge of by
analytical discourse . . . sex became a 'police' matter.[37]

This study suggests that by the mid-nineteenth century the analytic
zeal of the curious public descended upon the sexual and vocational
behaviour of working-class women. Scottish moral reformers were
preoccupied with the question of 'prostitutes'. By 1800 a public
discourse had arisen which escalated throughout the century. With
a view to discovering the 'truth' about the phenomenon moral
reformers actually created the 'prostitute', giving a history to the
individual women. Like the 'homosexual', the classification 'prostitute' was invented by moral reformers who attempted to impose an
alien interpretation on to the normal, or at least non-perverse,
activities of working-class women by labelling them 'prostitutes'.
Moral reformers exhibited a compulsion to 'know' this alien other,
the working-class woman, to define her activities along bourgeois
lines, and to police her. Unlike the 'homosexual', however, the
'prostitute' was both a sexuality and a vocation and has to be
examined on both counts. The thrust of discourses, however, was
not just repression or control but the moral regeneration of working-
class women. Finally, by using the Foucauldian paradigm to decon-
struct the aetiology of the 'prostitute' in the nineteenth century it
is possible to examine the process whereby sexualities have been
defined along class and gender lines.

According to Foucault it is through discourses that power and
knowledge are joined together. The object of analysis at the level
of discourse, therefore, is certain forms of knowledge regarding sex,
not in terms of repression or law, but in terms of 'power'. Foucault's
conceptualization of power is useful for three reasons. First, for
Foucault power is not exercised simply through a general system
of institutions and instruments of state for the subjugation of the
people. It does not reside exclusively in the state, and cannot be
reduced to class relations alone. Power is omnipresent. It is created

from moment to moment in relationships at all social levels. Second, power is not a negative concept and it does not exist only in the form of repression, censorship, or prohibition. On the contrary, 'power produces; it produces reality; it produces domains of objects and ritual truth'.[38] Finally, Foucault is interested in the power-knowledge complex, the way in which power operates through the construction of particular forms of knowledge. It is through discourses that power-knowledge is realized.

There are two problems with Foucault's theory of power that should be identified. First, as others have pointed out, his conceptualization of power is largely one-directional. And second, it underemphasizes the conflict between discourses. To address this, theorists like Christine Weedon and Diane MacDonell have incorporated Marxist theory which emphasizes that not all discourses carry equal weight or power: some are conservative and justify the status quo, while others are radical and challenge existing institutional practices. Discourses which challenge the status quo will either be marginalized by existing practices, dismissed, or lead to social change.[39] John Smail also addresses this problem by using Antonio Gramsci's notion of 'cultural hegemony'. Gramsci argues that the dominant social group not only controls the means of production but also the social, political, and ideological apparatuses that legitimate their control over the means of production. Ruling, then, is not simple oppression, but a process in which the discourse that defines the relations of domination plays an important role in the distribution of ideas, norms, and values. Often in the engineering of consent, a single discourse holds sway, but at other times this hegemony can be successfully challenged by a subordinate group with ideas of its own.[40] Put simply, discourses are historically and socially constructed. They are not neutral, but highly political, because the group with the power controls the dissemination of knowledge and therefore the discourse. No discourse exists by itself; each takes shape in relation to another, antagonistically, through the struggles which traverse various institutions and various apparatuses of the state. As such, there is a great deal of competition between discourses as each tries to establish dominance. The first step in any investigation of a discourse, therefore, must be to account for the social position of the speaker, the 'institutions prompting people to speak, and the social structures in which knowledge is shaped and produced'.[41] The trail, however, will not lead to the discovery of truth or pure knowledge; rather in the process of demystification one is most likely to find 'falsehoods, or ideology designed to conceal the truth'.[42] In sum, by modifying Foucault, recent contributions to discourse theory have created a theoretical framework that not only places discourse and power in relation to economic practices, but also directs attention to the relationship between the discourses and the potential for social change.

In the instance of prostitution, the struggle between discourses is most evident in the divergent discursive fields over its causes and control. As will be seen, it was the group that controlled the technologies of power that in the end controlled the discourse. Attempts to define the 'prostitute' were not just technical, but deeply political. In the context of this study it is necessary to emphasize that if the discourses on the prostitution 'problem' in Scotland in the nineteenth century are to be conceptualized as the engineering of bourgeois hegemony in the area of sexuality, this has to be treated as a process, and one that was resisted, rather than as an automatic consequence of bourgeois economic domination.

This brings us to Foucault's use of the concept of 'resistance', which has proved most fruitful in analysing the prostitution question. Foucault argues that power is produced from moment to moment in social relations at all levels, not because it embraces everything, but because it comes from everywhere. Power, therefore, can come from below. It is by virtue of this that he argues that where there is power there is resistance, or the operation of a 'reverse discourse'.[43] This is when the evaluations implicit in a discourse are reversed, for example in the 1960s slogans 'black is beautiful' or 'glad to be gay'. Foucault suggests that just as there exists a multiplicity of force relations which produce power, there also exists a multiplicity of relations that resist it. Points of resistance are present in every power network. Hence, there is no single locus of 'great refusal',[44] and, likewise, there is no single locus of control. However, this raises questions about the nature of resistance. If power is everywhere it is difficult to understand how it can be resisted. Or, conversely, if power always breeds resistance, why is there such stability in relations of domination? What are the conditions in which resistance occurs, and what form does it take? In this study I examine these questions by exploring forms of resistance and the extent to which the women labelled as 'prostitutes' were affected by the development of policies and institutional practices directed toward controlling their behaviour throughout the nineteenth century. The idea that women are passive objects of social policies is too simplistic; therefore I have emphasized women's capacity for agency (although this is difficult to demonstrate) by focusing on indicators of women's 'choice', whether they accepted the definition of themselves as 'prostitutes' and chose to reform along bourgeois lines, or resisted the bourgeois moral code and its limits on their sexual and vocational behaviour.

It should now be clear that once the sociopolitical and historical construction of the category 'prostitute' is recognized, a naturalistic or empirical study of prostitution and 'prostitutes' is extremely problematic. This study differs from other studies of Victorian prostitution in so far as the 'prostitute' is not treated as a valid observational or subject category with numbers to be counted, characteristics investigated, and history documented, but as an emerging label or censure. It was, however, a frequently contested category, whose boundaries were continually being redefined. For the purposes of this research the term 'prostitute' has been conceptually defined as a censure applied to women whose dress, behaviour, physical appearance, or vocation caused them to be labelled as 'prostitutes' within the framework of the discourse, as defined by middle-class observers. The term 'prostitute' appears in quotation marks throughout the book in formal recognition of the fact that it is a label and not an objective form of human behaviour.

This approach is informed by discourse theory and has, therefore, the advantage that it avoids the dilemma in certain areas of feminist historiography of portraying women either as the agents or victims of their time. As feminist historians have demonstrated, two trends currently exist within the field of women's history. The first is to chart the course of sexual inequality and the oppression of women. The second is to look to the past for evidence of women's power and autonomy rather than subordination. The problem with the first approach involves the question of agency: it fails to recognize women as full participants in the historical process capable of making their own history. The problem with the second approach is that by emphasizing women's culture and power it risks losing sight of the social inequalities which have marked women and which have been the basis of patriarchal and class relations. Second, while emphasis on agency is by far the more useful perspective, it is also the most difficult to demonstrate empirically with the sources available.[45]

This book has been divided into three parts, each of which examines the contributions of three discursive fields: the medical profession, organized philanthropy, and the local state. Part one looks at the relationship between social medicine and the state. Chapter one, which looks at legislation designed to control prostitution and venereal disease between 1497 and 1800, is intended to provide an historical context from which the changing penal reform systems and the ideologies of social medicine can be judged. Chapter two looks at the debate around the establishment of lock hospitals for women with venereal diseases. It is an example of the new technologies of social disciplining that were directed at women. Chapter three points to the existence of a discourse that runs contradictory to that of the reform-minded segments of the bourgeoisie.

Part two looks at the relationship between social medicine, the state and philanthropy as it evolved through the activities of the female penitentiary movement, and the establishment of magdalene homes. Chapter four looks at the internal management of these institutions in Edinburgh and Glasgow between 1797 and 1850. It is suggested that this period is distinguished from other periods in that it is characterized by a 'cult of sentimentality' around the figure of the 'prostitute'. Chapter five examines a shift in the discourse away from perceiving the 'prostitute' as an innocent victim of social injustice towards analysis of the causes of prostitution, which focused on the consequences of women's employment in the 'public sphere. Chapter six looks at the impact of the changing definitions of the causes of prostitution on the institutional practices of magdalene asylums throughout Scotland.

Part three forms the case-study portion of the book by looking at one technology of power in detail. It is argued that the deployment of discourses is, in this case, most significantly embodied in material practices. For example, the establishment and operation of the Glasgow system of police repression represents a moment in which one account of the prostitution problem and one strategy to control and reform the 'prostitute' became dominant. Chapter seven examines the components of the Glasgow system. It is suggested that although these agencies stressed their voluntary efforts, they were much readier to use the instruments of the state to enforce their code than had been true for earlier reform efforts. The final chapter identifies the approaches for policing prostitution used in the nineteenth century. As parts of the United Kingdom adopted the C.D. Acts to contain the spread of venereal disease, which also meant controlling prostitution, Glasgow developed a system of police repression which was designed to stamp out prostitution altogether. In the conclusion, it is argued that throughout the nineteenth century working-class women were overwhelmingly the targets of discourses on prostitution; an adequate explanation of this must incorporate a dual focus, on gender as well as class.

Part one

The birth of social medicine and the state

Steps taken towards the control of major epidemic diseases such as syphilis are amongst the earliest Scottish attempts at social medicine.[1] The birth of social medicine was largely the result of developments in the scientific community and the discovery that many diseases were not 'scourges' from God, but curable, or at least controllable. Venereal disease and its link with prostitution is an example of this. The medical interest in prostitution grew out of the public health movement. Though public health is usually associated with contagious diseases and sanitation problems it is also concerned with social issues.[2] The history of the surveillance and control of venereal disease and prostitution in Scotland from the late fifteenth to the early nineteenth century enables us to see how the antecedents of the nineteenth-century discourses on prostitution and their technologies of power were rooted in the theories of social medicine which date back centuries.[3]

From the outset attempts to control the spread of venereal infections were based on a double standard of sexual behaviour: legislation intended to control syphilis amongst the general population was often directed at women only. Examples of this process appear in the Kirk Session and Town Council records between 1497 and 1800. By reviewing this legislation it is possible to illustrate that the shift away from medieval forms of punishment for sexual offences such as fornication, prostitution, and adultery does not indicate a relaxing of the moral code or a move towards permissiveness.[4] Although social medicine rapidly focused its attention on the living arrangements of the urban poor, and this attention appeared to derive its impetus from 'class fear', early medicine had its own internal dynamic and a history which is not immediately reducible to economic and political class relations.[5] It was, however, reducible to patriarchal gender relations, in so far as both the local state and the medical initiatives had a direct moral message for women. Through early theories of disease, germs, and contagion the medical discourse created a new area of professional expertise. Sexual immorality and sexual disease were among the first targets for the new professional physicians, who rapidly developed a medical knowledge, language, theories, and specialist hospitals, such as lock hospitals, for the control and regulation of their affected clientele.

The Scottish lock hospitals and female penitentiaries that were established by 1800 are examples of the new technologies of social disciplining and systems of incarceration which continued to evolve in the nineteenth century. They differed from existing institutions of physical punishment or medical cure because they focused on the surveillance and regulation of the individual's moral character and not just their physical health or behaviour and they were intended exclusively for women. Sexual behaviour did not become more repressed by the nineteenth century, however. Historical evidence taken from contemporary accounts of the size and structure of nineteenth-century prostitution and the brothel systems, plus an analysis of popular literature indicates that the nineteenth century did not usher in an age of sexual repression. On the contrary, by the nineteenth century sexual behaviours which had always been punishable began to be spoken of, regulated, and policed in new ways.

Chapter one

'Harlots, witches and bar-maids'
Prostitution, disease, and the state, 1497–1800

The history of venereal diseases presents a challenging medico-social problem and many questions regarding the genesis of the disease remain unanswered.[1] There are two main schools of thought on the origin of syphilis in Europe: the Unionist and the Columbian. Unionists argue that it was a mutant form of an old disease which suddenly became more virulent as a result of changing social conditions, living habits, or climate. Columbians, on the other hand, claim that syphilis was a new disease brought to Europe by Columbus and his men upon their return from the Americas in 1493. A lesser known school of thought, the astrological school, was founded by Peter Pinctor in 1500. Pinctor demonstrated the precise date and time of the emergence of the disease astrologically, to the satisfaction of himself and other astrological physicians of the day. He proved that the 'new scourge' first appeared with the conjunction of Venus with Jupiter, Mars, and Mercury in October 1493.[2] Whichever school one follows, the deadly effects and the inability to treat the new disease is well documented.

The first appearance of syphilis in Scotland is less controversial. The first recorded cases coincided with the arrival of Perkin Warbeck, masquerading as the Duke of York, the younger of the two princes who was murdered in the Tower of London. Warbeck sought the help of King James IV and through his support he was able to invade England in 1460. His motley band of foreign mercenaries, numbering 1,400, was described as 'thieves, robbers and vagabonds', who desired 'only to live off robbery and raping'.[3] Historians suggest that Warbeck's soldiers, many of whom resided in Aberdeen between 1495 and 1497, brought the first recorded cases of syphilis to Scotland. During this time the first attempts to

control 'glengore' or 'grandgore', common Scottish names for syphilis, were incorporated in two edicts: the Edict of the Town Council
of Aberdeen, dated 21 April 1497, and the Statute of the Privy
Council of Scotland, dated 22 September 1497.[4] These attempts to
control syphilis are among the first experiments in Scottish social
medicine. The legislation, however, took the form of forcible isolation and harsh repression and there is little evidence of any con-
structive attempt to establish causes or cures, or to remove the
conditions responsible for its spread.[5]

Although the connection between syphilis and sexual intercourse
was not made until the next century, early legislation was based on
a double standard which contained a moral bias against women.
The engineers of the Aberdeen Act were quick to accuse 'licht
weman' of spreading the disease, and readily put their opinions into
action.[6] The Act demanded that 'all light [loose] women . . . dicist
from thair vices and syne of venerie' and work for 'thair support
on pain of being branded' or banished from the town.[7] Apart from
its being the earliest political notice of syphilis in Scotland, this
edict is of interest in that before 1500 no medical authority had
ever hinted that it had any connection with the 'syne of venerie'.[8]
This does not necessarily mean that Aberdeen medical men were
more astute, it may just mean that they were eager to blame women
for spreading a disease that was little understood and greatly feared.
What is clear, however, is that the attempt to control the spread of
contagious diseases among the general population by controlling
women's activities was by no means an eighteenth- or nineteenth-
century phenomenon. It is difficult to determine whether authorities
perceived the real problem to be the sexual promiscuity of Scottish
women or fear of syphilis, but it is evident that the link between
women and dangerous diseases was established long before it was
proven that the disease was communicated through sexual intercourse. In fact, until the sixteenth century it was believed that
syphilis spread via contact with clothes, personal possessions, baths,
kissing, and especially breath.[9]

The Statute of the Privy Council issued in Edinburgh was far
more detailed, having been drawn up by King James IV himself,
who took a personal interest in this new disease, partly because he
was a student of the medical arts and a lay-practitioner of leechcraft.
The King ordered the transportation of all infected individuals to
the Island of Ichkeith where they were to be treated.[10] The edict,

known as the Glengore Act, also contained an open invitation to anyone who could cure the disease: interested applicants were to be deported also. The whole operation was to be completed within two days, after which the cheeks of the 'uncured' were branded before they were banished so that they would be easily recognized if they dared to return.[11] This edict reflects the belief that the disease could be communicated by air (miasma) as well as via third parties. Edinburgh authorities were anxious about the health of medical attendants who undertook to cure the infected. In order to make them easily identifiable they decreed that physicians who worked with the disease should be branded with a 'marking irne'.[12] This attitude should explain why little headway was made in finding a cure until well into the nineteenth century. The more respectable members of the medical profession refused to work with venereal patients, so sufferers were left to the 'mercies of barbers, quacks and old women'.[13]

In 1507, two additional edicts were passed in Aberdeen. They, too, demonstrate the fear that the disease was passed by air. The first attempted to quarantine syphilitics by confining them to their homes, and the second banned them from entering the vicinity of butchers, bakers, brewers, and launderies.[14] In 1549, a special meeting of the provincial council of the Scottish clergy was held to inquire into the sexual incontinence of ecclesiastics and an edict was passed by the Edinburgh Synod to protect themselves against syphilis. It exhorted the clergy to keep away from their illegitimate children, prohibited their promotion in the church, and forbade their endowment with dowries or property out of the church's property.[15]

Throughout the remainder of the century efforts to control epidemics of syphilis failed. Public notices of its presence continually appeared at different times in various cities and districts, notably Aberdeen, Edinburgh, Glasgow, Stirling, Linlithgow, and Ayrshire.[16] By 1560, the authorities shifted their attention toward experiments in preventive medicine. In Edinburgh, an Act was passed which gave uninfected 'whoremasters and harlots' two alternatives: either confess their conversion to a new way of life or face penalties, depending on the number of previous arrests, ranging from public rebuke and carting to branding and banishment or torture and death. The segregation of syphilitics was confined to women only, as the Act directed that all 'whores', whether infected or not, were to be banished from the town and suburbs.[17] There was, however, no mention of punishment for the men who frequented these women. In 1561, for example, an order was passed by the Council commanding Lady Jane Stonehouse to remove herself from the 'toune' on account of her indecent behaviour. This order is notable considering the rank of the person against whom it was issued.[18]

Between 1561 and 1566 there were at least seven other similar enactments issued by the magistrates and councils. Queen Mary herself issued an Act 'to punish committers of fornication'. This is not surprising in view of the fact that medical archaeologists maintain that Mary's second husband, Lord Darnley, and probably her third, Bothwell, had syphilis.[19] The Queen also questioned the health of the high church dignitary who was appointed to baptize her son, James. She said that 'she would not have a pokie priest to spet in her child's mouth'.[20]

By 1587, the persecution of women for sexual behaviour intensified. In Glasgow female chastity was perceived to be so low that the Kirk Session enacted severe disciplinary measures. Punishments depended on the woman's social rank and the number of past offences. 'Harlots' were to be carted through the town, ducked in the Clyde, and put in the juggs* on a market day. Female servants were either fined £20 for each breach of chastity or sentenced to eight days in prison, where they were fed on bread and water, after which they were put in the juggs for a day. 'Honest men's daughters' were also included, but their fines depended on the discretion of the Kirk.[21]

In 1591, a year of escalated persecution of witches, fear of venereal disease was so intense and the public so wrathful that in cases where witchcraft and syphilis were linked, condemned women were not strangled before burning as usual, but were burned alive. One case in which the 'disease' is alluded to is the trial of a lady of wealth and station, Euphame Macalzane. The daughter of Lord Clifton, she was taken to Castel-Hill in Edinburgh and burned at the stake.[22]

By the sixteenth century magistrates appear to have made a connection between the evils of sex, women, and alcohol. In 1580 'A Most Strict Proclamation' was issued against female servants in

---

*The juggs (jougs) were an instrument of punishment similar to the pillory; the criminal was fastened to the wall or a post by an iron collar around the neck.

taverns, 'because of fornication and filthiness that is committed by them, as the occasion of intissing youth.'

> ... in past times the iniquity of women taverners in this burgh [Edinburgh] has been a great occasion of whoredom, insomuch that there appears to be a brothel in every tavern; therefore all vintners of wine may engage women taverners before the next Martinmas hereafter were to be certified, that if their women committed any immoral fault they should have to pay £40, except if they deliver the offender into the hands of the bailie, to be banished, according to the law, as soon as the offence comes to their knowledge.[23]

The fine remained at £40 until 1699, when it was raised to £100 scots. and the Town Council urged churchmen to police their respective parishes regularly so that they might discover 'guilty' female servants and punish them accordingly.[24]

Only two additional Acts relating to prostitution were passed between the seventeenth and eighteenth centuries in Scotland. The first, in 1650, prohibited brothel-keeping and ordered the guilty to be 'carted and scourged for their vileness, and banished ... under pain of shame [and] disgrace'. In the second, an army officer was dismissed for keeping a 'whore'.[25]

There is every reason to believe that the brutal sentences contained in the various Acts were carried out, though, fortunately for the 'guilty', historians claim that they often fell into disuse shortly after their enactment. Judging from the severity of the sentences it is clear that sexual offences were considered to be of sufficient importance and magnitude to merit serious attention and interference.[26] If these punishments appear exceedingly savage or harsh, it should be emphasized that at the time they were actually regarded as mild sentences. Mild punishments generally ranged from branding, mutilation, and banishment (often preceded by public whipping), to penance in the Kirk, being chained in iron rings, or wearing a helmet with a spike jabbed into the mouth to prevent speech. The pillory or stocks and banishment, usually by excommunication to the next parish, were also used. For more serious crimes such as murder, death penalties were carried out by beheading, hanging, drowning, or burning. Preliminary tortures included wrenching of the head with cords, tearing off the nails with pincers, scourging with branding, cutting out the tongue, or cutting off the ears and hands.[27] Drowning was the commonest method of executing women, being considered more respectful than hanging. In 1530, for example, Katherine Heriot, accused of theft and bringing a 'contagious sickness' from Leith, was drowned in Quarry Holes at the Greyfriars' Port. In cases of particularly heinous crimes, such as treason and witchcraft, burning at the stake was considered more appropriate.[28]

In medieval Scotland prisons had a custodial rather than a reformatory function. When offenders were imprisoned it was only until the proper sentence was determined. The very idea of imprisonment – feeding and clothing the offender for ten or twenty years – would have appeared absurd to the authorities. Rehabilitation was a luxury and the authorities had neither the time nor the inclination to try to make 'useful members of society' out of offenders.[29] Post-Reformation discipline exercised by the General Assembly and the Kirk Session altered this pattern somewhat. Their definitions of crime widened from violence and offences against property and the state to include crimes against religion and morality. The Kirk was extremely astute in hunting down fornicators, adulterers, blasphemers, sabbath-breakers, and drunkards. They also began to use incarceration in unprecedented ways. After the Proscription of Popery by Parliament in 1560 one of the first acts of legislature was to impose a penalty for the 'filthy vice of fornication'.[30] The powers of the authorities to enact new and harsh legislation was not questioned.[31] Although incarceration was used more it continued to be expensive, and throughout the 1700s prison sentences were often waived or shortened whenever fines could be paid. Similarly, banishment, which was the cheapest and easiest punishment of all, remained popular.

The last significant Act against prostitution passed in Scotland prior to the nineteenth century was issued in 1700. It appears that, by this time, Town Councils were less concerned with the abolition of prostitution than with its recognition and control and the segregation of the women involved from the general population.[32]

> The Bailies reported, notwithstanding the great care and pains taken by them to punish common whores and thieves, and banish them from this city, yet they are still found within this city and suburbs, having no mark or distinction to make them known from other inhabitants; and therefore were of the opinion, that, to

conform to the custom of the other places abroad, these common thieves and whores should be marked upon the nose, by striking out a piece of the left side of the nose with an Iron made for this purpose.[33]

This legislation was considerably more than just an attempt to suppress prostitution. It reveals an acceptance of it as an inevitable aspect of social life. The reference to the 'custom of other places' is significant, as it was around this time that European countries began the policing and medical inspection of 'prostitutes' and brothels. On the other hand, perhaps the Town Councillors were simply afraid to enact further legislation. Probably because they had already found it necessary to inflict punishment on the 'Burgesses for their licentious behaviour', the baillies and members of council themselves would be the next parties to be charged with the crime; and rather than persist in contriving punishments which might soon be inflicted on themselves, they perhaps thought it better to desist from interference. Their efforts, therefore, were redirected towards the suppression of behaviours usually associated with prostitution, such as street disorders, and the apprehension of blasphemers, drunkards, card players, Sabbath-breakers, and other 'lewd persons'. In addition, a by-law was passed in Edinburgh which prohibited 'respectable females from wearing plaids and other parts of dress' that were likely to confuse them with street-walkers.[34]

The shift away from physical torture as punishment for sexual offences does not indicate a relaxing of the moral code or a move towards a permissive society. Foucault argues that if the severity of the codes relating to sexual offences diminished considerably by the nineteenth century, it was because in many areas the law deferred to the expertise of the medical profession.[35] The authorities turned their attention towards isolating problematic populations, in this case women labelled as 'prostitutes', from the respectable members of the community, and to this end the expertise of the medical profession was summoned. In 1592 the Glasgow Kirk Session directed 'that the house beyont the Stable Green Port for women affectit with the Glengore be looked efter'.[36] This was not the first quarantine hospital to be built in Scotland, however, as hospitals for lepers were used in Dundee, Edinburgh, Glasgow, and Haddington.[37] What is significant about the hospitals for venereal patients is that, unlike cases of leprosy and the other epidemics which swept through the country, it was only women who were singled out for hospitalization. In 1600 a special meeting of the Session was announced to examine 'how the infection of glengore within the city may be removed.' All the 'chirurgeons and professors of medicine' were expected to attend.[38] The hospital mentioned above was not built until 1805, but the problem did not disappear, and the medical profession was increasingly looked upon for a solution.

As suggested above, rudimentary efforts at sanitary control were not just limited to the control and surveillance of prostitution and venereal disease. Evidence suggests that other areas of social hygiene were developed by the new medical profession. Attention was focused more and more on the living habits of the working class who were migrating from the countryside to the cities by the thousands. Medical attention focused on the problem of destitution as a chief cause of increasing misery and disease[39] and physicians began to publish advice manuals and public health information. Employers, for example, were advised to strip and examine servants from the Highlands carefully for signs of infection before they were hired. Farmers were advised to supply a separate spoon and fork for every servant, even a casual labourer, or to refuse to engage servants who could not supply their own eating utensils. The one-bed household was discouraged.[40] The family structures of the poor were also attacked. In 1769, William Buchan, an Edinburgh-trained physician and the author of *Domestic Medicine* (subtitled 'or the Family Physician, being an attempt to render the Medical Arts more generally useful, by showing people what is in their own power both with respect to Prevention and Cure of Diseases'), argued that the primary cause of infant mortality was parental neglect. He suggested that the proper management of children should be made the principle part of female education.

> It is their province [the mother], not only to form the body, but also to give the mind its most early bias. They have it very much in their power to make men healthy or valetudinary, useful in life or pests to society.[41]

Upper-class women were warned against allowing strangers to kiss their children and not to suckle any infant whose health was uncertain. The background of wet-nurses was to be carefully investigated.

Buchan indicated that it was not just women who should be concerned with the health of children. The father had an equal

interest in his children's welfare and ought to assist in the improvement of their minds and bodies. He also had a word for the physician: he stressed that child management should cease to be the
sole province of old women. He encouraged the profession to take
up studies in childhood illness and to raise midwifery from an old
wives' pastime to a science practised by medical men.[42]

By the eighteenth century the spread of epidemics was attributed
almost totally to the customs of the poor. This argument was used
to explain why epidemics were most frequent in the autumn when
the countryside was overrun by migrating agricultural gangs, a class
notorious for promiscuous eating, drinking, sleeping, and smoking.
These were the avenues along which diseases such as syphilis were
believed to pass, and avenues from which the upper classes could
not escape. An unclean glass in a wayside tavern might be the
vehicle through which the disease was inadvertently transmitted
between classes, and the custom of employing wet-nurses for their
children was a continual menace. 'The possibility of contagion
through sexual connection was often overlooked, sometimes
asserted, sometimes denied'.[43] It is important to note, however, that
strict controls adopted by the bourgeoisie by the nineteenth century
were not immediately or directly imposed on the working class; on
the contrary, 'the most rigorous techniques were formed and, more
particularly, first applied, with the greatest intensity, in the econ-
omically privileged and politically dominant classes'.[44] It was the
sexuality of bourgeois children that was first problematized and
bourgeois women were the first females to be medicalized.

> The bourgeoisie began by considering that its own sex was some-
> thing important, a fragile treasure, a secret that had to be disco-
> vered at all costs . . . [T]he first figure to be investigated by the
> deployment of sexuality, one of the first to be 'sexualized', was
> the 'idle' woman. She inhabited the outer edge of the 'world', in
> which she always had to appear as a value, and of the family,
> where she was assigned a new destiny charged with conjugal and
> parental obligations. Thus there emerged the 'nervous' woman,
> the woman afflicted with 'vapors'; in this figure the hysterization
> of women found its anchorage point.[45]

For the most part, at this stage, the working class escaped the
deployment of 'sexuality', while the bourgeoisie policed themselves.
But evidence of an increasing effort to control the sexual behaviour

of the working class can be seen throughout the nineteenth century. The escalation of the effects of urbanization, in the form of overcrowding, epidemics, prostitution, and venereal diseases which threatened the safety of the bourgeoisie, was necessary before the working class was recognized as possessing a 'sexuality' that could be effectively colonized. Successful colonization required a whole technology of control apparatuses to make it possible to keep them under surveillance.[46]

> Schooling, the politics of housing, public hygiene, institutions of relief and insurance, the general medicalization of the population. In short, an entire administration and technical machinery made it possible to safely import the deployment of sexuality into the exploited classes: the latter no longer risked playing an assertive class role opposite the bourgeoisie; it would remain the instrument of the bourgeoisie's hegemony.[47]

To summarize, legislation relating to venereal disease in Scotland was based on a double standard of sexual behaviour which contained a moral bias against women. As will be seen in the next section, however, by the nineteenth century special attention was directed at the moral regulation of working-class women. Although by the end of the eighteenth century 'prostitutes' were no longer dragged through the town, dunked in lakes, or whipped and branded, prostitution remained a punishable offence. Punishment was simply administered in new ways. The best example of this process is the lock hospitals and female penitentiaries, which were two of the agencies for control and surveillance of women developed by the beginning of the nineteenth century. In institutions such as these, 'prostitutes' were isolated from respectable community members. Medical cure was combined with long periods of physical and moral discipline, directed toward the punishment of the soul rather than the body, which was clearly more in tune with nineteenth-century evangelicalism.[48]

Chapter two

A medical model of immorality
The Glasgow Lock Hospital

The connection of venereal diseases with leprosy made by the medieval authorities alluded to above, reveals their inability to distinguish between the ulcerous conditions of venereal disease and those of leprosy.[1] The term 'lock', was derived from 'loke', a house for lepers. According to William Acton the origin of the term 'lock' was in the French word 'loques', meaning rags, bandages, and lints. Lock hospitals acquired the name because the first one was located on the site of the medieval leper house in Southwark.[2] Walkowitz suggests that 'prostitutes' became the social lepers of the industrial revolution as syphilis replaced leprosy as the symbol of social contagion and disease.[3]

The founding of lock hospitals reflected three trends within the late eighteenth-century social reform movement. First, the awakening of philanthropic concern for the problems of illegitimacy, prostitution, and moral and physical contagion. Second, the need to provide medical care for patients rejected by other hospitals.[4] And finally, the larger eighteenth-century medical and moral crusade to improve the conditions in prisons, workhouses, and hospitals. Social reformers' concern at the problems of criminality, poverty, and disease was not limited to the exercise of harsh laws; they erected new technologies of power in the form of institutions for disciplining these troublesome populations. The new strategies of incarceration implemented by the social reform movement were simultaneously medical, hygienic, and moral.[5] The new 'structures of confinement' (asylums for the mentally ill, orphanages, female penitentiaries, etc.) embodied the principle of the exclusion of 'social deviants'. They did not stop with physical incarceration: reformers were equally concerned with reforming the moral character of the inmates.[6]

But unlike other forms of 'deviance', the moral regulation of 'sexual deviants' was targeted at women. Similarly, unlike other forms of disease where both sexes were quarantined, with syphilis it was women only who were subjected to segregation from the community in lock hospitals and subsequently in female penitentiaries where they were to be morally reformed.

The medical isolation of 'prostitutes' in lock hospitals is one example of the process of moral regulation. It set up structures for a wide range of related social demarcations. These included dichotomies such as the distinctions between the deserving and undeserving poor made by philanthropists throughout the nineteenth century.[7] Strategies for reforming 'prostitutes' in lock hospitals institutionalized more than just the double standard by only punishing women. It was also a class and gender strategy, which crystallized the distinction between 'pure' and 'impure' women. Lessons in personal hygiene and moral training stressed class differences and a belief that a 'prostitute' could regain her correct place in the female labour force, but this required hard work and religious training.[8]

The question of sexual immorality was at the heart of the early discourses of social medicine. Its goals, however, reached beyond containing epidemics or disease. As historians have indicated, the reformers established an extensive network of social policing with a view towards the colonization of urban working-class culture in the first stages of industrial capitalism.[9] The medical profession became an influential pressure group in campaigns for moral reform and provided the intellectual and scientific rationale for state intervention in working-class culture. The process is illustrated most effectively in Buchan's *Domestic Medicine*, introduced in the previous chapter, which was aimed at the educated laity, local gentry and their wives, the clergy, professionals, and others who would spread enlightened ideas regarding preventative medicine. The book contained sections on the treatment of common diseases (fevers, ague, pneumonia, whooping-cough, measles), a section on industrial diseases, and a section on infant and child care. Buchan believed strongly in the potential of the social hygiene movement, but without the support of a proper medical police funded by local government he feared that nothing could be accomplished.[10]

Physicians also had a personal stake in the public-health movement. Frank Mort suggests that the period witnessed the beginning of a distinctive professionalization of medicine. Previously, the social status of the local doctor lay between the trade origins of the barber-surgeons and the superior rank of the legal profession.[11] Buchan blamed the medical profession for the aura of superstition and quackery which surrounded it. In order to establish scientific credibility he exhorted physicians to abandon their pose of mystery.

> The affection of mystery may, for a while, draw the admiration of the multitude, but will never secure the esteem of men of sense . . . Every attempt therefore to monopolize or conceal any thing related to the preservation of health or cure of disease must not only be injurious to the interests of society, but likewise detrimental to the medical art. If medicine be a rational science, and founded in nature, it will never lose its reputation by being exposed to public view.[12]

Social medicine enabled professionals to carve out a distinctive sphere of expert knowledge within the emergent culture of the bourgeoisie. Physicians secured their ascendency through institutional politicking and by claiming an intellectual monopoly over key explanations of human affairs and social progress, notably the rapid cultural transformations taking place in urban society. As a result, medical research rubbed shoulders with moral philosophy and political economy.[13] This process is clear in the debates over the causes of prostitution and the institutions best designed for its surveillance and control. It is evidenced in the debate surrounding the establishment of the Glasgow Lock Hospital in 1805, which can be followed in a series of letters to the editor of the *Glasgow Courier* which appeared regularly from January to August 1805.

Before examining this debate it is necessary to state that since the Reformation there had been little institutional hospital provision, in the modern sense, for the sick in Scotland. Sufferers of diseases of any kind were likely to have been treated as outcasts.[14] The first modern hospital, the Edinburgh Infirmary, which opened in 1729, had accommodation for only six patients. In 1741 a new hospital opened with accommodation for 228. This remarkable increase in provision for the care of the sick was brought about largely through the support of subscriptions by the Town Council and contributions from the Church of Scotland.

Glasgow exhibited the same zeal in its civic leaders. In 1733 a Town's Hospital opened, which was supported by the Town Council, the Merchants House, the Trades House, and the general Kirk Session, which contributed to it in specified proportions. In Aberdeen a similar plan was put into operation and hospital accommodation for eighty patients was available by 1750. Other towns in Scotland followed the lead: Dumfries and Galloway Infirmary (1776), Montrose Royal Infirmary and Dispensary (1782), Dundee Infirmary (1798), Paisley (1805), Greenock (1807), The Northern Infirmary at Inverness (1799), Gray's Hospital at Elgin (1819), and Perth in 1838. Although these hospitals were described as voluntary, it is significant to note that they resembled municipal institutions in their foundation and management. The subscriptions which supported them were akin to voluntary taxes; the same methods were employed at the time to raise money for roads, bridges, and harbours.[15]

Prior to the establishment of lock hospitals at the turn of the century, venereal diseases were either treated in wards of these infirmaries, or in separate buildings on the grounds, or in special wards of workhouses. The patients in lock hospitals were poor working-class women who were presumed to be 'prostitutes'. The medical authorities, who reflected the attitudes and prejudices of the community at large, regarded venereal diseases as vile and loathsome, and were ambivalent about treating these cases. Many general hospitals would not admit female venereal cases without a character reference or other proof of 'respectability'.[16] In lock wards and hospitals in-patient facilities were reserved for women, while working men and sailors were usually treated as out-patients, with the exception of Greenock, where the population of sailors was so great that hospital provision was made in the Infirmary for more serious cases. Finally, wealthy men and women were treated privately in their own homes.[17]

The debate surrounding the consequences of establishing a lock hospital in Glasgow was based on two underlying issues: first, the medical-scientific versus the religious fundamentalist understanding of the meaning of disease; and second, the community's responsibility for the provision of hospitals to cure it. It should be stressed that the hospital was intended to be exclusively for women; at no point in the debate was it ever suggested that men should also be admitted.

The most frequent objection to the lock hospital involved a struggle amongst those who maintained a religious fundamentalist perception of disease as God's punishment of sinners. Fundamentalists maintained that diseases were Acts of God, in the shape of divine retribution against sinful people. In this case it was God's retribution against sexually promiscuous women: a direct 'scourage of the crime, inflicted by the Deity to diminish its frequency'.[18] Fundamentalists objected to both medical intervention and a hospital in which women were cured of syphilis on the grounds that it interfered with the will of God. They argued that the lock hospital would encourage illicit sexual activity and increase the number of 'prostitutes' by breaking down 'the barriers between virtue and vice'.

Supporters of the lock hospital rejected the fundamentalists' claim that hospitals which treated 'vicious diseases' would increase the amount of prostitution by diminishing 'women's horror' of it. They regarded themselves as progressive thinkers and, like Buchan, they had abandoned the retribution theory for a more scientific understanding of the causes of disease. They did not abandon the language of the Old Testament or the Christian world view, but rather combined them with three modern perspectives: environmentalism, hereditarianism, and evangelicalism.[19] The result was a pre-Darwinist understanding of the nature of human progress, which juxtaposed representations of the primitive and ancient world with the problems of contemporary society.[20] They argued that Biblical doctrine and ancient history proved that the notion of 'disease as punishment for sin' was irrational and unscientific. For example, fear of disease could not logically be used to prevent or punish sin.

> The progress of vicious habit among individuals in an advanced state of society, is neither to be checked nor regulated by fear, and least of all by the fear of a contingency . . . We are not now to be governed as children or savages, solely by the dread of the lash. The Spartan youth were educated through fear, and discovery and punishment were but incentives to fresh acts of cautious depredation.[21]

They indicated that it was just this sort of thinking that pulled civilizations backwards. It was only through a rational investigation of knowledge that Christian truths would be revealed and humanity ascend to new heights.[22] Only through education, for example, was it possible to influence the mind and thereby change the animalistic behaviour that led to sexual promiscuity and disease. First, however, it was necessary to cure the body.

As environmentalists, they combined their commitment to education and scientific investigation with attention to the brutal effects of the rapid industrialization of the cotton industry, which brought great affluence to the middle class. They feared that this newly acquired affluence would reduce men to their most brutish and animalistic level, which would inevitably lead to the decline of civilization if the morality of the masses was not kept in check. They pointed to the fall of the Roman Empire as an example of what lay ahead. They identified the problem as industrialization, which, 'engrafted in poverty and filth, was the chief cause of vice, wretchedness and disease'.[23] It was for these reasons that the new medical profession turned their attention to the living habits of migrating men and women, whom they regarded as sources of infection, licentiousness, and disease.[24]

As hereditarianists they were also concerned with the question of 'biological responsibility' with regard to the species. They recognized the debilitating effect of congenital syphilis and argued that if 'allowed its scope in the present generation, however viciously acquired, [it] poisons in a future one'. They argued that society had a moral obligation to cure syphilis, not so much for their own sakes as for the sake of future generations.[25]

Hospital supporters believed that the 'vice of prostitution' could be diminished, but before that could be accomplished it was imperative that the community accept the responsibility for curing the victims. One writer argued that the cure was the responsibility of the benevolent, the moralist, and above all the politician, who must be interested because the 'primary supports of every state are the health and strength and activity of its citizens'.[26] The early nineteenth-century tendency to equate nationalism with the citizen's sexual behaviour, identified by Foucault,[27] is evident in the demand for a lock hospital. It was seen not simply as a moral or a medical issue. Rather, it reflected a deep concern for the political might of the nation. Supporters argued that the security of the country did not depend as much on its financial resources, as on 'the virtue, the vigour and the activity of its citizens, which render the state invulnerable'.[28]

Finally, in addition to a fear of genetic deterioration, there was an evangelical emphasis on moral regeneration. The nineteenth-century Christian physician had a moral obligation to relieve human suffering. Unlike fundamentalists, who argued that suffering was a suitable penalty for sexual transgression, evangelicals were concerned with the state of the victim's soul. Rather than allowing them to suffer unattended, one advocate argued that the ideal time to attempt the moral reform of 'unhappy females' was while they were suffering from the 'fatal effects of dissipation'.

> In such a situation, oppressed with disease, uncertain of life, and looking forward with a tremendous anxiety to another world, she listens to exhortation, and is alive in every hope. Then is the time to remove the load that oppresses her heart and disturbs her peace ... He beseeches her to reform, and turn to the paths of virtue. She is convinced; she is changed; and becomes, in place of a burden, a comfort to society.[29]

Fundamentalists did not believe that a lock hospital alone could accomplish moral regeneration. They accused supporters of calculating to 'lessen the pains of wickedness'[30] by producing clean 'prostitutes' who would return to the streets 'unimproved and unreformed, prepared to run a new course of debauchery'.[31] The fundamentalists argued that the 'radical defect' of the plan was its single-minded concern for the cure of the body. It stopped at the very point it should 'proceed with redoubled vigour'. They asked the hospital supporters: 'Is that all? After having cured the body, is there no provision to be made for the mind? After having relieved the miserable wretch from the tortures of disease, is she again to be left to herself?'[32]

In the end it was concluded that the lock hospital should not be constructed without some provision being made for a female penitentiary or magdalene home. Representatives of both sides of the debate agreed that there was a civic responsibility to make some provision among the charities for a home for repenting 'prostitutes', where 'serious penitence should be cherished and confirmed'.[33] The possibility of a magdalene asylum made the idea of a lock hospital more palatable to its opponents. It was also seen as a necessity by hospital supporters, who, incidentally, were not all in agreement as to whether the lock hospital and the magdalene asylum should be established together or as separate institutions. Nor was there any agreement as to which institution was the more urgently needed or the more effective. In terms of sheer numbers one writer argued that a lock hospital was more urgently needed because of the overall ineffectiveness of female refuges. He argued that in the last seven or eight years the magdalene asylums in Edinburgh and London only claimed to have reformed ninety-eight 'prostitutes' between them, whereas the London lock hospital near Hyde Park 'cured' 300 women annually. He concluded that in the present state of society, where vice could never be totally suppressed, it was preferable to control disease in lock hospitals in order to ensure that new victims of 'debauchery and artifice' were not required to replace the sick and diseased.[34] The bottom line, however, was that there should be no cure without reformation of the patient's moral character.

In 1805 the hospital supporters were victorious and the Glasgow Lock Hospital opened on August 7th. It was the third to be opened in Britain. The first two were in London (1746) and Westmoreland (1792), followed by Newcastle (1813), Manchester (1819), Liverpool (1834), Leeds (1842), Bristol (1870), and Birmingham (1881).[35] Glasgow's Lock Hospital was first located in a house in Rottenrow, which had been purchased and converted into a hospital. Initially it had eleven beds, but by 1810 the number was increased to twenty. In 1846 a new site in Rottenrow was acquired. The new hospital had seven wards with forty-five beds, extendable to eighty beds should they be required.[36] Although the hospital had no legal power to detain patients against their will, in its management practice and style it resembled a reformatory or prison.[37] In the first fifteen months, fifty-four patients were admitted, forty-two were dismissed as cured, and three patients were dismissed as 'irregular'.[38] The latter category meant that they either demanded their release before the doctors considered them to be cured or were forced out owing to their own misconduct. Applicants were admitted without charge unless they were of the 'superior class' who could afford to pay a guinea. In 1870 thirty women paid; in 1881 only eight could afford to do so.[39] Similarly, individuals who applied for admission more than twice were expected to pay a guinea on their third admission. Many who could not afford to pay went to the lock ward in the Edinburgh Infirmary where no such regulation was enforced.[40]

For over 400 years mercury was the principal treatment for syphilis and gonorrhoea, which were regarded as the same disease until 1793. In fact, it had been 'proven' by John Hunter, a renowned Scottish surgeon. Hunter believed that the symptoms, either urethral discharge or genital ulcers, depended on the site of the infection. To prove his hypothesis he inoculated himself from a patient who had both syphilis and gonorrhoea. His syphilis, although nobly acquired, caused his death in 1793. The same year in Edinburgh, Benjamin Bell succeeded in separating the two conditions. Wiser than Hunter, instead of inoculating himself, he inoculated his students. But it was not until 1879 that the bacteria could be isolated in a laboratory and the diagnosis of gonorrhoea was placed on a 'scientific' basis.[41]

As stated, treatment for venereal diseases was generally mercury in ointment or tablet form. It was most effective against syphilis, but care had to be taken as to over-use. Between 1806 and 1868, a number of syphilitic patients were re-admitted to the Greenock Infirmary with mercury poisoning,[42] which often caused the loss of teeth, destruction of the nasal cavity, blindness, and kidney complications.[43] Although these health risks were recognized mercury continued to be used throughout the nineteenth century.[44]

Unlike Glasgow, which supported a separate lock hospital until the Second World War, the main provision for venereal patients in Edinburgh was the Royal Infirmary. Even this minimal provision was eliminated for a brief period between 1835 and 1847, when a fever epidemic put such pressure on the hospital that venereal patients were forced out to make room for fever patients.[45] Female venereal patients were excluded from the Infirmary from the time it opened until 1750 when a ward containing twelve beds was put aside.[46] Although a separate lock hospital was not established until 1837, there were many citizens who argued that a properly managed lock hospital would be the best possible preparation for the Edinburgh Magdalene Asylum, which had been open since 1797. Andrew Duncan, Professor of Medicine at the University of Edinburgh, for one, had been campaigning for a separate lock hospital since 1825. Although his reputation was indisputable, his motives are questionable and they reveal the logic behind the operation of the double standard of sexual behaviour. He argued that in order to 'afford protection to impudent youth' it was important to get infected 'prostitutes' off the streets as 'speedily as possible'. He obviously believed that a young man should be able to sow his wild oats unencumbered by fears of disease. Further, he explained that a lock hospital would make it possible to separate the newly fallen victims of 'artful seduction . . . from the most abandoned of their [female] species'. He claimed that

> by appropriating a Hospital to this disease alone, where each female might, during the whole progress of her cure, be kept in solitary confinement, such a Lock Hospital would be a house of reformation'.[47]

It was not until 1835 that a suitable location for the Edinburgh Lock Hospital was acquired, through philanthropic initiative, in Surgeons' Square. When the fever hit Edinburgh in 1837 the hospital received the boost it needed to start admitting patients. Although supported by a prestigious list of subscribers, the hospital remained small; at its busiest it only accepted forty patients a year. After only twelve years it was closed and provision was made again at the Royal Infirmary for sixteen patients, who were given the most inferior accommodation.[48] In 1881 Francis Cadell, lecturer on syphilology at the Edinburgh School of Medicine, complained that merging the lock patients with others in the Infirmary led to a deterioration in the care of venereal patients.[49] In 1885, twenty additional beds were made available for female patients. Two rooms were prepared in the basements of the central medical pavilions, access to them being obtained from the wards immediately above by a spiral staircase. The rooms were to be used as sleeping quarters only and patients continued to attend clinics and eat their meals in the old ward. These basement rooms became known as the 'Duck Pond', because in order to reach their sleeping quarters each evening the women were paraded along the corridors. The nurses found the nightly procession of women 'waddling through the ward in single file . . . loosely clad, their feet shod with heelless slippers' so amusing that they were nicknamed 'ducks' and the lock ward became known as the 'Duck Pond'.[50] Although many patients would have found this treatment humiliating, this sort of stigmatization was not uncommon. In cities without lock hospitals, where venereal diseases were treated in the workhouse, 'disorderly and profligate women' were made to wear yellow dresses. Thus the female wards of workhouses were often called the 'canary wards'.[51]

To summarize, it is important to re-emphasize that the control of venereal diseases was based on a double standard where women were singled out for surveillance and control. Unlike cases of leprosy and other diseases, where both sexes were quarantined, with very few exceptions in cases of syphilis it was women alone who were segregated from the community. The isolation of indigent women in lock hospitals (wealthy women were treated privately in their own homes) reflects more than just the double standard whereby women are punished for behaviour engaged in by both sexes. It established institutional structures which distinguished between 'pure' and virtuous women and those who were dangerous and 'impure'. Finally, the lock hospital debate demonstrates that lock hospitals were only regarded as the first step in moral reform. The board of directors at the hospital argued that many of these women had 'some principles' remaining and with the proper training in a magdalene asylum 'might be rendered virtuous'.[52] Before examining the institutional practices of Scottish magdalene homes it is necessary to point to the presence of another discourse on prostitution, which differed radically from that promoted by evangelical physicians, philanthropists, and the local state.

Chapter three

Familiarity with the illicit

Two types of interpretation are offered in histories of human sexuality. The first suggests that in each period a culture of puritanism, discipline, and prudery is followed by one of permissiveness and sexual liberation. The alternative to this view is typified by surveys conducted by Alfred Kinsey, who claims to have demonstrated the opposite. Kinsey argues that there is little difference in the sexual behaviour between one generation and the next.[1] Similarly, recent studies in social history provide little evidence to sustain the claim that sexuality became more repressed by the nineteenth century. Moving outside models of repression and liberation, however, is Foucault's account. According to Foucault, by the nineteenth century sexual behaviours, such as fornication, adultery, and prostitution, which had always been punishable, began to be spoken of, regulated, and policed in new ways. For Foucault, the nineteenth century is characterized by the emergence of a multiplicity of discourses produced by a whole series of mechanisms operating in different institutions.[2]

Although a rational fear of contagious diseases like syphilis, which were barely understood and generally incurable, led to brutal punishments and repressive legislation, especially in venereal cases, sexual activity itself was not repressed. Throughout the centuries fear of contamination coincided with a somewhat light-hearted and jovial attitude toward sex and infection, as well as a casual acceptance of extramarital sex, prostitution, and the local brothel. Historical evidence from Scotland and other parts of the United Kingdom suggests that in the early nineteenth century certain sectors of the community displayed 'tolerant familiarity with the illicit'.[3]

A satirical view of syphilis and sexual promiscuity is not confined to the late eighteenth and early nineteenth centuries. Various sarcastic allusions to syphilis and the moral laxity of the court, clergy, and commoner can be found in the work of fifteenth- and sixteenth-century poets William Dunbar and David Lindsay, and historian Hector Boece's *History of Scotland*.[4] These illustrations suggest that contemporaries perceived the morals of the community to be lax, but it also raises the question of how closely personal behaviour is reflected in the literature and writing of the period. By the late eighteenth century epidemics of syphilis are well documented and commentators suggest that the number of brothels in some Scottish cities was rapidly increasing. The author of *Reminiscences of Auld Ayr* boasted that there were only two known brothels in Ayr at the beginning of the nineteenth century and no street soliciting.[5] In Edinburgh, however, where syphilis was euphemistically referred to as a 'pair of Canongait breeches',[6] the number of brothels had increased from five or six in 1763 to over twenty times that number by the end of the century. An inhabitant of Edinburgh claimed that he could no longer walk between Castle Street and Holyrood Street without being accosted as 'every quarter of the city was infested with multitudes of streetwalkers'.[7]

Historically, British prostitution was always less institutionalized than it was on the continent, where the system of regulation fostered police corruption, women's dependence on pimps, and organized brothels.[8] Walkowitz identifies three distinguishing features of British prostitution in the nineteenth century. First, most 'prostitutes' worked independently of pimps and third parties who had a vested interest in keeping them on the streets. Scottish evidence supports this, as contemporary observers recorded very few pimps among Scottish 'prostitutes'.[9] The second distinguishing feature of nineteenth-century prostitution is the presence of a strong female subculture, as evidenced by the fact that the majority of brothel- and lodging-house-keepers were women. Although not all of these women were 'professionals' or ran full-service brothels, it was in their interest that their female lodgers sought out male clients, thus enabling them to charge more rent. Besides lodging single women, formal and informal brothels were also operated as family businesses by women who needed to support their dependents. Rather than being hardened professionals, the majority of these women, who would have been classified by the authorities as brothel-keepers, were poor working-class women who, like the 'prostitutes', were trying to earn a living.[10] Finally, Walkowitz argues that nineteenth-century prostitution can be distinguished from later periods because brothels were informally tolerated by the poor working-class community.

Most studies of prostitution describe the 'prostitute' as a silent victim of social injustice.[11] Walkowitz, however, argues that not all 'prostitutes' conformed to this stereotype. These women were not 'dehumanized or defenseless vagabonds', but poor working women trying to survive in towns that offered only low wages, unstable employment, and hostility to independent young women. She argues that 'prostitutes' were an integrated part of the working-class community, and their general economic and social profile differed little from that of the rest of the community. Their choice of prostitution was in many ways a rational choice given the set of unpleasant alternatives open to them.[12]

The term 'brothel' commonly referred to a place where more than one 'prostitute' resided.[13] One observer divided Glasgow's brothels into three classes, based on the social status of the men who frequented them. He stated that by 1843 there were 450 brothels in total. Sixty were first-class brothels, supported by wealthy merchants, military officers, and 'gentlemen who moved in the higher circles of society'.[14] These brothels were certainly not found in the poorer districts of Glasgow, but in the more respectable parts of the city. There were 180 second-class brothels, frequented by businessmen, clerks, and shopmen, and were the busiest when university term was in session and large numbers of the students were in the city.[15] In second-class brothels the women were highly visible and identifiable by the flamboyant bonnets they wore. They generally walked the streets in an effort to entice men back to their houses. There were 210 third-class brothels, frequented by farmers, mechanics, apprentices, soldiers, and sailors. In third-class brothels women could expect to earn one shilling per customer, of which the mistress claimed half; the women therefore depended on what they stole for their survival. Theft was not allowed in first- and second-class houses unless the visitor was a 'passing stranger' or intoxicated, and in such cases they were only allowed to pilfer part of the contents of his purse, in addition to their 'present', as the wages were called. In better brothels this ranged from five shillings to five pounds.[16]

In contrast, an observer from Edinburgh arranged the classes of 'prostitutes' from that city on the basis of their living arrangements alone. Those with the highest social status had houses of their own, followed by those who lived in rooms of their own, or in private lodgings. Next came those who were lodgers in public brothels or lodging-houses, and finally there were those of no fixed address. He calculated that there were about 200 brothels in Edinburgh by 1840. This number included all houses where 'improper' conduct between the sexes was tolerated by managers of the establishments, such as taverns, ginger-beer shops, eating-houses, lodging-houses, and public brothels where larger numbers of women were boarded and lodged.[17] As will be seen in part two, the broad definition of a brothel corresponds with the broad definition of 'prostitute'.

The manner in which brothel-keepers made their money is of interest. The girls who earned the money entered these houses on the condition that they pay a grossly excessive sum for their board and lodgings, in addition to half of their 'presents'.[18] Board ranged from ten shillings to £1 per week depending on the respectability of the house and the rank of individuals who frequented it. The wages in the most respectable houses ranged from £5 to £35 per week. Unfortunately this did not mean that the girls and the mistresses both became rich. In most cases crafty mistresses managed to cheat the girls out of most of their share. In order to keep up the respectability of the house all girls had to be gaily attired; and it was the prerogative of the mistress to suggest and furnish them with these articles of dress. The clothing was rented by the girls at the most exorbitant rate. From the time the girls entered the house until they left it their clothes were provided in this way. It was by this dress system that they were always kept in debt to their mistress. Other methods adopted by mistresses to squeeze money out of the girls, while at the same time trying to attract visitors to their houses, were the practices of taking an 'airing in a coach', or attending public promenades and entertainments, bathing quarters in summer, and the races. The expenses of these displays were not defrayed by the house, but charged against the girls' earnings.[19]

In lower-class brothels, the dress required was plainer and mistresses did not furnish them in the same manner. The house had an extensive wardrobe, from which girls rented the items they required for the evening. The sum charged for the loan depended on the traditions of the house and the quality of the article. For example, the loan of a 'blouse for one night, 6d.; for an umbrella, 6d.; for a bonnet, 4d.; a petticoat, 4d.; a shawl, according to the value'; and so on with the other articles.[20] In addition to the sum paid for clothes, they also paid the mistress from twelve to fifteen shillings for their board per week, plus half of the wages and half of what they stole from clients. Because 'prostitutes' were in debt to the mistress, they were prevented from moving on when they chose to leave. If a girl demanded her release or decamped in the night then she was inevitably forced to leave without her possessions, which were either kept by way of compensation for the debt by her mistress or locked up, and therefore inaccessible. It is not improbable that the habit which brothel-keepers had of keeping the clothes was their only insurance of keeping these lodgers.[21] Most women worked independently, however, and either resorted to full-time prostitution when unemployed or as part-time or 'clandestine prostitutes' to supplement their low wages. These reports, however, paint the blackest picture of nineteenth-century prostitution and probably only describe the most cunning and craftiest 'professional' brothel-keepers, who controlled only a small percentage of the trade. Brothel-keepers and 'prostitutes' alike were generally poor working-class women whose activities represented survival strategies in times of economic hardship.

The male associates of brothel-keepers were known as 'spoony men' or 'fancy men'. A spoony man was an individual who provided the financial backing or granted financial assistance when required. In contrast, a fancy man was either partially or wholly supported by a brothel-keeper or 'prostitute'. The latter was most often a husband or lover, whereas the former was only a business partner. Lower-class brothels seldom had spoony men but almost all had fancy men, who generally served as 'bullies' to the establishment. The office of 'bully' was to settle by physical force disputes which arose between the girls and their clients. Bullies were more common in cities like London and Paris than in Edinburgh and Glasgow. London bullies were described as the 'most desperate characters', who 'spend the day in the public houses, and the night in brothels, in which they assist in robbing and often murdering their victims'. Where the brothel was a family business, men and children either lived in the house or in a separate dwelling. In some instances neither the husband nor the children were permitted to visit the brothel.[22]

This was also the age when a visiting gentleman could purchase a copy of *Ranger's Impartial List of the Ladies of Pleasure in Edinburgh*[23] for one shilling. This little journal contained an annotated list of the names, addresses, and ages of fifty 'ladies of pleasure'. Miss Inglis, for example, resided at Miss Walker's in back of Bess Wynd. She was described as 24 years old with short black hair and bad teeth.

> She is foolishly good-natured, and many a one takes the advantage of her upon that account. Notwithstanding, she is no novice at the game of love, for she is remarkably fond of performing on the silent flute, and can manage the stops extraordinary well. She twists round you like an eel, and would not loose a drop of the precious juice of nature, not for a kingdom.

Peggy Alexander, at Monteith's Close, was described as a

> smart genteel lass, about 20 years of age, dark hair, good teeth, fine skin, and extremely good-natured. It is something very odd, that this Lady, although admired by most of the male sex, is universally hated by the sisterhood. She has got a very agreeable squint, which sets her off to great advantage. And when she's in action, she heaves her little Cupid's kettle-drums with great agility, and her languishing eyes speak very forcibly the language of love. She can accommodate any gentleman in a genteel manner at her own house.

The editor of *Ranger's List* revealed that prostitution flourished in the courts, the senates, in the halls of justice, the churches, the navy, and the army. He regarded it as harmless as long as a gentleman was cautious and selected a woman who had been careful to avoid 'the contaminated embrace'.

In Glasgow around 1820 a complete list of the names, addresses, prices, and descriptions of the 'sporting ladies' who would be in the city during the Glasgow Fair was printed on a broadsheet.[24] Broadsheets were a form of cheaply printed popular literature and were very much a part of the street culture of Scottish towns.[25] This list was basically the working class's equivalent of *Ranger's List*, catering to the tastes and pocket-books of working men of all ranks. For the skilled tradesman there was Miss McNab from Edinburgh, 'who charges high, but she is willing, before she wants – to take a shilling'. Next came Meg from Aberdeen. 'Her price is only half-a-crown, and when she is paid she quick lies down'. Also, 'Bet, Jean, Kate and Polly' who ne'er thought shame to blaw the coal, for to increase the lewd desire of men, and then their buttocks fire. Their price is low, if that's your mind, they swear they're not a jot behind, The rest; although their price is scant, they'll take a gill before they want.

Finally, there were the 'sporting drest' ladies from Greenock, 'a large assortment of the best, And if the hire you cannot pay, they'll trust you to another day'. A similar list of 'bonny ladies' by the same author could also be purchased in Edinburgh during the week of the Musselburgh races. The author identified the addresses of the main brothels as: Canongate and Blackfriar's Wynd, Shakespeare's Square, James Square, South Bridge Street, and the High Street.[26] Other sources report that it was common for annual social events such as these fairs and races to attract large numbers of women from all over Scotland and parts of England and Ireland. William Tait claimed that there was a large migration during the Musselburgh races, but the women did not stay long, as they usually followed the horses on to Ayr.[27]

The subject of venereal disease appears to have found a more sobering outlet in poems and street ballads. A broadsheet dated September 1828, recounts the unfortunate adventure of a 'young inexperienced farmer . . . who fell in with a dandy young lady, that took him to the famed battery, in the Canongate'. It appears that after a night of whisky, dance, and frolic the lad awoke to find that he had not only been robbed:

What if my mammy should ken, that I lay all night wi' a hen, that picked my pockets so complete, my mammy I dare not meet . . .
The doctor says I am not well, with that he gives me a pill [mercury]. It's night and morning for to take, swallow that or your life's at stake . . . It was the first time I was in Edinburgh town, I never thought to meet such a loon. All her promise she was to fulfill, but now I see it was all for my ill. All young men take from me, from lewd women keep yourself free. They are like subtle serpents crawling on the ground, for in their tail a sting is to be found.[28]

Such misfortune was not confined to Edinburgh. A broadsheet

published in Glasgow tells the story of an encounter between two young gentlemen:

> As I was walking down by the Lock Hospital,
> As I was walking one morning of late,
> Who did I spy but my own dear comrade,
> Wrapped up in flannel so hard is his fate.

CHORUS

> Had she but told me when she disordered me,
> Had she but told me of it in time,
> I might have got salts and the pills of white mercury,
> But now I'm cut down in the height of my prime.

> I boldly stepped up to him and kindly ask'd him,
> Why was he wrapped in flannel so white,
> My body is injured and sadly disordered,
> All by a young woman my own heart's delight.[29]

In addition to prostitution and venereal diseases, the subject matter of popular street songs, poetry, and broadsheets included tales of murders, disasters, suicides, crimes, sentences, and executions.[30] One example is the account of the trial and sentencing of that 'wicked and cruel woman Mary McKinnon, who kept an infamous house on the South Bridge of Edinburgh for the horrid and barbarous murder of William Howat by stabbing him with a large carving knife'.[31] Other popular themes included tales of seduction, adultery, abortion, and infanticide; those with 'fallen' women themes were especially appealing. For example, there was the sad tale of Ann Smith, who was executed for the 'cruel and inhuman' murder of her sweetheart, John Williams, who refused to marry her after she was with child by him.[32] And the story of the Grassmarket servant girl who 'hung herself with a napkin' in Edinburgh on 29 October 1823, for the sake of the china salesman from England who deceived her.[33] Finally, there was an interesting account of a virgin who gave birth to a baby boy on her wedding night. After carefully reviewing her case a group of 'learned physicians' concluded that 'a woman might have a child without the concurrence of a man; which notion was firmly supported by a great many women'.[34]

To summarize, it should be emphasized that the majority of these broadsheets were produced purely for entertainment and sold in the streets. Their content is of interest because they reveal the existence of another discourse on public morality; not one of the new specialisms, but a 'popular' view, which challenges those contemporaries who wanted strict moral reform. Moreover, it demonstrates that a familiarity and openness on the subject of sex was an integral part of both working-class and middle-class culture. Thus an analysis of the discourses on prostitution should consider the point that there is no direct evidence that sexual behaviour became more repressed by the nineteenth century or that the century ushered in an age of sexual repression, but there was a multiplicity of discourses on the subject of sex. By the nineteenth century sexual behaviours which had always been punishable began to be spoken of, regulated, and policed in new ways. If there was ever only one discourse on sex, it had vanished by the nineteenth century with the emergence of a whole series of mechanisms operating in different institutions, 'in an explosion of distinct discursivities which took the form of demography, biology, medicine, psychiatry, psychology, ethics, pedagogy and political criticism'.[35]

It should now be clear that legislation relating to venereal disease and prostitution in Scotland was, from the outset, accompanied by a moral bias against women. For a man venereal disease was, at the least, a nuisance, at the most, a sign of depravity. For a woman it was a crime, which explains why legislation directed at controlling the spread of the disease was largely directed at women. Although by the end of the eighteenth century 'prostitutes' were no longer dragged through the town, dunked in lakes or whipped and branded, prostitution remained a punishable offence. Punishment was simply administered in new ways. By the nineteenth century traditional techniques shifted from emphasis on punishing the body toward punishing the mind.[36] The new object was not to 'punish less, but to punish better, to punish more deeply into the social body'.[37] Efforts to enforce disciplinary measures against 'harlots', 'witches', servants, and bar-maids, as well as titled women and 'honest men's daughters', indicate that legislation was initially directed at women of all social ranks. By the nineteenth century, however, special attention was paid to the moral regulation of working-class women. The best examples of this process are the lock hospitals and female penitentiaries that began opening by the end of the eighteenth century. The isolation of indigent women in lock hospitals marks the introduction of an identifiable class component in the debate on moral regulation with its emphasis on working-class women as 'polluters'. Similarly, it established institutional structures which distinguished between 'pure' and virtuous women and those who were dangerous and 'impure'.

As stated, the founders of the lock hospital intended it to have a broader scope than just the treatment of venereal diseases, which was only the first step in moral rehabilitation. The reformers agreed that there should be no provision for curing the body without also making some provision for reforming the mind. To accomplish this, social medicine found its chief ally in the philanthropic activities of the prison reform movement, which was responsible for setting up the first magdalene homes in Scotland. Like early social medicine, the clergy, middle-class women, businessmen, and local state representatives who made up the ranks of the philanthropic movement were deeply influenced by environmentalism, hereditarianism, and evangelicalism. This is seen most clearly in the origin and development of the female penitentiary movement in Scotland from the late eighteenth to the late nineteenth century. It is to the activities of the philanthropic movement that we shall now turn.

Part two

Philanthropy, piety, and the state

Throughout the nineteenth century British journals and the popular press were marked by a proliferation of debates about the social problems of the growing cities. Indeed, a concern had developed on the part of segments of the bourgeoisie to tackle or at least contain the problems, either through legislation or voluntary initiative and philanthropy. The massive urban growth of the first decades of the century made already existing social problems appear more prominent than ever before. By the 1840s Glasgow was by far the largest city in Scotland and the second largest in the United Kingdom. At 275,000 in 1841, the population of Glasgow was twelve times larger than it had been in 1775, and between 1831 and 1841 it grew by more than one third. Edinburgh, at 138,000, was only half Glasgow's size, and Aberdeen, Dundee, and Paisley were each only half the size of Edinburgh.[1] Historian C. A. Oakley claims that life in general changed more in these years than in any other decade in Scottish history.[2]

Scottish industrial cities had their fine, airy, and healthy quarters that compared favourably with any in England. In contrast with middle-class neighbourhoods, however, the poor in Scotland, particularly in Edinburgh and Glasgow, were described as 'more wretched than the poor in any other district in the United Kingdom'.[3] In Edinburgh the contrast between the 'brilliant aristocratic quarter in the New Town' and the 'foul wretchedness of the poor in the Old Town' was 'striking'.[4] Similarly, in the heart of Glasgow, south of the Trongate and west of Saltmarket, as well as in Calton and off the High Street, there were endless labyrinths of narrow lanes into which debouch courts were formed by decaying, ill-ventilated, unsanitary, and overcrowded houses.[5] In 1839, J. C. Symons, an assistant commissioner on the official inquiry into the conditions of the handloom weavers, wrote of Glasgow:

> I have seen human degradation in some of its worst phases, both in England and abroad, but I can advisedly say that I did not believe until I visited the wynds of Glasgow, that so large an amount of filth, crime, misery, and disease existed in one spot in any civilized country.... In some of these lodging rooms we found a whole lair of human beings littered along the floor, sometimes 15 and 20 in number, some clothed and some naked men, women and children all huddled promiscuously together. Their bed consisted of musty straw, intermixed with ambiguous rags, of which it was difficult to discover any other feature than their intense dirtiness.... Thieving, and prostitution constitute the main sources of the revenue of this population.[6]

These districts, which sheltered Scotland's 'residuum', the pauper class, did not escape the notice of the social reformers and philanthropists, who in their writings defined the problem in terms of the conditions of 'pauperism' – the condition of individuals – rather than poverty, a condition of capitalism inflicted on exploited workers.[7] By implication, then, pauperism was seen as a consequence of an individual's chosen lifestyle: idleness, drunkenness, irreligion, imprudent marriage, and sexual promiscuity. Philanthropists' writings on poverty, public health, and housing also linked these concerns with prostitution, which was perceived as another consequence of 'sinful' living.

The public discourse on the prostitution problem, composed of a stream of tracts and essays, formed a central part of the debate. Reading this literature one is struck by the authors' disgust at the unseemly behaviour of the urban proletariat. One receives the impression that they were exploring a dark continent peopled by a class who, in their culture and number, were as dangerous as 'foreign savages'. The threat of the urban proletariat was compounded by increased trade union activity and Chartist demonstrations during the 1830s and 1840s, which suggested to the bourgeoisie that 'Armageddon might be just around the next bend'.[8] With the defeat of Chartism in 1848,[9] the dangers which the proletariat represented were no longer overtly threatening to the legitimacy of bourgeois domination, but they continued to represent a threat of a different kind. The fear that the military force of the Empire might be weakened by venereal disease continued to play a part, but this alone cannot explain the extent of the reaction, or the range of emotions which encircled the complex figure of the 'prostitute' who, in an important sense, was only born out of the arguments about her sexual and vocational behaviour. For a number of different social groups, and in different ways, the 'prostitute' signified the underside of both the Christian social order and industrial capitalism, which the bourgeoisie claimed to represent and uphold. Thus, whether the 'prostitute' was seen as victim or polluter, she was a living violation of bourgeois notions of female sexual propriety. This section of the book is devoted to an examination of the role of organized philanthropy in the discourses on the prostitution problem as it unfolded throughout Scotland in the nineteenth century.

Chapter four

An invitation to discourse

The initial connection between philanthropists and 'prostitutes' lay in the former's activities in the prison reform movement. Developments in the penal system throughout the preceding centuries led to an increase in the number of people incarcerated for a wider range of offences, many of whom would have been reprimanded, fined, whipped, or sent back to their masters and not imprisoned earlier in the century.[1] The increase in the prison population led to the problems of overcrowding and an inability to classify prisoners by age and sex or the seriousness of the crime and number of previous offences. From these problems emerged a growing concern about the role of prisons and poorhouses in controlling young female paupers, orphans, and misdemeanants. Authorities claimed that the poorhouse was the worst place for impressionable young girls, whose morals would be corrupted if they were left to associate with older women of 'low character'. They predicted that without their intervention poorhouse girls would grow up to be 'prostitutes' and thieves, or by producing illegitimate children would become chronic burdens on the parish.[2] In addition to being critical of the impact of poorhouses on the moral development of young females, philanthropists were also critical of the penal system for its part in 'hardening' young female offenders, particularly those charged with first offences and sexual misconduct. They argued that bringing young female offenders before the court and subjecting them to prison sentences aided their corruption. This does not mean that reformers were losing faith in the reformative potential of detention; on the contrary, they fully endorsed detaining 'fallen' women, provided that they were not incarcerated with 'criminals'. Their solution was to establish separate and non-statutory institutions called magdalene homes, which would divert young women away from prisons and poorhouses. They adopted what criminologists now call a 'decarceration strategy',[3] to entice women charged with sexual misdemeanours into direct care early in their careers, and personally to supervise their reformation. This involved persuading a woman to commit herself to a long period of 'voluntary' incarceration in a magdalene asylum, where she would undergo a strict regime of moral education and industrial training, and be expected to conform to middle-class standards of femininity.

Through their crusade to prevent young working-class women from being corrupted by bad associates in streets, public houses, prisons, workhouses, and cheap lodging-houses, many moral reformers became familiar with brothel and street life and the plight of the 'fallen' women. In their attempt to establish homes in which these women might be reclaimed and rendered useful members of society, they faced opposition similar to that encountered in the lock hospital debate. To begin with, although female penitentiaries were common throughout Europe[4] – the first opened in Paris in the thirteenth century – they were regarded with hostility and suspicion in Britain. Britons were reluctant to undertake institutional rescue work because of its popular association with Roman Catholicism. The public were suspicious of female penitentiaries because they resembled 'popish convents'.[5] The Scots also shared this suspicion and were hesitant about supporting institutions where internal transactions were concealed.[6] In addition to prejudices against female refuges in particular, reformers were also faced with the challenge of breaking down the public's hostility towards the 'prostitutes' in general. In order to generate funds to build female penitentiaries it was necessary to shift public opinion away from hostility towards sympathy and compassion for 'fallen' women.

This chapter explores the activities, debates, and discourses on prostitution throughout the nineteenth century. The first section examines the first part of the century. It is suggested that in order to cast the 'prostitute' as a suitable object of charity and compassion reformers generated what Edward Bristow calls a 'cult of sentimentality' around the figure of the 'prostitute',[7] whom they featured as a helpless victim of seduction or social injustice, 'more sinned against than sinning'. The second section focuses on the second half of the century. The social groups that were the most influential in the debates are identified as the reformers in the medical profession, philanthropists, and Owenite socialists. In the final section it is suggested that by the middle of the century the image of the 'prostitute' as victim returned to a portrait of her as a threatening social problem. This required a wider analysis of the causes of prostitution which included working-class women's roles in the 'public' sphere. Like pauperism, recruitment to the prostitution trade was analysed in terms of individual character flaws: employment in the 'public' sphere; frequenting working-class entertainment; or greed, vanity, and love of finery. Only a passing acknowledgement was paid to contributing social factors like poverty, unemployment, and a lack of education.

It is difficult to explain exactly why there was a change in attitude by the middle of the century. There is no direct evidence that prostitution was actually changing its character or increasing, or that venereal disease was becoming more widespread. Indeed, it is probably a mistake to look for a 'real' cause, in that sense, because it probably had as much, if not more, to do with changing bourgeois sensibilities – what Beatrice Webb called the 'new consciousness of sin' among men of intellect and property,[8] – than any material change in the sexual behaviour or the health of the nation. Foucault argues that throughout Europe, by the middle of the nineteenth century, sexual matters had become characterized as much more than sporadic activities to be either condemned or tolerated. Sex had become something which needed to be managed and regulated 'for the greater good of all'. It was no longer something which individuals judged from a safe distance: 'it was something to be administered . . . It had to be taken charge of by analytical discourse . . . sex became a "police" matter'.[9]

THE CULT OF SENTIMENTALITY: 'MORE SINNED AGAINST THAN SINNING'

The struggle to cast the 'prostitute' as a worthy object of charity and compassion is most evident in the activities of the directors of the Glasgow Lock Hospital and Stevenson MacGill, Professor of Divinity at Glasgow University and secretary of the Glasgow Society for the Encouragement of Penitence (1801). With the support of Edinburgh's evangelical iron-monger and secretary of the Philanthropic Society, John Campbell, they were among the first to deploy a sentimental portrayal to generate financial support for magdalene homes.[10]

To begin with, the directors of the lock hospital had never regarded hospitalization as anything but the first step in moral reform and they 'regret[ed] the total want of a Magdalene Institute or of some fund to prevent the necessity of females returning to their former immoralities' after leaving the hospital. They admitted that although the patients were 'reduced by their own misconduct to the lowest state of poverty and disease' they were still the proper objects of commiseration and charity. The directors were concerned because most of the women had been abandoned by their families and owing to their previous misbehaviour, found it difficult to find respectable employment. They argued that many of these women had 'some principles' remaining and with proper training in a magdalene asylum, 'might be rendered virtuous'.[11]

MacGill, a pioneer of Scottish prison reform, had strong views on the reformation of juvenile delinquents which prompted his interest in the plight of 'magdalenes' and the necessity of an asylum for their reformation.[12] His work is of particular interest because it reflects the Glasgow Magdalene Asylum's initial attitude toward 'prostitutes'. In his effort to convert a suspicious, if not hostile public, he became a spokesman for these 'unhappy individuals', for whom he believed the public should feel only pity. MacGill did not approach the public with a description of the living habits of the city's 'fallen' women or brothel life, fearing that they would find them so 'loathsome and shocking' that they would be deterred from supporting the asylum.

> I shall not attempt to describe to you the miseries of those who are sunk into the lowest depths of profligacy. They present a picture of human depravity and wretchedness, too deformed, loathsome, and shocking for the public eye; from which retreating, sickened and appalled, your dread and abhorrence might be apt to overcome the workings of compassion.[13]

Instead, he summoned the public to consider what these women 'have been, and what they possibly still may be'. In reference to their personal histories, he implied that many had only recently 'fallen' and were still capable of 'feeling guilt and shame';[14] emotions which others believed vanished with the loss of 'virtue'. MacGill attempted to arouse public sympathy and moral and financial support for a magdalene asylum by portraying 'magdalenes' either as the unfortunate daughters of the 'respectable' working class, who had been forced to leave the 'counsel and protection' of their families by coming to the cities in search of employment, wherein they fell 'into the society of the wicked'; or as innocent servants who had been seduced by the 'devilish machinations of the unprincipled and callous profligate'. In either case, according to MacGill, the final outcome was predictable:

> From one step to another, and by a process easily conceived, they pursue their course of depravity. . . . In drunkenness, debauchery, theft, the riot and noise of shocking passions, and with a rude levity ill concealing the misery of a diseased body and a wretched mind, they spend those days which once were passed in innocent pursuit. . . . Yet though they have fallen, they think of former days, their former prospects, their father's home, and the hopes of their parents.[15]

He reminded the public that a magdalene asylum was the only way forward for females who desired reformation.

> But how shall they return? Is it not the situation of thousands, who wanted only to hear some encouraging voice, to see some ray of hope, to discern some opening pointed out by a friendly hand and to receive some assurance of shelter, some chance, though at a distant period, as a hired servant, of being admitted into their father's house[16]

According to MacGill all a 'fallen' woman really desired was to be reunited with her family or employed as 'a hired servant'. The emphasis on service is significant for many reasons. Domestic servants formed the largest class of self-supporting women, the majority of whom were unmarried and lived in the houses of middle-class families, who feared them as a source of 'contagion and corruption'. Throughout the century the tracts and essays on prostitution were laden with tales of wet-nurses who communicated syphilis to respectable people's children.[17] Reformers had ample opportunity to observe their servants' habits, manners, and morals and regarded themselves as experts on the subject. In many cases, contact with their servants was the only contact they had with working-class women, and through their roles as employers they had considerable power and influence over them.[18] Finally, over the first half of the century the majority of women who applied to magdalene homes were former servants, many of whom claimed to have been seduced. This provided grounds for concern about their behaviour, especially their sexual behaviour. As one reformer, later in the century, wrote:

> Incontinence prevails extensively among the class of domestic servants. . . . Like illegitimacy, or prostitution, statistics prove unequivocably the immorality in that class upon which much of the happiness of the community depends. . . . To the domestic servant all our fingers point. They tell us that our maids fill the country with illegitimate children, and swarm the streets as prostitutes.[19]

Other statistics from magdalene homes indicated that the majority of inmates were sexually active teenagers who were either orphans or from broken homes, a trend which persisted throughout the century. These factors raised disturbing questions about the nature of Scottish 'manhood' and extramarital sex[20] and caused many to comment on 'the unmanliness, the unutterable baseness of some men's pleasures'.[21]

It should be noted that portraying 'prostitutes' as the daughters of 'respectable' working-class families who had been either drugged or duped by artful rakes, or as helpless servants who had been led astray and then abandoned by their lovers had a strategic importance. Defining 'prostitutes' as victims individualized the problem. Lynn Nead argues that defining 'prostitutes' in terms of their own guilt was an effective way of disarming them of their power. The image of the 'prostitute' as a pathetic outcast 'ravaged by feelings of remorse and shame' was an attempt to deflect the power and threat of working-class women.[22] As a fund-raising strategy it appears to have been effective, as magdalene homes opened in Edinburgh in 1797 and in Glasgow in 1815. By the middle of the century, however, seduction was no longer accepted as the primary cause of prostitution. A new generation of moral reformer had emerged with a wider definition of the problem and their attempts to determine the causes of prostitution were not merely descriptive. They believed that establishing the causes was only the first step to amelioration.

MID-CENTURY DISCOURSES: THE MORAL STATE OF
THE NATION

By the middle of the century moral reformers' analyses of the causes of prostitution focused on predicting which vocational or leisure activities and personality traits would lead to a woman's downfall. Although evidence of a public discourse on prostitution existed throughout the century, the discussion intensified in the 1840s around the time the Registrar General began to publish statistical inquiries into the living conditions of Scotland's poor. These studies defined many of the traditional rural and urban working-class living arrangements as 'social problems' and aroused a wave of social consciousness in many who awoke to what they called 'the moral state of the nation'. The Scottish establishment, which had long claimed moral superiority over their neighbours in England and on the continent, were seriously shaken by statistical exposés of illegitimacy and infanticide, prison convictions and intemperance, and above all studies which appeared to reflect badly on the sexual behaviour of women.[23] Of these, prostitution became one of the most popular and studies were frequently replicated. Inspired by Parent-Duchatelet's study of prostitution in Paris (1838), Scottish moral reformers attempted to reconstruct the number and nature of the country's 'prostitutes'.

Between 1840 and 1890 three distinct groups contributed regularly to the public debate on the prostitution problem in Scotland and other parts of Britain. The first two, philanthropic citizens and reformers in the medical profession, were heavily influenced by evangelicalism, which distinguished them from the third, the Owenite socialists, because the former emphasized the necessity for the resocialization of individual women, while the latter stressed the need to reorganize society itself. In Scotland, evangelicals never ceased to be orthodox Calvinists and Presbyterians; they were fervently religious, puritanical, and anxious to see their ideals adopted by society as the accepted norms. Nineteenth-century evangelical reformers first wished to transform individuals, and to help each personally to make his or her own way to the 'throne of Grace', and only secondly did they want to reform society in order to ease the individual's path to salvation.[24] The stance of Scottish philanthropy remained ameliorative and at no time did evangelical reformers challenge the legitimacy of the existing social hierarchy.

Yet this does not mean that there were not reformers who were disturbed by the living conditions and deprivation of the urban poor,[25] but their goals remained the identification of 'dangerous' populations and the salvation of souls.

The philanthropic and medical discourses represent many branches of voluntary initiatives to reform the 'fallen'. The former was elaborated by lay individuals and many Scottish clergy, most notably Ralph Wardlaw, who along with William Tait opened the mid-century campaign against prostitution. In 1840, the same year that Tait published *Magdalenism*, Wardlaw, a respected Congregationalist minister in Glasgow, was petitioned by '38 ministers of the gospel' and '11,000 fellow citizens of all religious persuasions' to give four lectures on female prostitution. These were delivered first in Glasgow before an 'exclusively male audience', including the Lord Provost and Town Council. The lecture series was so popular that it was repeated some weeks later in Edinburgh for the newly formed 'Society for the Protection of Young Females'.[26]

Another prominent Glasgow philanthropist was William Logan, whose work represents the hands-on attempt of a churchman to collect 'moral' statistics. Logan was a city missionary between 1843 and 1870. Since his career began, his crusade to reform 'fallen' women had taken him through the lock wards of hospitals and workhouses and missions in London, Leeds, Rochdale, Manchester, Edinburgh, Dublin, Cork, and Bradford.[27] In Glasgow, Logan became a familiar visitor to first-, second-, and third-rate brothels, the lock hospital, the Female House of Refuge, the Magdalene Asylum and police offices. He noted little difference in the systems of prostitution between cities, with the exception that girls in Glasgow 'were more depraved' and their clients less ashamed of their conduct or afraid of their 'good name'.

> There is one respect particularly in which the harlotry of Glasgow is more debased and unnatural than in any other place of which I have knowledge; but so disgusting, that even amid the plain speaking of this publication it cannot be described. In England, there is at least an understood acknowledgement of the prohibition of nature. In Glasgow there is none. Can the harlots be more debased without their paramours sharing in the deeper debasement?[28]

Another member of this group was R.N. Somerville, who held

midnight meetings in the 1860s in an effort to draw 'prostitutes' out of their haunts and into the sphere of the church. In 1860 Somerville, of Anderston Free Church, broke the ice among his congregation when he announced his 'congregational plan' to aid 'fallen women' by introducing midnight meetings in Glasgow.[29] Midnight meetings were closely associated with other forms of rescue work and were popular throughout the United Kingdom. On the evening of a meeting volunteers from Somerville's church stood on street corners and distributed printed invitations to street-walkers.[30] The invitations promised free refreshments, usually tea, coffee, and cakes. As guests discovered, these were mixed with religious sermons. The purpose was to entice and subsequently reform as many 'prostitutes' as possible.[31] After the meeting and sermon the following proposal was made: 'If any person be willing to forsake her sinful life we shall aid her in every possible way'.[32] The organization promised to provide work and accommodation for women who were ready to begin a 'new life'. A constant welcome was extended at the church and volunteer ladies promised to visit the girls daily and to stand by them in all their needs. Over the first seventeen months, seventy-two girls were taken into the congregation, but only thirty-six displayed any signs of true 'penitence'.[33]

The final member of this group was J.D. Bryce, a merchant, who was on the board of directors of the Glasgow Magdalene Institution, the Female House of Refuge, and Female House of Shelter. Historian Olive Checkland argues that the 'philanthropy of piety' involved more than going out to the community and homes of those in need. There was also a range of challenges which required an alternative strategy which amounted to the provision of a 'substitute for home itself'.[34] The 'institutional approach' was directed at orphans, the physically and mentally disabled, and 'prostitutes'. The establishment of magdalene asylums, female refuges, and penitentiaries for destitute and homeless women and girls was the common response to the prostitution problem, which reflects part of a larger movement to 'colonize' the poor.[35] In these homes a 'problematic' segment of the female working class was isolated from the more respectable community, and 'voluntarily' underwent intensive resocialization, moral education, and industrial training, and was thereby restored to 'respectability'.[36]

The identification of prostitution and venereal disease – the two continued to be linked – as a particularly pressing problem is generally said to be what lay behind the implementation of the C.D. Acts in certain English and Irish ports and garrison towns by 1864. However, it cannot be concluded that there was no similar concern in Scotland, where the Acts were not implemented.[37] Scottish magdalene homes were among the first in Britain and many of the authors of the most influential accounts of the prostitution problem were Scottish. Their writings were not merely descriptive, but designed to awaken authorities and citizens to the dangers of what they had begun to term 'the great social evil'. The contributions of medical 'experts' to the discourse on prostitution represents three streams of thought within the medical profession during the mid-nineteenth century – evangelical, state regulatory, and moralist – though they were by no means agreed on the nature, causes, or remedies for prostitution.

The evangelical approach is typified in William Tait's 1840 survey of prostitution in Edinburgh, which is one of the earliest attempts to analyse and expose the problem, and which historian Helen Ware claims is by far 'the best description of early Victorian prostitution and the social and economic conditions in which it flourished'.[38] His position as the house surgeon of the Edinburgh Lock Hospital and the Midwifery Dispensary, and secretary of the Edinburgh Society for the Protection of Young Girls provided him with first-hand knowledge of the living conditions of Edinburgh's 'prostitutes'. He claimed to know 'more than three-fourths of all the common prostitutes in Edinburgh' by name.[39]

There are traces of evangelicalism in each of the physicians who contributed to the debate on prostitution, but Tait is distinguishable by his emphasis on 'prostitutes' as people rather than carriers of veneral disease.[40] Evangelical physicians like Tait condemned male sexual licence as a threat to the family and to conjugal love,[41] and promoted the traditional puritan ideal of a patriarchal 'marriage of affections' consecrated in the home, a zone of intimacy and refuge from the competitive world of work and politics. Like Tait, James Miller also demanded a single standard of sexual conduct and claimed that the powerful male sex drive, which was stronger than women's, could be kept under the control of a 'rightly balanced, duly principled, and well exercised mind'.[42] According to Tait, it was control of 'sexual passions' that separated 'civilized man from animals'. Men who allowed their sexual desires to dominate their natures were 'unmanly men'. In fact, he took the point so far as to argue that any man who could not control his lust belonged in a 'madhouse'.[43]

Evangelicals and physicians were also concerned with strengthening the patriarchal family and they sought to reimpose the moral and social authority of the father over extra-familial relations at a time when it was feared that the social and material basis of paternalism had been eroded.[44] They stressed also that while employers had the right to exact their 'quantum of labour' they ought also to appear as moral agents before their employees.[45]

> We maintain that the employer, while benefiting by the comparative cheapness of female labour, is bound to appear on the scene in a moral capacity. We attack the mere materialism of transactions, contracts, and engagements. The master . . . is not quit of his duty when he pays the stated wage.[46]

The 'prostitute' represented a threat to the patriarchal family, and was regarded as a source of pollution and a constant temptation to middle-class sons.[47] More threatening still to respectable society were the clandestine 'prostitutes' who as servants were able to infiltrate the sanctity of middle-class homes.[48] Tait cautioned young men to be on the look-out for crafty clandestine 'prostitutes' who ritually pricked their forefingers with needles in order to pass as 'respectable' seamstresses.[49]

William Acton, an English venereologist and crusader for the C.D. Acts, represents the 'sanitary approach', which was instrumental in generating an intellectual climate either sympathetic to the C.D. Acts or vehemently opposed to them. Acton's contribution to the debate is important because it became an important plank of the regulationist platform.[50] Acton, who campaigned for the Act of 1864 and its extension to the entire civilian population in 1866, became the target of anti-regulationist propaganda in Scotland. Acton stressed the need for a compromise between strict moral principles and the realities of social life. His task was to make state regulation palatable to a population whose ideas and values had been shaped by evangelicalism. He demanded the state regulation of prostitution which was already tacitly sanctioned by British society.[51] He argued that since the state already concerned itself with other epidemic and contagious diseases, venereal disease should be no exception.[52] He explained that he did not wish to make the 'path of sin less dangerous for the sinner'; it was probably an unhappy coincidence that curing disease also made prostitution less hazard-ous. However, he stated that the benefit to society and the thousands of 'miserable women' should not be abandoned merely because it entailed this consequence.[53]

Later evangelicals like James Miller, Professor of Surgery at Edinburgh University, exhibited a narrower and highly moralistic approach to the prostitution problem.[54] He did not regard 'prostitutes' with anything other than vile contempt. His writings on prostitution are characterized by a harsh condemnation of lower-class life and morality, and lack of sympathy and practical understanding of the life of the poor which distinguishes Tait's work.[55] By crusading against the C.D. Acts and the publishing of essays, moralists like Miller made full use of the public platform and press. Miller was also concerned with the state of public morality and argued that certain theatricals, the ballet, modern fiction, and plays pushed the moral tone of society downward.[56] He believed that only through education and religion would the masses gain the self-control and self-respect necessary for amelioration.[57] By focusing on intemperance, censorship, moral education, and sexual purity he diverted attention away from the material issues such as female unemployment and poverty which caused prostitution.[58]

Evangelical philanthropists and physicians dominated the public discourse on prostitution, but theirs was not the only voice raised in protest. There were other interested groups who were particularly sensitive about the sexual exploitation of working-class women by upper-class men. 'On public platforms and in their journals, working-class critics used the discussion of prostitution as a rhetorical opening to hammer away at the corruption of the old moral order and the exploitative character of class relations under industrial capitalism'.[59] By the 1840s a socialist view of prostitution, later endorsed by the Fabians and by Engels, had emerged in the writings of Robert Owen, described as an industrialist, 'cotton-spinner, socialist, social reformer, social scientist, and economist'.[60] He was also the founder of a model community in New Lanark, a few miles from Glasgow.[61]

Owen believed that an individual's character was strictly a product of his or her environment. Contrary to many of his contemporaries, who believed that poverty was the consequence of sin and part of the Divine Order, Owen thought that intemperance and ignorance were symptoms of poverty. As the masses were lifted out of poverty, as they were better fed, housed, and clothed, and given culture and education, so would their characters improve.[62] He developed this thesis early in 1800 and tested it in his model community at New Lanark. The community was based on co-operation rather than competition; he believed the latter led to poverty in the 'midst of plenty, and to a savaging of the relationship between man and man, between classes and between members of the same class'.[63] Owenites, therefore, were regarded with hostility by the ruling class who called them 'socialist and subversive'.[64] Although Owen had no direct interest in New Lanark after 1828, male and female Owenites, many of whom were also Chartists, were active in Scotland throughout the 1830s and 1840s.

Criticisms of the marriage system, particularly the late marriages of the rich and the 'careless and imprudent' marriages of the poor, existed in the writings of Tait, Acton, Wardlaw, Miller, and Logan, but no one attacked the institution of marriage as directly as Owen did in the 1820s. According to Owen the 'present marriages of the world, under the system of moral evil . . . are the sole cause of all the prostitution'.[65] The importance of the family in the nineteenth century is crucial to understanding the impact of Owenism. Owen saw the family as the main bastion of private property and the guardian of bourgeois individualism and self-interest, which he abhorred. Disharmony in society was rooted in the family. It isolated people and served as an organ of tyranny by which women were subjected to the rule of their husbands. Owenites demanded that the community replace the private family, and advocated the communal education of infants from the age of 2 in order to undermine familial influences. His ideas further inspired devotees in separate campaigns for woman's suffrage, divorce reform and birth control later in the century.[66]

Apart from Owen, little direct concern was given to the economic problems facing women until the work of Marx and Engels and Margaret Irwin became influential later in the century.[67] Concern for the sexual exploitation of working-class women, however, is evident in feminist and working-class agitation surrounding the C.D. Acts. One agitator was Robert Wilson, a Glaswegian who described himself as a 'bona fide working man, occupied ten hours a-day', and unshackled by the influences which 'froze the feelings', and sealed the 'lips of those who are falsely styled the noble and the great'. Wilson objected to the assumption espoused by regulationists that working-class men would not protect their wives and daughters from the abuses under the C.D. Acts. He stated that 'working men are honourable, and often more honourable . . . [and] love their wives and daughters as well, often better than many who call themselves gentlemen'.[68] In the name of 'patriotism and religion' Wilson demanded that the C.D. Acts be repealed. With the support of the Scottish Women's National Association for the Repeal of the C.D. Acts, working-men's leagues were formed early in the 1870s in Glasgow and Edinburgh. These leagues worked closely with the other branches of the Ladies' National Association throughout the campaign and both groups were extremely effective in distributing tracts and collecting signatures and their members were prominent speakers at public meetings.[69]

Although there was a considerable amount of overlap among discursants' political and religious persuasions, reformers used their roles as professionals to legitimate their participation in the public discourse. Dr Miller, for example, accorded the medical profession a vigilante role. He argued that the control of prostitution could only be accomplished with the expertise of the medical profession. 'With speculum in hand', he explained:

> The medical man must be conjoined with the policeman in this dirty and degrading work . . . he must go from brothel to brothel, and from door to door, examining patient by patient systematically . . . like a railway porter, with a hammer in hand, examining axle by axle in a newly arrived train, to see whether any may be heated or no.[70]

Similarly, Logan, Wardlaw, and Somerville claimed that it was the clergy who had the special role to play in the battle against prostitution. With the image of 'Mary Magdalene' to guide them, churchmen set out to reclaim the fallen. Logan stated that no other professional could, without damage to his character, attempt to rescue 'unfortunate females'.[71] From the pulpit they should warn of the 'snares of the devil'.[71] Parents needed to be warned to watch the morals of their sons, and he instructed masters and mistresses to keep a vigilant eye on their young domestics. Female domestics needed to be warned of flatteries, false promises, vanity, and the other numerous nameless arts of the 'liers-in-wait for their virtue'. Wardlaw urged parochial ministers and the pastors of dissenting congregations to augment their district schools in the poor locations of the city where literacy levels were lowest, to set up reading classes for young factory workers, and to teach the principles of religion which were most likely to safeguard virtue.[73]

Like the evangelicals, Owenite socialists manipulated the theme of prostitution for their own political ends, but in opposite ways. Owenites used their wide definition of the causes of prostitution, which included poverty and the deficient or maleducation of women and self-competition, to launch an attack on the corruption of bourgeois society.[74] Scottish clergy like Wardlaw and Logan, on the other hand, listed the influences of socialist ideology among their causes of prostitution, 'illegitimacy', and wife desertion. Logan accused socialists of seducing young female factory workers, and warned industrialists against hiring them as foremen.[75] Wardlaw used the occasion of his first lecture on prostitution to attack Owenite philosophy on the marriage question and defined prostitution as the 'socialism of brutes'.[76] Owenites retaliated by accusing Wardlaw of slander and 'gross misrepresentation of socialist views relative to the "intercourses of the sexes"', and challenged him to debate the socialist doctrines related to 'marriage and divorce'. Wardlaw, incidentally, refused to attend the debate 'in a hall of avowed Atheism'.[77]

To summarize, Scottish moral reformers used their roles as professionals to legitimize their participation in the public discourse on prostitution. As will be seen in the following section, which deals with the 'causes' of prostitution, there was a great deal of overlap in the points of agreement between reformers. With the exception of Owen, reformers accepted the importance of material causes but as environmentalists and evangelicals their cure lay in moral education. Education and reform, however, were only prescribed after the fear of physical contagion and political threat was diffused.

AN ARMY OF MAGDALENES: WOMEN IN THE 'PUBLIC' SPHERE

Before looking at the contemporary perceptions of the causes of prostitution and definitions of a 'prostitute' it is necessary to recall that the 'prostitute' was a label or censure, encompassing a constellation of women's behaviour which moral reformers found objectionable or threatening. The significance of recognizing that they are socially constructed categories enables one to see that the debates over who was and who was not a 'prostitute' were not just technical, but deeply political. Through these discourses the 'prostitute' was given a history, a past, a childhood, and a character. There may be valid psychological theories which account for the bourgeois male's fascination with the subject, but this is beyond the scope of this study. What is clear, is that by the nineteenth century the bourgeoisie could not easily ignore the presence of large numbers of women in the streets, whose dress, physical appearance, occupation, or behaviour led to their being labelled as 'prostitutes'.

By the middle of the century seduction was no longer regarded as the only cause of prostitution. As stated by the editor of the *North Briton* in 1864, the idea that 'prostitutes' are victims of seduction was very 'sentimental' but 'erroneous'. He accepted that some women 'on the town' had been seduced, but they were exceptions to the general rule. He stated that prostitution in Edinburgh was a trade to which girls served an apprenticeship in the same way as they would have done when learning millinery or shoebinding.[78] Accordingly, 'prostitutes' and brothel-keepers were regarded as the 'aristocracy of Edinburgh's closes' and little girls fought with each other for the 'honour' of running messages for them. They grew up familiar with the language, the manners, and the 'morale' of the brothel. From childhood they were reared in the midst of 'crime and vice' and when they reached womanhood they became journey-women and walked the streets on their own account.

> These girls are the young recruits who are continually swelling the ranks of our Old Town prostitution. As the little boy ties his toy sword to his side and sighs for the day he will be able to enlist as a soldier, so do little girls study to imitate the prostitute, as they sigh for the day in which they will, like her, have money to spend. They look forward and upward to the time when they will enter on their teens, and walk the streets like those who they envy.[79]

Although this is obviously an exaggeration, it supports Walkowitz's suggestion that moral reformers were unable to construct a cultural model that would make a poor woman's move into prostitution comprehensible within the terms of her social and cultural world. For bourgeois moralists, working-class culture represented a totally negative culture. From their point of view, only a 'degenerate social milieu that spawned an alienated, anti-social personality would explain a woman's entry into prostitution.'[80]

In their attempts to arrive at the true causes of prostitution reformers focused on the presence of women in the 'public' sphere. Thus, they did not always distinguish between 'prostitutes' and mill-girls, or any of the other groups of working-class women who, unescorted by men, regularly congregated on the streets.[81] Similarly, unmarried mothers and prostitution were not necessarily seen as mutually exclusive because it was believed that an unmarried mother had 'taken the first step in prostitution', not just because she was unchaste, but because it was virtually impossible for a woman alone to support herself and her child.[82] Although there is evidently some truth in this, the remark was a moral censure and not based on an analysis of political economy. What is most striking about mid-century attempts to define 'prostitutes' and prostitution therefore, is that there was so little attempt to systematize it. Apparently observers felt quite confident in their ability to recognize a 'prostitute' if they saw one.[83] For example, Chief Constable McCall of the Glasgow Police stated that the 'test of a prostitute is, that the woman is known to be going about the streets by the police, following no other occupation, and earning her livelihood in that way'.[84] On the basis of McCall's definition a 'prostitute' was any woman found in the streets who could not give a satisfactory account of how she earned her living. This could easily have included the unemployed and casual labourers.

The situation was not so very different for women who could give a satisfactory account of how they earned their living. By 1870, the percentage of servants in magdalene homes began to fall, but those from other occupations rose. The records of the Glasgow Lock Hospital suggest that between 1870 and 1890, 33 per cent of the patients were mill-girls and 25 per cent were servants. These were followed by machinists, washerwomen, and needlewomen.[85] The surgeon at the lock hospital stated that although only one in ten of the women admitted gave 'prostitute' as her occupation, all were either 'regular avowed prostitutes' or young women who had 'more or less given way to immoral practices'.[86] The hospital maintained the following definition of a 'prostitute':

in the vast majority of those cases the patients were prostitutes of one kind or another, that is to say that they were women consorting with more than one man.[87]

Although Alexander Patterson recognized that many of the factory labourers worked at their occupations during the day and in the evenings took to the streets to supplement their low wages, his attitude indicates that he defined many women as 'prostitutes' who would not have defined their own behaviour as prostitution; unfortunately, there is no direct evidence of what the women themselves thought. It can be concluded then, that one indicator of whether a woman was considered to be a 'prostitute' was whether or not she had an occupation. Proof of employment, however, was not enough. Other variables, such as her behaviour in public and feminine appearance were also included in the labelling process. The following account of women at the annual Glasgow Fair holiday was echoed in many descriptions of female behaviour at other working-class leisure activities like dance-halls, theatres, public houses, and other places where 'respectable' women with 'feminine sensibilities' were not supposed to go.[88]

> The ground was teeming with street girls, some of them might be mill-girls – several mill-girls were under the influence of drink . . . [and] many of them were successful in their attempts to lead lads and boys away with them, two gaily dressed girls picked up young men and went off to the Green [park]. . . . Saw thirteen couples lying on the Green; two couples of whom were in the very act of prostitution. [89]

> Saw 94 prostitutes, also a large number of very young girls like mill workers, scarcely distinguishable from prostitutes in their conduct. Saw 5 young prostitutes squatting on the grass in a very immoral manner; also one couple lying on the grass. (We speak confidently of the purpose, because a policeman on the Green assured us . . . that no woman went to the Green after a certain hour, save for that purpose[90]

The apparent disgust at the unseemly behaviour of the mill-girls barely conceals a tendency to eroticize these young women. Recalling the humbler days of his youth as a shop-hand in a flaxmill, James Myles reported that after enquiring as to where some of the mill-girls learned the 'immoral' song they had been singing, '[t]hey burst into a shrill wild laugh – a laugh that can only be given by mill-girls – seized me, pulled me down on the floor, and proceeded to maltreat me in a manner which was neither modest nor merciful'.[91] Similarly, Tait's writings reveal that 'disgust' was not the only reaction to the presence of 'prostitutes'. They were also thought of as 'fascinating' and 'seductive'. Tait feared that for as long as 'prostitutes' were allowed to roam the streets, men, young and old, would be tempted.

> From boyhood to manhood his life is one continued fight against it . . . he cannot pass along the street in the evening without meeting with, and being accosted by women of the town at almost every step. Their fascinating smile – their artful and familiar conversation, are sure to attract his attention. The freedom with which they approach him, the affection and friendly manner in which they ask after his health and invite him to their lodgings, together with their handsome figure and beautiful appearance, are too much for any one whose conduct is not governed by powerful religious principles.[92]

Moral reformers regarded these women as 'unfeminine'. They correlated certain forms of working-class behaviour which offended bourgeois norms – rough voices, garish dress, drinking and swearing – with another: sexual promiscuity, although there was no evidence that this lifestyle led to prostitution. Furthermore, unlike the servant, whose activities were confined to the 'private' sphere, female factory labourers were seen as a potential political threat. Sharing the same working conditions as men, they were often involved in the same political movements.[93] Historians argue that in some areas female industrial action had a significant impact on trade union development[94] and Scottish women were prominent among the Chartists and Owenite socialists.[95] In the eyes of the bourgeoisie, female factory workers had one foot in the 'feminine' sphere of home and family and the other in the 'masculine' world of social production. Because they were financially independent and in some cases relatively well paid, they were perceived as not fulfilling the 'natural' role of the female sex, that of dependence on and ministering to men.[96]

Throughout the nineteenth century the expansion of the market economy and the commercialization of traditional female tasks transformed women's household-based methods of earning a living. Traditionally, women earned money through such activities as sewing and washing, which had never caused alarm as they were seen as supplementary to domestic chores. By the nineteenth century, increasing numbers of women left their families and villages to find wage-earning employment in Scottish factories, cotton mills, and other industries. The changing pattern of women's work challenged the division of labour dictated by the doctrine of separate spheres because it undermined the foundations of the patriarchal family.[97] Controversy over the presence of working women in the 'public' arena, therefore, became an integral part of the public discourse on the prostitution problem.

Reformers recognized the economic hardships these women faced. They noted that during depressions in the trade cycle, when unemployment was high there was an increase in the number of 'prostitutes' on the streets.[98] They agreed that the unstable market for semi-skilled and unskilled female labour and low wages were common causes of prostitution. But they were at a loss as to what should be done about it. Their faith in private enterprise and the Poor Law committed them to the belief that anyone who was prepared to earn an honest living could do so if they tried.[99] Tait demonstrated that this was not true. In order to combat female poverty he suggested that many of the 'male' occupations such as shop assistant, tailor, furniture polisher, engraver, or coppersmith be done by women. Similarly, he recommended the implementation of a price-fixing board which would guarantee seamstresses a minimum wage,[100] but his suggestions were ignored by his contemporaries, who devoted their attention towards rating the female occupations in order of risk. They concluded that the chances of a woman 'straying from the path of virtue' was intimately linked to her choice of occupation. The most dangerous occupations were those in mills, shops, theatres, public houses, and agriculture, and work as seamstresses and message and flower girls.[101] Reformers admitted that the low wages paid in these trades frequently drove women from 'cruel and biting poverty' to prostitution. However, they also claimed that 'vicious inclinations' acquired in childhood and bad associates were just as likely to expose a woman to temptations as her occupation.[102] In order to prevent women from resorting to prostitution the majority of reformers recommended moral education and training in domestic service and other forms of work that were subject to direct patriarchal supervision or parental discipline.

To summarize, moral entrepreneurs frequently used the mill-girl to typify the status of women who worked in the 'public' sphere. They worked outside the home, many alongside men or in direct competition with them in areas which, unlike domestic service, defied the doctrine of separate spheres. Thus, whether a woman was driven to prostitution by poverty or 'unsexed' by paid labour, she was regarded as unfeminine. To stress this, reformers did not always distinguish between 'prostitutes' and mill-girls, or any of the women who congregated in the streets. Moral reformers defined women who worked in the 'public' sphere as potential 'deviants' or 'prostitutes'. This is not to suggest that all working-class women were regarded in this way, but that they engaged in behaviours that were seen as causes of prostitution. They defied bourgeois notions of 'femininity' because their life-styles did not conform to middle-class standards. Because of the realities of working-class life, especially among the poor, the 'unfeminine' woman would always be found among the poor, where overcrowding, poverty, and lack of education meant that they were excluded from the 'position and education' which confirmed the 'character' of higher-class girls.[103] Reformers stressed that the working-class girl had to be taught that chastity and virginity were the

> priceless jewel in her honour – however plain her person – however humble her rank may be – which, without the deepest shame and detriment, she dare not give away.[104]

If the criteria for classifying women as 'prostitutes' appear ambiguous it is because reformers were more concerned with practical control than systematic, academic, or philosophical discussions.[105] They were not satisfied with simply analysing the causes of prostitution; their primary concern was reforming the women who were recruited to the trade and to this end they looked to the magdalene homes as refuges where offending women were placed under a harsh regime of moral education and training and expected to conform to middle-class notions of sexual and vocational propriety.

Chapter five

The domestication of 'fallen' women

English and Scottish philanthropists had some degree of success in their attempt to cast 'fallen' women as suitable objects of charity. The first female penitentiaries began to appear in the late eighteenth century. The first was the Magdalene Hospital which opened in London in 1758, followed by the Lock Asylum (1787), the London Female Penitentiary (1807), the Maritime Penitent Refuge (1829), and the London Society for the Protection of Young Females and Prevention of Juvenile Prostitution (1835).[1] By 1900 there were over seventy female refuges throughout the United Kingdom, of which at least twenty were in Scotland.[2]

Scotland's first non-statutory female penitentiary, or magdalene home was opened in Edinburgh in Canongate Street by the Philanthropic Society in 1797; called the Edinburgh Magdalene Asylum it was originally designed for women of all ages who were recently discharged from prison, but after a four-year trial it was concluded that many were too old, and 'from their inveterate habits', generally intractable. The directors concluded that they would have a better success rate if they focused on younger women, who had not been on the streets long enough to develop serious drinking problems or connections with the criminal underworld.[3] Within a year of its opening a Ladies' Committee was formed to oversee inmates' work, dress, and conduct.[4]

MacGill did not succeed in drumming up enough support for the Glasgow Magdalene Asylum until 1815. Before this time the Glasgow Society for the Encouragement of Penitents[5] sent suitable candidates for reform to Edinburgh. In 1815, through the 'scanty benevolence' of the Congregational, Episcopalian and parish churches, enough money was raised to build an asylum on Parliamentary

Road. Unlike the Edinburgh asylum, it was located in the country.[6] The building was surrounded by an acre of 'properly enclosed' land, where inmates were occasionally permitted to walk.[7] It provided accommodation for thirty-four inmates. The dormitory, 'fitted up in a plain, but handsome manner', contained sevènteen bedrooms, each designed to accommodate at least two inmates. It also contained apartments for the superintendents, four working and eating rooms, and a chapel.[8] A formal Ladies' Committee was not established until 1861, and women were not permitted to sit on the Board of Directors until 1913.[9] The asylum in Glasgow was called the Magdalene Asylum until 1840, when, as will be seen in the next chapter, it was converted into the 'House of Refuge for Females' by the activities of the reformatory school movement. Although a magdalene division continued to exist throughout the period, it was not a separate institution again until it was re-incorporated as the Glasgow Magdalene Institution in 1860.

The emphasis of this chapter is on the management practices of these magdalene homes. In an attempt to demonstrate how the discourses introduced in the previous chapter were manifested in the changing material practices of these institutions, it is argued that a contradiction emerged between the directors' prejudice against women's employment in the 'public' sphere and the institutions' dependence on women's wages for the running of the institution. This contradiction was resolved by shifting ideologies of moral regulation: ideologies were frequently altered in class-specific definitions of femininity. The first section of this chapter examines the daily regime used by the institution to encourage moral reform. The next section explores the relation between ideologies of moral reform and material realities and the creation of what Bristow calls a 'sanctimonious sweatshop'. The final section looks at the impact of moral regulation on inmates who successfully completed their training and offers suggestions regarding those who rejected the institutions' efforts to impose limitations on their sexual and vocational choices.

'WHOLESOME, PATERNAL, CHRISTIAN DISCIPLINE': SCOTTISH MAGDALENE HOMES

The Glasgow Magdalene Asylum was modelled on the one in Edinburgh.[10] Both were charitable institutions which relied on voluntary subscriptions and support. They also relied on the co-operation and willingness of inmates to conform to the rules of the establishment because they lacked the statutory power to detain them against their will.[11] The purpose of a magdalene asylum was to rescue and reform. According to the directors, the official objectives of the Glasgow asylum were:

> to provide a refuge for those destitute and unhappy females, who have trespassed against the laws of purity and virtue, but who feel a desire to forsake their profligate course of life; – to be enabled by instruction in the arts of female industry to support themselves in an honourable manner – and to be taught that knowledge of their Maker and of themselves, which the Scriptures of Truth alone contain.[12]

Similarly, the only 'prerequisite' for admission to the Edinburgh asylum was that 'she be sincerely sorry for her past delinquencies and desirous of being reformed'.[13]

Those they intended to rescue were not professional 'prostitutes' with long criminal records, but young female misdemeanants, paupers, and vagrants.[14] While it was hoped that they would come voluntarily, women were usually brought to the institutions' attention by magistrates, missionaries, the police, and the lock hospitals, because either through unemployment, extreme poverty, or illness they had committed sexual offences or had engaged in full- or part-time 'prostitution', as defined by the institution. In Scotland the lock hospitals and magdalene asylums were separate institutions, but they played complementary roles. Asylums refused to admit women with signs of venereal disease and hospitals lacked facilities and resources to pay much close attention to patients' moral rehabilitation; therefore, they depended upon each other for the exchange of inmates.

The institutions favoured women under the age of 24, who were neither pregnant nor diseased at the time of admission, and who were of reasonable intelligence and willing to submit to discipline. Inmates who received a clean bill of health from the asylum's physician were selected after a lengthy interview, during which it was up to them to convince the directors of their sincere desire to reform. It was possible to fool both the committee and the physician. Inmates were frequently sent back to the hospital for a 'course of mercury',[15] the nineteenth-century cure for venereal disease, or to the poorhouse when pregnancies became obvious.[16] Others, like Jess Wood, were sent on their way shortly after admission as it became clear that they would be 'highly dangerous to the Institution'.[17] Still others, such as Margaret Richie, with warrants for their arrest, were carted off by the police when their whereabouts became known.[18]

The interval between the application and full admission was known as the probationary period. A new inmate's conduct was carefully monitored by the directors, matrons, and the Ladies' Committees for up to three months. The Edinburgh directors claimed that it was 'so difficult to eradicate the taint of moral contagion that the period of probation [was] seldom less than [three] months'.[19] Acceptable inmates were classified according to their past education, behaviour, and marketable skills. In Edinburgh, inmates were confined to their rooms for the first months and permitted contact only with the staff and the Ladies' Committee.[20] Part of the asylum was appropriated for women of a 'better order than the others. . . . These were women who had been seduced or lived as kept mistresses, but had never 'been on the town'.[21] Inmates who passed the probationary period were fully admitted to the institution, where they were expected to stay for two years. Those who completed the programme were given a certification of character and guaranteed the protection of the institution for as long as they behaved and received favourable reports from their employers.

Life in a magdalene home was organized around the premise that inmates could only be reformed if order was put into their lives and a strict regime of 'mild, wholesome, paternal, and Christian discipline'[22] was enforced. Accordingly, the day was punctuated by work, prayer, and strict discipline.[23] After admission inmates were expected to take a 'hot or cold bath', and were given a uniform.[24] Their own clothes were cleaned, ticketed, and laid aside and would only be returned in case of dismissal. The cost of the uniform was deducted from the wages inmates earned from their employment in the institution. The daily routine, which varied little throughout the century, was designed on the principle of an efficiently run home, characteristic of 'respectable' family life in the households of the directors. The only exception was that inmates were prohibited contact with anyone outside the institution. The management believed that inmates were more likely to internalize the reformatory's teachings about how women like themselves ought to behave if they were isolated from contradictory examples.[25] This applied particularly to inmates with family and friends, whom the institution regarded as troublesome.

The directors rapidly discovered that although the majority of inmates with previous work experience were former servants, a great percentage had never held a steady job. In fact, many were unskilled and illiterate. The Glasgow directors observed that 'several of the women have everything to learn' not only had they been idle, but were totally 'ignorant of useful employment'.[26] This was compounded by general bad health, malnourishment, and a range of complaints such as physical disabilities, poor eyesight, epilepsy, and other health problems that were common to the population in general. The directors' descriptions of inmates' behaviour and characters ranged from 'naturally dull, thoughtless and high minded, childish, vulgar, uncouth, and stupid'; to 'willing to work, diligent, a strong desire to do her duty, behaves with propriety and professes religion'.[27] Rather than a true indication of the inmates' characters, however, these descriptions are as much a function of the directors' expectations, the monotony of institutional life, and the psychological effects of institutionalization.

On a typical day in the Glasgow asylum, inmates arose at dawn. Washers began work at 5.30 a.m., laundry workers at 6.00, and sewers at 7.00. The sewers took turns doing domestic chores around the asylum.[28] Before breakfast, the 'sisters' gathered with the matron for 'family worship'. Breakfast (porridge) was between 8.00 and 9.00, after which the inmates resumed their revenue-generating employment in the laundry or sewing room. Dinner was between 1.00 and 2.00 and supper between 7.00 and 8.00. In Edinburgh meals were prepared from a recipe book published by the Society for Bettering the Condition of the Poor, which the Ladies' Committee recommended for its cheap dishes and useful suggestions, such as substituting rice and barley porridge for bread.[29] After supper there was 'family worship' again. It was not unusual for inmates to work for an hour or two after supper. One hour was set aside each day for the education of inmates who could not read, and each girl was given her own Bible as soon as she was able to read it. The entire inmate population was examined regularly in reading and reciting portions of scripture. Throughout the day the staff were expected to take every opportunity to instruct inmates in the principles and duties of religion.[30] Bed-time was at 10.30, making the average working day at least ten hours. With only minor exceptions the regime was the same in Edinburgh.

The programme was strict and the rules numerous. The directors expected a high standard of conduct from the inmates, who were expected to observe a 'becoming silence at all times.' No 'snuff . . . no letters, or parcels, or messages' were allowed in the house[31] and felonies such as swearing, fighting, and lying (which were always a problem) were punished either by expulsion, solitary confinement, or hard physical labour. Mary Buchan was put in solitary confinement twice for insolence and the bad quality of her work.[32] Margaret Reid was rebuked for striking Robina Miller on the side of the head,[33] whereas Jean Marshall was given a week's confinement and a week washing the stairs for a similar offence.[34] Between 1833 and 1835 discipline in the Edinburgh asylum was so bad that the directors resorted to shaving inmates' heads in order to suppress the desire to get out. Head shaving was also practised in the London Magdalene Hospital and the Dublin Lock Hospital, but was less common in Glasgow. The directors in Edinburgh found it extremely effective:

> by the adoption of the practice alluded to, an advantage has been gained, as no woman likes to leave the Asylum without her hair; and, before it has grown a proper length, she has become habituated to her situation, and by instruction and example, made to see the sinful course she had been pursuing. This effect has failed in only two out of fifty cases![35]

Although women came voluntarily and the institutions could not detain them against their will, once admitted it was rather difficult to leave.[36] It was against the asylums' policies to release anyone before she demonstrated that she was capable of a 'change of life', whereupon she was either reunited with her family if the directors approved of their character, or placed in domestic service.[37] Country service was always preferable because many of the inmates were too well known to be returned to their former communities. Inmates who desired to leave before being formally discharged were required to give a month's notice and were frequently put in solitary confinement to think it over. After that time, those who could not be prevailed upon to stay were reprimanded, scolded, had to turn in their uniforms, and were dismissed.

A similar procedure was followed in cases where inmates rebelled against, or resisted the institutions' attempt to control their behaviour. In cases where inmates were expelled for misbehaving they were reprimanded in front of the other women and a copy of the report was sent to the police. Nelly Sutherland and Bell Evans were dismissed in this way for deliberately setting fire to their bedroom,[38] and the Council Chambers were informed when Betty Semple was dismissed 'at her own desire and under suspicion of being accompany of a theft committed by Jess Dow, [who] stole her clothes'.[39]

Inmates who were so anxious to leave that they ran away, were charged with the theft of their uniforms, forfeited any money they had earned, and were prohibited from readmission. When Margaret Peat ran off, she was brought back to the asylum under guard and sentenced by the magistrates to two months in the Bridewell;[40] Ann Robertson was given six months for the same offence. Circumstances were better for Ann Wallace, however, who 'ran away with the Society's clothes. Mrs Coutts [the matron] met her on the street 2 days afterward and brought her back to the Asylum . . . took her clothes . . . and turned her away; and she having promised to go to the harvest; they gave her 1 [shilling] to buy a Hook'.[41] Although the merit of each case was carefully weighed against the circumstances, the rules were strictly followed.[42]

Recent studies[43] of statutory and non-statutory female penitentiaries have demonstrated that these institutions developed a variety of social-control strategies intended to domesticate inmates, and thereby make them suitable and submissive domestic servants. The first step in the process was the initial act of detention, or 'voluntary incarceration'. Incarcerating women for sexual misconduct was used to protect them from being further corrupted, or from becoming hardened 'prostitutes'. At the same time, it was intended to protect society from the spread of corruption and contagious diseases.

The situation in Edinburgh reveals that the work of reforming 'prostitutes' did not have full community support. The following examples of opposition and subversion reveal the presence of the conflicting discourses suggested in the previous chapters. The asylum's unfortunate location in the centre of town and lack of a proper chapel[44] meant that inmates were regularly subjected to harassment from unsympathetic members of the community. In 1799 the windows on the west side were nailed shut and painted white to keep out prying eyes.[45] On 21 June 1802 Thomas Pentland Smith was charged by the Canongate Magistrates with having 'followed two of the girls on their returning from Church and . . . [with] behaving in the most outrageous manner'.[46] In 1821, the directors built a Porter's Lodge by the gate to serve as a gatehouse, to prevent the girls from escaping late at night.[47] In 1835, 'for greater seclusion', half the windows in the house were boarded up[48] and the fence had to be raised to prevent 'improper persons'[49] from speaking to the inmates. In 1836 a bottle of whisky was 'thrown over the wall', and 'partaken in by . . . Betsy Miller and Margaret Cammeron'.[50] Sexual harassment was less of a problem in Glasgow because the asylum was in the country. MacGill had argued that only away from the corruption of the city could women practise their penitence undisturbed.[51]

Voluntary incarceration was also intended to ensure the 'disruption of family ties', which was the second step in the process of moral regulation. In cases where an inmate's family and friends were judged to be an unsuitable influence, the institution endeavoured to establish itself as a surrogate family.[52] To ensure that the good work of the institution was not undone by the corrupting influence of relatives and friends, and the inmates tempted to return to their old ways, the asylum encouraged the women to sever all ties with their past.[53] Cases such as the request of Catherine Culbertson's mother to have her back in Haddington were blocked by the directors 'lest she should fall into bad company again'.[54] And the matron was warned never to allow any of Helen Mortimer's family to enter the asylum as they were all 'people of bad character'.[55] The inmates were also discouraged from contacting former inmates and two girls were never allowed to go to service in the same household.[56] Relatives wishing an appointment had to meet with the matron's approval. If successful, the meeting took place in her presence.[57]

In addition to incarceration and disrupting families two other strategies for moral regulation were developed: moral education and industrial training. The directors believed that both could be accomplished through a regime of hard work and Bible reading. One historian states that religious indoctrination in magdalene asylums had one overriding aim: to replace deceit and pride with guilt. The directors found nothing more disturbing than an inmate's unwillingness to confess her sin.[58] Their policy was that each inmate would receive her own Bible as soon as she had learned to read.

The scriptures would reveal the extent of the inmate's sin, defilement, and guilt and she would learn to accept herself as a 'sinner'. Therefore, her punishment took the form of penitence and prayer combined with periods of solitary confinement. This was part of the new philosophy of punishment that emerged in the prison reform movement between 1775 and 1840. The new form of corporal discipline, directed at the mind with large dosages of scripture and hard labour, replaced a cluster of punishments directed at the body such as whipping, dunking, and branding used in the previous centuries. According to Michael Ignatieff, the significance of solitary confinement was that it offered the perfect reconciliation of humanity and terror. It epitomized a punishment so rational that offenders punished themselves in the 'soundless, silent anguish of their own minds'.[59] Furthermore, by individualizing punishment, the directors glossed over the consequences of the class inequalities, poverty, and hypocrisy which were responsible for the inmates' troubles.[60] Finally, through Bible stories, inmates were taught a morality centred on self-sacrifice and duty. Through the Christian chain of command which paralleled the Victorian social-class hierarchy and which sanctioned female inferiority, self-abnegation and duty, each inmate learned her appropriate gender role and social-class position.

Finnegan argues that the fierce religious indoctrination used in female penitentiaries was often unnecessary because it placed additional strain on the inmates, who, for whatever reason, were so desperate to abandon their former lifestyles that they entered an institution. It resulted in frequent run-aways, dismissals, and letters from former inmates who were reduced to spiritless demoralized creatures, entirely lacking in self-confidence and betraying a morbid sense of dependence on the matron.[61] Many of the letters sent to the matrons in Edinburgh and Glasgow suggest that feelings of humility, subservience, and loneliness dominated these women's perceptions of themselves and their situations, which was probably the reason that their letters were selected for display in the annual reports. It was interpreted as a sign of deep 'penitence' and true reformation.

> Dear Miss Nott [Glasgow Matron]: I have a letter from my brother, telling me that his wife and himself freely forgive me, and if I do what is right that they will make me their sister, as I ought to be; so you see I have much to thank God for – the

only friends of my own that I want to think of me are going to love me as a sister. And see the other friends that I have got. I want you to pray for me every day, that I may not get proud of my sinful self because my friends are so kind to me. I want to make everybody like me, but I want to be very humble.[62]

In addition to religious education inmates were provided with secular education, which ranged, as the literacy level of the general population improved, from basic reading and writing early in the century, to special classes in geography, arithmetic, music, and weekly lectures on 'homely and interesting' subjects and Gospel Temperance meetings as the century ended.[63] Education classes were intended to be a pleasant break from the other activities of the day, and it was believed that it was important for inmates to develop their minds.

With the exception of the paid labour, what is striking about the evening curriculum and special events is the overall 'gentility' and similarity to the manner in which middle-class women might spend their evenings. The emphasis on gentility reflects how closely penitentiaries associated middle-class manners with reform. It was not intended that inmates become learned, or 'ladies', but rather they should appreciate the values associated with being a 'lady',[64] in order to make them better servants.

Education was supplemented with training for domestic service so that inmates would be able to support themselves after they left the institution.[65] The directors intended to return inmates to their families where ever possible, but in cases where they were orphans or the family was unsuitable, inmates were returned to the 'private' sphere as competent and submissive servants. Domestic service was regarded as the principle form of paid employment for women that did not break with the feminine role. Thus inmates could act out their femininity by becoming servants, which conveniently enabled bourgeois women to protect their own femininity.[66] This letter from a former Glasgow inmate illustrates this nicely.

I have a good situation, and I am doing the very best to give satisfaction. . . . The one baby is [18] months old, and the other [5] months old, and very delicate, but my mistress says the young baby has grown this last week. I am coming to see you on Thursday evening first to get a lesson in shirt-ironing. I got all the washing done up nicely. I did the collars and cuffs, but I was afraid of the shirts, so they were sent out. . . . Mrs S. said to me last night, I hope you will not be going away and leaving me, for she knows very little about housekeeping and less about children, so I am going to be the baby's mother[67]

The directors were prejudiced against women in 'public' paid employment and preferred to place inmates in situations, such as domestic service, where they would be dependent upon others for food and board, and where they hoped the girls would be closely supervised by 'respectable' members of the middle class. Nicole Rafter argues that the very concept of an institution dedicated to the rescue and reform of women over 18 was rooted in the perception of women as child-like creatures.[68]

An inmate was considered to be morally reformed when she displayed a 'change of heart', which was believed to indicate her conversion to middle-class standards of feminine propriety. The directors claimed that the two-year residence in the institution provided inmates with a 'fresh start' in life. They hoped that the education and moral training plus the 'elevating' influences of the Ladies' Committee would provide inmates with a surrogate for the family so many lacked.

> When the girl . . . is once more out in the world, the Homes have a new function to discharge for her help and benefit. To them she turns as indeed a home, and to the Matron as indeed a mother, without this tie maintenance of the cure would in many cases be followed by relapse.[69]

What the institutions intended for the futures of 'fallen' women and the social position to which they could properly aspire was, however, directly related to class. The directors believed that with proper help and guidance it was possible for a former inmate to regain her previous place in the female labour force as a domestic servant and to rise to a respectable position within the working-class community. Furthermore, the opportunity to serve 'respectable' people was implicit in what they meant by a 'fresh start'. If the directors felt any concern about sending inmates into service, the same situation that got so many of them into trouble in the first place, they soothed their consciences with the belief that the moral education inmates received would neutralize and fortify them against 'evil influences and temptations'.[70]

85

By the middle of the century the number of former servants applying to magdalene homes began to drop and there was a marked increase in women, especially those from Glasgow, with previous work experience in mills and factories, who refused to be placed in service. The directors regarded the former factory workers with a certain degree of frustration and disillusionment.[71]

> [W]ith this class, who are too often the offspring as well as the associates of the low, the drunken, the dissolute, who have not ever had the elements of religious or moral training, and who have previously been employed as field-workers, mill-workers, charwomen, hawkers etc., the directors have some difficulty, as they are manifestly unsuited for domestic service[72]

In the early days, girls such as Betty Finlay, who declared that she 'could not bring her mind to that kind of employ [service]',[73] were sent to David Dale's cotton mill at Lanark.[74] This is ironic because, although the directors applauded Dale's system of patriarchal paternalism under the influence of Dale's son-in-law, Robert Owen, and the Owenite Socialists in the 1830s, reformers attacked the community at New Lanark and charged socialism with causing prostitution.

With respect to the changing ideologies of moral regulation and gender, by 1835 the Edinburgh directors observed that much of the behaviour displayed by former factory workers, which they described as 'discontent and riotous behaviour', could be controlled by moving inmates from sewing to washing. They discovered that those inmates who were used to 'roving' would not conform to sedentary work, and concluded that this energy could be 'harnessed' in the laundry room.[75] By the mid-century more emphasis was placed on industrial training in laundries, which had proved to be the most financially profitable activity anyway. Through training in the laundry the directors promised to turn out a highly skilled and well disciplined industrial labour force.

To summarize, the system of moral regulation developed in these institutions depended on moral education, religious training, and strict discipline. In addition, however, the directors had to develop strategies other than corporal punishment for dealing with inmates who resisted their programme. Their solution was to try to manage 'discontent and riotous behaviour', in other words, 'resistance' by shifting 'troublesome' inmates from sedentary work to active labour.

They argued that certain inmates, generally those with previous employment in the 'public' sphere, were 'manifestly unsuited for domestic service'. In this light, they developed two streams for moral regulation. The first was designed for inmates who had never been 'unsexed' by employment in the 'public' sphere. These would be returned to the 'private' sphere as competent and submissive domestic servants. The second stream transformed inmates, mainly those with prior employment in the 'public' sphere, or those who refused to be deferential, into well disciplined industrial labourers.

THE 'SANCTIMONIOUS SWEATSHOP'

The ideologies of moral regulation were frequently altered to meet economic pressures in the institution and in the community. Behind the directors' idealized image of the morally reformed female proletarian lay the material realities of reproducing the institution: paying the bills and possibly making a profit. This resulted in a contradiction between the need to maintain the institution, on a day-to-day basis, endemic to all charities, and the moral reform of the women, unique to magdalene homes. Similarly, the directors recognized that by the middle of the century there was a demand from the community for female labour in industry and more women expressed a preference for that work. The directors astutely resolved this contradiction by constantly shifting their ideologies of moral regulation, a process which can be observed in a series of experiments in Edinburgh and Glasgow throughout the century. It should be emphasized that these were charitable institutions and at no time in their histories did subscriptions pay for more than a fraction of the administration cost. The directors were therefore faced with the dilemma of how to create the right balance of 'work and religion'. Training in needlework and laundry were central to these homes because they generated an income.

Although the directors recognized that prostitution had many causes, they attributed it to the inmates' previous unwillingness to work. In order to re-proletarianize the inmates, the institution operated in what sociologists of education now call the 'long-shadow of work',[76] basing their regime on training in deference and subordination, qualities the inmates would need as suitable servants or labourers. The organizational structure of magdalene homes was based on a paternalist model, which recast elements of the factory system in the image of the patriarchal family, thereby reproducing the patriarchal and class order of society.[77] The 'fatherly' male directors reigned supreme as the chief disciplinary officers. The 'motherly' matrons, usually middle-aged spinsters or widows, acted as the subordinates of the male directors and role models for the inmates. The other members of staff, also unmarried women, were expected to set an example of cleanliness and tidiness in their own person and to see that inmates did the same. They were also expected to maintain a professional distance from the inmates and to report any signs of 'levity, or any thing on the part of inmates at variance with good order'.[78]

Upon admission the inmates were separated according to their past employment records and education, as well as moral character. Those who had been 'seduced' were segregated from the more 'depraved', who had actually been 'on the street'. Women on probation were strictly forbidden to communicate with the other women; even during family worship they sat 'behind a screen', separated by staff members who sat between them.[79] Once fully admitted to an institution, inmates were then further segregated on the basis of the status of the employment they performed. The higher status workers such as sewers were segregated from the kitchen help; the washers, manglers, and glazers were segregated from 'the other classes above stairs'; and the laundresses from 'the other classes above or below stairs'.[80]

Early in the histories of the asylums the directors discovered that getting a good day's work out of the inmates would be a continual battle. Many had never held a steady job and others were totally unskilled and illiterate. This was compounded by general bad health and physical complaints. Even among the 'able-bodied', getting work out of them was a challenge. In order to induce the inmates to 'industry' the Edinburgh directors decided to give each inmate a daily quota of work and the surplus value, roughly one-third, would then be given to them as wages for clothes. Those who failed to meet the quota only received one-quarter of the profit.[81] Allowing inmates to keep part of their wages would teach them the value of 'honest' labour, plus the diligence and thrift they would need in the work force.[82] In contrast, the Glasgow asylum did not pay its inmates for the quantity of work produced, but gave one shilling to inmates who behaved for six months after leaving the institution.

The opportunity to earn a little money for clothes, however, inspired few inmates. They were frequently reprimanded for the insufficient amount of work they produced. This resulted in stricter rules in Edinburgh. In 1800 a few looms had been purchased so that inmates might be taught a trade. In order to force inmates into taking an interest they stressed that 'any women who left the loom without permission would be dismissed'.[83] Furthermore, idle inmates were always publicly reprimanded and rule violations were punished with solitary confinement.[84] For example, when Margaret Reid refused to do the laundry she was given '3 days solitary confinement to think it over'.[85] In addition to corporal punishment, the directors recognized the value of positive reinforcement and gave inmates material rewards for good work and moral behaviour. Special dinners and 'dishes of tea' were regarded as rewards for 'diligence',[86] and a few positions, such as messenger and door-porter were reserved for girls of merit. These tasks were to be viewed as a means of 'exciting a spirit of emulation amongst the rest, that they also may be put in places of trust'.[87] Finally, 'as a means of promoting emulation', inspirational tracts and books were awarded to the best scholars.[88]

The directors' strategies for reforming inmates frequently had to be altered to meet the financial needs of the institution. For example in the 1800s, when the treasurer's report was favourable, the Edinburgh directors responded to complaints about their high prices by lowering them. In 1843, however, a time of acute financial stress, they responded to another series of complaints about their high prices by developing an elaborate argument. They claimed that they could not reduce their prices without reducing the value of the labour of 'honest and industrious' females in the community, who from poverty would be forced into 'vice and crime'.[89] Although there is obviously truth to this argument, it was motivated by the institution's need to make a small profit and not an analysis of political economy.

Similarly, when the institution was in financial trouble they changed their views about the moral significance of profit-sharing. In 1833, for example, the Edinburgh Asylum was £650 in debt,[90] and the directors were faced with either reducing the inmates' stipends from one-quarter to one-sixth or abolishing them all together. After learning that the Glasgow asylum did not pay their inmates directly,[91] the Edinburgh directors abolished the girls' allowance and decided to give them some clothes when they left instead.[92] In the more affluent 1850s, the directors felt free to reinstate their profit-sharing system, but this time the highest paid inmates only received one-twelfth of the profits. The washers and kitchen maids only earned a sum equal to the average earnings of the best sewers, whereas the glazers could earn the average of the best sewers plus 25 per cent.[93] The directors had high hopes for their experiment, but with the free-enterprise system there were a number of unforeseen consequences. First, it did not increase the productivity as expected and it resulted in a decrease of the quality of the work because women rushed to get as much done as possible. Second, the girls became dissatisfied with tedious work which did not pay well. Third, the inmates refused to help one another. And fourth, it promoted 'individuality and made it difficult to arrange work tasks collectively'.[94] After two years the experiment was abandoned and replaced with a series of 'reward tickets'[95] which had no direct cash value.

In 1877, the Edinburgh asylum boasted that the 'long hours of work had been shortened' in order to give time for 'intellectual and moral training'. On closer examination, however, it turned out that the matron had found another money-making scheme. She converted the 'odds and ends of time . . . to good account' by getting inmates to knit stockings. In total they earned four guineas for the 150 pairs of stockings 'in time which might otherwise have been wasted, while their hands have been trained in work, which is essential to domestic economy and comfort'.[96]

By the middle of the century the managers discovered that laundry work was the most profitable and easily learned of the trades tried in the institution. It was, however, a problem in Edinburgh, where the institution was located in the centre of the city. The clothes were frequently damaged by the soot from the Gas-Light Company and had to be rewashed, which 'required double quantity of soap'. The patrons complained of stains being left in the clothes, and the matron was afraid to 'mention gas as the cause of it, as families might be disposed to withdraw their employment'.[97] On 14 August 1821 a whole greenfield of clothes was destroyed by the gas and the institution sued the Gas-Light Company for damages, while two girls worked around the clock scrubbing out stains with 'salts of lemons'.[98] Consequently, the laundry in Edinburgh never really got off the ground until 1864 when the asylum moved to the country.

In contrast Glasgow's laundry, which employed forty women by

1867, was a booming success. The directors boasted that their institution was

> not only a refuge to unfortunates, but what is of still more conse-
> quence, it is a training school for them in good conduct and
> in some homely branch of usefulness and of what many prove
> remunerative occupation.[99]

The popularity of laundries among rescue homes not only helped to cut the cost of an inmate's confinement. Laundry work served a symbolic function: through daily laundry work women performed a cleansing ritual.[100] They enacted 'penance for their past sins and purged themselves of their moral contagion'.[101] It is not surprising then, that in 1877 the directors of the Glasgow institution imbued laundry work with great moral significance. They regarded it as 'not only more healthful and more remunerative, but, in its moral tendencies, far superior to needlework . . . [which] is monotonous and less profitable'.[102]

Glasgow experienced a trade depression between 1877 and 1883[103] and the difficulties women faced finding employment together with the clamp-down on street soliciting resulting from the amended Police Act meant that many were driven to the institution to escape poverty and police harassment. The depression also decreased the amount of laundry work available by increasing competition between commercial laundries and other charities; the Magdalene was not the only charity that did laundry work. Nevertheless, throughout the 1870s and 1880s laundry work became an increasingly important part of the annual revenue of the institution. The directors boasted that it paid for two-thirds of the cost of maintaining the home, and also played an indispensable part in the training of girls for 'future usefulness'. Prior to 1886 work had been done by hand, but as a result of steam technology it became clear that modernization was necessary if they were going to compete with commercial enterprises. In order to finance this, the directors actively solicited funds. They claimed that at least £2,000 was needed to modernize the machinery and extend the plant. They explained:

> It would be no kindness to the inmates to give them the shelter
> of the Home for a given period, and to keep them in semi-idleness,
> the condition of idleness having been the bane of many of them

in the past. On the contrary, an endeavour is made to impress them with the dignity of labour, and to teach them self-respect and independence, thus raising them to a higher moral platform, to breathe a purer and nobler atmosphere.[104]

The loyal patrons responded and the money was raised within a year. The plant acquired a steam engine, a boiler, and washing and calendering machines. The directors were beginning to regard the laundry more and more as a competitive business and began to advertise in annual reports and charity pamphlets. In order to pass this entrepreneurial spirit on to the inmates and to entice them into taking a more active interest in the 'domestic and industrial' work, they introduced a system of profit-sharing. Premiums varying from one to seven shillings were allocated to girls according to merit, conduct, industry, and the class of promotion obtained. Thus, every inmate would be made to feel that the 'prosperity of the Homes, [was] her prosperity in which she ha[d] a direct personal interest'.[105] By 1909 the directors observed that a laundress had become a highly skilled occupation. 'Such great strides had been made in the laundry trade', since the

> time when it was thought that any female could wash and dress clothes. It has become a skilled industry that can only be success-fully pursued after a period of prolonged and careful training; and to bring such women as the inmates . . . up to this high standard is not an easy task.[106]

This remark was made the same year that the residence requirement was under review by less sympathetic board members. Since these magdalene homes opened, the two-year residence requirement had been a regular source of controversy. There were many who argued that they could reach more girls if residency was reduced to four months. But the goal of the majority of directors was to create an industrial labour force and many argued that keeping inmates for shorter periods would be too expensive because by the time an inmate was physically and technically capable of earning her keep, she was likely to leave the institution. Financial motives and the need to make profit out of the inmates' labour, therefore, lay behind the two-year residence requirement, which is another example of reform ideology being shaped by economic realities. In short, although the directors never ceased to espouse the claim that these were voluntary organizations, subtle incentives such as the premium scheme and the promise of material goods, which were reinforced by the activities of the Edinburgh and Glasgow police and magistrates, served to keep inmates in the homes until the directors were satisfied that they were morally reformed, and until they had produced a significant income for the institution. Economic necessity, therefore, reinforced ideology in the 'making of a sanctimonious sweatshop'.[107]

This analysis of the goals and objectives of the magdalene homes in Edinburgh and Glasgow tells us as much about nineteenth-century perceptions of women's roles in the home, at work, and in society as it does about the institutional practices themselves. The directors of these institutions never ceased to promote the virtues of domesticity for women and preferred to return inmates to their families and friends where they would continue to have a dependent status, or as domestic servants where they would be supervised in 'respectable' middle-class households. Their efforts to reform working-class women, however, collided with social reality in ways they had not anticipated. These institutions were subjected to social, political, economic, and internal pressures that prohibited them from becoming a 'rehabilitative utopia'.[108] By the middle of the century the increase in the demand for female labour in industry, plus inmates' preference for this work meant that the directors shifted their emphasis from training in domesticity to industrial labour. Similarly, behind the institutions' programmes of moral regulation lay the contradiction between the material reproduction of the institutions themselves and moral regulation of working-class women. The strategy the directors developed to resolve this contradiction was to attach a moral significance to certain kinds of work. The challenge then, was not simply a matter of re-socializing women for service or factory work, but a moral mission. The directors assigned a moral meaning to certain forms of female labour, thus through their programme of moral reform they not only created women fit for work, but work fit for women. As the century progressed, and more women resisted employment in the 'private' sphere as domestic servants, the directors were able to resolve their bias against placing women in the 'public' sphere. But, before they could make the fact that women worked in the 'public' sphere palatable to themselves and the middle-class patrons they had to convince themselves that these women had been properly socialized. Although the first goal of the magdalene home was training in domesticity, the increased emphasis on industrial training was rationalized as its second goal but it was equally important for the acquisition of appropriate working-class gender roles. In an attempt to assess the impact of the magdalene homes on the lives of inmates it is necessary to examine how they were placed when they left the institution.

PROLETARIANIZATION: THE IDEAL WORKING-CLASS WORKER AND WIFE

In order to ease the shock of transition upon leaving the institution, which the directors acknowledged was considerable, especially in the light of the problems many of the women had with alcohol, the directors established an informal parole system. The conditions of probation, which was supervised by representatives of the Ladies' Committees, were really only practical in cases where inmates found employment in domestic service, factories, and warehouses in the vicinity of the asylum. Inmates were expected to remain in employment and to keep in touch with the asylum for a full six months and were invited to come back to the home for advice or assistance in case of difficulty. Representatives of the Ladies' Committees made regular visits to girls in their new situations and paid bonuses to those who 'behaved' for at least six months. Clearly, then, there was at least a financial incentive for remaining in contact. A great deal of evidence suggests, however, that many former inmates returned to the institution for advice and assistance in times of need. Those who left their native communities wrote regularly to the institutions to inform the matrons of marriages, the birth of children, career success, general well-being, and of course to collect their bonus. The 'bonus', incidentally, was really just the balance of the money earned in the laundry or sewing room.

[Mary Douglas] called for the purpose of getting one of the Superintendents to go with her to purchase a dress and some other articles she wanted. Her mistress when paying her wages (£4), engaged her for the next half-year, and said she was quite sensible that she had done her utmost to please. This being the end of the first year since she left the House, she has saved £1, which entitles her to the premium given by the directors, and another £1 saved from her earnings while in the Home: making in all £3, which sum is now lodged for her in the savings bank.[109]

Table 5.1 Breakdown of satisfactory dispositions in the Glasgow Magdalene Institution and Edinburgh Magdalene Asylum, 1860–1890.*

	Glasgow		*Edinburgh*	
	N	%	N	%
Restored to family or friends	1022	51	222	23
Domestic service	696	35	687	72
Other employment†	271	14	47	5
	1989	100	956	100

Source Calculated from the Annual Reports of the Glasgow Magdalene Institution and the Edinburgh Magdalene Asylum.

Notes
*Data for 1882–3 missing for Glasgow; data for Edinburgh are for 1861–90.
†Includes those placed in public laundries, mills, warehouses, factories, and other employment.

Between 1860 and 1890 35 per cent of the Glasgow inmates who were placed to the directors' 'satisfaction' were employed in domestic service. During the same period the Edinburgh asylum placed 72 per cent in service (see table 5.1). Finnegan states that reformed 'prostitutes' were regarded as cheap labour and many had little to look forward to other than a life of loneliness and exploitation.[110] Given that their stay in the asylum was only temporary, and many of the inmates were difficult to place, the directors occasionally sent inmates to families who were not 'Christian philanthropists'. Considering the status position of a 'magdalene' and the fact that the Ladies' Committees were frequently popping in, an inmate's past could have been the source of gossip throughout the household, where she may have been regarded with suspicion and hostility and victimized by other members. In a letter to the matron in Glasgow a former inmate wrote:

> I was glad to hear that some of the girls got situations, which I trust will be good ones. . . . You say in your letter you hope I had a good cause for leaving my last place. I will explain to you someday the reason. I used to blame the girls for running away from their place. . . . God helped me, and I was restrained from doing wrong[111]

In a more extreme case Isobel Nesbit had to return to the Edinburgh asylum after only a few months in service because her master's son 'without laying to her charge and material fault kicked her to the door in a very unreasonable and brutal manner'.[112]

In addition to domestic service, however, they also returned inmates to their families or to friends whenever they were considered to be suitable. The Glasgow directors sent 51 per cent of its suitable placements back to their families, whereas the Edinburgh directors sent 23 per cent home (see table 5.1). They often assumed the position of unpaid servants or nurses in the homes of relatives. Household service and kinship obligations overlapped a great deal in the nineteenth century and it would not have been regarded as unusual to expect a young woman with no marriage prospect to spend her life looking after ageing relatives.

> Dear Miss Weir [Glasgow matron] . . . I was glad to hear that you are all doing well, and enjoying Christmas as usual. I have not much news as everything here is so dull. My aunt had been very ill, but she is better now. Remember me to all my friends[113]
>
> [Jess Ross] taken out of the house by a respectable cousin of her own in 1852, to attend his wife who was then in delicate health, and who subsequently died, [J.R.] conducted herself with so much propriety, and was so kind and attentive to his children, that he had since married her, and she is now making an excellent wife.[114]

In relation to the question of marriage, extracts in the matron's registers and letters to the institutions indicate that many former inmates married in the years following those spent in the homes. The Ladies' Committees regarded these marriages with some ambivalence. They were obviously uncertain of the suitability of 'fallen' women for marriage and possible motherhood. In one case, the Glasgow Ladies' Committee assured the subscribers that the man in question had 'been honestly dealth with . . . Nothing [was] concealed from him that he ought to know'.[115] On the whole, they accepted that inmates would marry and raise children, and they made no attempt to conceal it from the subscribers, but they preferred that intended marriages were properly contracted. In reference to the eight women who eloped in Edinburgh 'without warning' between 1866 and 1867, the Ladies' Committee remarked that 'when it is considered what the history and habits of the class are, an immediate acquiescence in the restraint of a life of usefulness and religious training is more than can in all cases be expected.[116]

It should be noted, however, that these elopements were triggered by an irregular set of circumstances. In 1866 a thorough painting of the asylum had been ordered, which required the 'necessity of the presence of numerous workmen'. It was then that 'symptoms of a desire to return to evil courses became visible'. During that period four inmates eloped, five were 'dismissed as incorrigible', and eight more eloped later in the year.[117]

In general, they suggested that after receiving the 'benefits' of the institution, former inmates made ideal wives for working-class men. The case of 'E.K' is typical of this attitude. The matron was 'pleased' to report that she

> lived comfortably with her husband, making a tidy wife and mother. She has frequently called at the Home since, and it is quite a pleasure to see how respectable she looks and how nicely she and her little son are dressed. Both herself and her husband are in full communion in the Church.[118]

As stated previously, these asylums were aware that not all inmates would make suitable domestic servants or candidates for the marriage market, so they included industrial training in their regime. In the process they promised to turn out a skilled and well disciplined industrial labour force. Of the total number of inmates who were found employment by the Glasgow institution, table 5.1 shows that 14 per cent who were 'satisfactorily' placed were found work in factories and mills, warehouses, and public laundries. In Edinburgh only 5 per cent were found other forms of employment. These 'success' stories clearly demonstrate what the directors had in mind for the inmates and the future of the working class.

> [Eliza Roberts] After remaining in the Home 15 months, and having been taught to operate on a sewing machine was sent out to a situation in a warehouse, where she earns about 12s per week. She attends Church regularly as well as a Sabbath evening class. Is residing with her parents, to whom she has been sent on leaving the Home. She puts a portion of her weekly savings in the savings bank.[119]
>
> My Dear Miss Weir, I have commenced to wash and iron for myself, and I am doing very well. Any young woman can get from 25 to 30 shillings a-week. I have not regretted coming to this colony [Australia] I would advise any young woman to come

out here; they would do so much better than at home. . . . There is nothing but white clothes worn in the summer.[120]

In order to ensure that newly released inmates were not reunited with unacceptable acquaintances, the directors arranged for some of them to emigrate to the colonies and North America, where they hoped that away from the corruption of the overcrowded cities, inmates would have the opportunity to live respectably. Emigration therefore replaced the transportation of convicts, undesirables, and surplus populations in the nineteenth century. In Ann McIntyre's case, the directors arranged her passage to a new life on a female convict ship which was headed for New South Wales via Van Diemen's Land.[121] Emigration was, however, only a limited option. In 1848, the Colonial Emigration Society informed the Edinburgh directors that they were hesitant to send many more girls to the colonies because they had received an 'abundance of applicants of unblemished character'.[122]

Finally, other inmates were placed in employment in Britain in 'respectable' homes far from their families. Without their own families it was hoped that inmates would continue to identify with their 'surrogate' family in the institution. This ensured that they were not exposed to contradictory value systems or tempted to return to their old ways. In the following case the writer was obviously aware of the contradiction and wanted to ensure that the matron realized that she was attempting to deal with it.

Dear Miss Nott . . . my father was down seeing me on the Fast-day. When they came and told me I was quite suprised to seen [sic] him. He told me that the way [sic] that he did not write he was out of town working, and he was wishing to come and see me. I am glad that he is not drinking any now. . . . The master and them all was quite suprised to hear that he had come to seen me. I thought that I would just write and let you know that I had seen him.[123]

The asylum's efforts to become a surrogate family, and in the process to break down traditional working-class values and support networks, is an example of what Jacques Donzelot describes as a 'familialist strategy'. In this context, Nancy Wood, following Donzelot, describes rescue work as an attempt to depoliticize poor working-class communities, at the same time that it effected an increasing insinuation of non-familialist agencies into the family nexus.[124]

Table 5.2 Disposition of inmates in the Glasgow Magdalene Institution and the Edinburgh Magdalene Asylum, 1860–90.*

	Glasgow		Edinburgh	
Disposition	N	%	N	%
Satisfactory†	1989	40	956	55
Diverted to other institutions‡	1192	24	120	7
Unsatisfactory**	1741	35	624	36
Died or sent abroad	49	1	31	2
	4971	100	1731	100

Source Calculated from the Annual Reports of the Glasgow Magdalene Institution and the Edinburgh Magdalene Asylum.

Notes
*Data for 1882–3 missing for Glasgow; data for Edinburgh are for 1861–90.
†Includes those who were restored to family and friends (Glasgow 21%, Edinburgh 13%) and placed in domestic service (Glasgow 5.5%, Edinburgh 2.7%)
‡Includes those who were sent to the House of Refuge or similar institutions, poorhouses, Lock hospitals, infirmaries, or insane asylums.
**Includes those discharged as intractable, disobedient or insubordinate, those who went off clandestinely or absconded, and those who left voluntarily.

ACTS OF RESISTANCE: DEFIANCE OF THE MORAL CODE

Despite the strict rules and regulations hundreds of women applied for admission to the asylums in the first decades of the nineteenth century. Statistics from table 5.2 indicate that of the 4,971 women admitted to the Glasgow Magdalene Institution between 1860 and 1890, 40 per cent were placed in situations more or less acceptable to the directors. The Edinburgh Magdalene Asylum had a slightly better success rate, where, of the 1,731 women admitted during the same period, 55 per cent were satisfactorily placed. These figures do not include the 'problem cases', which were diverted to other institutions, such as the hospital, insane asylum, and poorhouse. The Glasgow directors, for example, sent 24 per cent of their inmates to other institutions and Edinburgh sent 7 per cent (see table 5.2). Magdalene asylums attracted a large number of inmates who, although willing to work hard and accept the rules, were described as either mentally or physically incapable of contributing much to the institution or their own upkeep, and therefore very hard to place. Inmates such as Elizabeth Anderson, whose health was too bad for her to be sent to service, yet not bad enough for hospitalization, or Mary Danskin, in 'want of the proper uses of her faculties', or Jess Forbes, in the institution for three and a half years, who was 'weak in her intellect, but would suit a family where there was no great confusion of work', and many others, were burdens on the institution. The directors were often vexed about how they could get rid of them. They frequently sent inmates to households which were totally unsuitable[125] or paid relatives and friends small sums to take an inmate off their hands, or gave the woman a few shillings and sent her to the poorhouse. Pregnant inmates were also given a shilling or two and sent to the poorhouse and only invited to return after their confinement if they left their babies in the poorhouse.[126] Finally, there were a few cases, such as the following, who were chronically or terminally ill and were allowed to remain in the asylum until their deaths, because they simply had nowhere else to go.

> [Mary Campbell] had in all events, a very poor up-bringing, and when admitted she was extremely ignorant, of a rather unamiable temper, and made little response to the kindly treatment she met with. . . . After being ill sometime in the Home she was, by medical advice, sent to one of the city hospitals. She was there only about 10 days, when she asked to be allowed back to the Home. She was found by the van-man sitting resting by the road-side, for she was then very weak – and on being asked by him where she was going her reply was that she was 'gaun hame to Lochburn to die' . . . And so she continued in the Home . . . and if death-bed testimony of faith in Christ may be regarded as in any case hopeful or satisfactory – and who shall venture to reject it? – then we had that testimony from M. . . . She was enabled by faith to say – and she said it repeatedly – that the Lord Jesus was her only Saviour, and in that faith she died.[127]

Finally, out of the total number of inmates admitted to the institutions 35 per cent of those in Glasgow and 36 per cent of those in Edinburgh were the objects of the greatest concern to the directors (see table 5.2). These were the inmates who were recorded as having left the institution of their own accord or clandestinely, or who were dismissed as intractable and insubordinate. These statistics suggest that approximately one-third of the inmates chose not to accept the path of reform offered by the institutions. They left before they had completed the two years' residence and therefore did not receive a certification of character from the directors. The directors explained the large proportion of these cases by reminding subscribers that many had only been in the institution a few days. Further, they emphasized that every inmate was received on her own voluntary application and that the matrons, who had no power over them, did not attempt to detain anyone against her will. The directors maintained that past experience had proven that unless inmates had reached the state of 'true sorrow for sin' and a 'settled desire to amend had been reached', real reformation could not be expected.[128]

The high drop-out rate does not imply, however, that these institutions failed because the directors did not rescue enough inmates, or because they possessed a naive analysis of the causes of the problem. Nor does it imply that a large percentage of the inmates could not cope with or rebelled against irksome rules or that they were genuinely intractable, as Finnegan's study of the York penitentiary suggests. Indirect evidence suggests that rather than judging these inmates as 'failures', their refusals may be interpreted as acts of resistance to moral reform and surveillance. Resistance, in this case, may have meant the refusal to accept the magdalene institution's definition of the problem because not all inmates saw themselves as subjects of the discourse as 'magdalenes', 'fallen' women, or 'sinners'. Foucault describes this by suggesting that wherever there is power there is opposition and resistance or the operation of an alternative discourse or subculture with its own definitions and norms of behaviour.

Historians have argued that 'chastity' may not have had the same social meaning for working-class women, whose courtship and marriage customs differed from those of middle-class observers.[129] Many women who moved into occasional prostitution through economic necessity had previous sexual experience, and, similarly, the distinction between occasional sex with a lover and clandestine prostitution for money, food, or drinks may have remained fluid.[130] In regions where premarital sex and pregnancy and prostitution became common, working-class communities accepted them as normal.[131] Generalizations about subjective attitudes toward sexuality are always difficult to make, but in this case it is possible that these women would not have recognized themselves as subjects of the discourse, although they may have recognized that it applied to other women. The important point to keep in mind, then, is that moral reformers defined certain women as 'prostitutes' who would not have defined their own behaviour as prostitution, and who would not have perceived themselves as potential clients of the magdalene home.

To summarize, these asylums developed a variety of social-control strategies to encourage an inmate's moral reform. Techniques such as incarceration, the disruption of family ties, infantalization, moral education and industrial training, emigration, and diversion to other institutions where problem cases could be kept more or less permanently, were used to get inmates to conform to middle-class notions of feminine propriety. These activities reflect the notion that a 'fallen' woman could regain her character, but this required intensive resocialization and moral education. Through moral education and industrial training the directors attempted to create competent domestic servants. The social-control strategies were also designed to reform inmates' sexual behaviour. This entailed the socialization of inmates to conform to middle-class codes of class and gender. Reformers hoped that inmates would embrace middle-class values such as family, cleanliness, chastity, domesticity, and appropriate feminine gender roles.[132] Philanthropy, as Ignatieff points out, was not just an innocent pastime of a bourgeoisie with too much time on its hands, it was an act of authority that created a dependent relationship between rich and poor.[133] It was therefore a political act. As Walkowitz argues, the desire to protect working-class women was part of a larger programme to control their threatening sexual and vocational behaviour, and reflects a desire to impose a middle-class social code on working-class women.

Chapter six

Friendless, fallen, and inebriate women: the transformations

By the middle of the nineteenth century the idea of incarcerating women for sexual offences, either through formal channels which landed them in state prisons or through informal channels which led them to magdalene homes, could no longer be considered new. The general philosophy of early magdalene asylums in Scotland and England did not vary significantly from institution to institution, but by the middle of the century the reform strategies they used to achieve these ends began to shift. Critics of rescue work emerged and either developed new institutions and societies or struggled to gain control over older ones. They argued that rescue workers had to do more than merely provide refuges. They incorporated the penitentiary principle within their wider aims as they adopted a more aggressive style and missionary methods. New organizations carried rescue work beyond the provision of refuges for repenting women and career training. They extended their activities to seeking out and saving the 'fallen'.[1] Building on chapter four which examined the 'ideas' or discourses of Scottish moral reformers, the purpose of this chapter is to examine their 'activities'. The first section looks at contemporary criticisms of magdalene homes in general. The next section identifies some of the new institutions that opened in Scotland.

The attack on female penitentiaries began in 1840 with the publication of Tait's *Magdalenism*. Tait had recently become the secretary of the Edinburgh branch of the newly formed Society for the Protection of Young Females and the Prevention of Juvenile Prostitution, which the directors of the Edinburgh Magdalene Asylum regarded as too 'aggressive':

A kindred society has been lately formed in Edinburgh, and it may be thought by some that on that account the Magdalene Asylum will be unnecessary. The directors observe that the object and character of the 2 institutions are quite distinct. The new society . . . is aggressive in its character being designed to prevent the crime of prostitution, by adopting measures for pulling down those haunts of vice to which females are decoyed. The Magdalene Asylum is simply penitentiary in its character, being designed for reception, training and religious instruction.[2]

Tait attacked the administration of the asylum in Edinburgh for its complacent attitude, for its outdated punitive management practices, and for its location. He claimed that it looked more like a madhouse or prison than a refuge for the penitent, and its location in the centre of the city greatly inhibited its ability to perform its work since it was impossible to institute a full service laundry because the smoke from the surrounding factories contaminated the clothes. Similarly, the privacy of the yard was disturbed by the surrounding dwellings, which meant that the inmates could not work or walk in the yard without being watched by the neighbours. Tait claimed that before anything could be accomplished an asylum had to be located in the country with sufficient space for a laundry and a garden where the inmates would be removed from the temptations of the crowded town and have 'free exercise and employment in the open air'.[3]

Tait also objected to the administration's dependence on violent control measures such as head-shaving, solitary confinement and other forms of corporal punishment. He regarded head-shaving, which served no other purpose than repressing the desire to get out, as cruel; it put the institution on the same level as a prison.[4] Logan shared this criticism, stating that it had a 'bad effect on the mind of depraved females: self-respect is lost as a consequence'.[5] Tait was also very critical of the lengthy probationary period and solitary confinement. He saw no advantage in isolating new inmates from the other residents, as 'nothing depresse[d] the human spirit more than solitary confinement'.[6] Separating inmates was cruel, it threatened their love of society and friendship, and resulted in a high percentage of runaways. He urged the asylum to adopt the 'familialist' model developed in the London Penitentiary, which used positive reinforcement rather than shock treatment to encourage good behaviour. The best way to gain an inmate's confidence, he pointed out, was through flattery rather than force. Inmates should not be overly constrained and ought to be encouraged to make friends. Newcomers should be assigned a couple of older inmates to act as 'big sisters'. The value of this was that women with similar backgrounds and past troubles, who had been in the institution for a while, and had 'seen the error of their ways', would have a much more positive influence on a newcomer than the matron, superintendent, or Ladies' Committee.[7] The expediency of depending on peers to socialize newcomers to conform to the norms and expectations of the institution should not be overlooked, neither should its similarity to the boarding- or finishing-school systems, which had become an important part of middle-class girls' experience of femininity by the middle of the nineteenth century.[8]

As was seen in the preceding chapter Tait's suggestion had a minimal impact on the administration of the Edinburgh asylum, with the exception that it moved to a rural location in Dalry in 1864 and for a brief period in the 1870s, hired social workers to recruit more inmates. In 1874, Miss H. Kent was employed as a female missionary. In addition to her work on the streets she visited two poorhouses, the lock wards, the jail, and the maternity hospital.[9] In 1877 she was replaced by Miss Purves, who extended the duties to visiting 'poor fallen girls' in the brothels, picking them up in the streets, and waiting on them in the police cells.[10] Within a year she was so well known among the city's 'fallen' that she reported that of the twenty women brought before the police court in one day, only three were unknown to her.[11] In the final analysis, however, the Edinburgh asylum remained one of the most conservative of all the Scottish institutions throughout the nineteenth century.

In Glasgow, J.D. Bryce, a philanthropic merchant and the secretary of the magdalene division at the House of Refuge, which replaced the Magdalene Asylum in 1840, was more successful in his bid to shape the direction of the magdalene home. Circumstances in the Glasgow asylum had changed by 1840 as a result of the reformatory school movement. In 1837 a house of refuge for boys had opened to aid boys discharged from prison. It was seen as a preventative measure to divert boys who, from destitution or exposure, were at risk of becoming juvenile delinquents. By 1840 it had proved

105

itself to be so effective in reducing the cost expended on the prosecution of juveniles that the city established a similar house for girls. To minimize costs the magdalene asylum was renovated for that purpose.[12] In 1841 an Act of Parliament placed both institutions under one board of commissioners, provision being made for their common support by a tax on the city, (one penny in the pound on rents of £12 and above). The resulting institution was called the House of Refuge for Females; the 'Magdalene' as a separate institution ceased to exist,[13] and its name disappeared from the list of city charities until 1860.

The formal dissolution of the magdalene asylum does not mean that Glasgow's philanthropists terminated their crusade to reform the 'fallen'. The directors only agreed to the merger on the condition that room would be reserved for forty 'prostitutes', under the age of 25. The remaining 120 places were for children and adolescents who, after being charged or convicted of a crime, 'consented' to go there as an alternative to prison.[14] A few places were also allocated to destitute girls and orphans who were considered 'at risk' of falling into crime.[15] The Act, however, did not prevent the directors from continuing to admit suitable young women of their choice or rejecting referred cases if they regarded them as unsuitable.[16] The Magdalene Asylum and the House of Refuge were combined for twenty years, but by the late 1850s this arrangement was under attack. The introduction of the Youthful Offenders Act in 1854 was the last straw. Under the terms of the Act, the magistrates acquired the power to commit offenders under the age of 16 to the refuge without the consent of the offender or the consent of the directors. In addition, the Act made it imperative that every offender sentenced to the reformatory first complete a mandatory fourteen-day prison sentence. Once admitted to the refuge, the detention ranged from two to five years. According to Bryce and the other directors of the magdalene division the Act had many advantages for children, but it altered the character of the institution considerably.

They argued that the presence of juvenile offenders gave the institution a penal character. They maintained that there was a qualitative difference between a 'magdalene' and a 'criminal'.

[It] was offensive and irritating to the women, as it gave their department a penal aspect, quite opposed to its real character, for, notwithstanding the stigma of the name common to both, the two branches differed entirely.[17]

Bryce pointed out that in order to simplify the classification of inmates, rather than placing girls charged with sexual offences and public order crimes (vagrancy, disturbing the peace, or petty theft and vandalism) in the juvenile division, girls charged with both offences were placed in the magdalene division. In many cases this meant they were punished for their sexual behaviour rather than the crime for which they had been sentenced by the court. This outraged J.D. Bryce, who argued that 'magdalenes' should not be forced to associate with the 'criminal element'.[18] Bryce believed that a separate penitentiary should be established for 'prostitutes', as such, catering to women who were not yet associated with the other forms of deviance encountered in the House of Refuge.[19] Bryce's solution, which had been suggested by Wardlaw ten years earlier, was the establishment of the new Magdalene Institution which opened in 1860.

Bryce was one of the last moral reformers to be driven by an idealized image of 'fallen' women. He was not interested in reforming criminals or hard-core 'prostitutes', and argued that energy should be directed towards sexually promiscuous young women who needed only to be taught the conventional code of female propriety.[20] He believed that there was a 'better' class of 'prostitute' on the street whom the Magdalene Division, while it was connected with the House of Refuge, had been unable to reach.

> Of old there was much in the manner of admission to deter the best class from coming to the Home. There was the ordeal of an examination by the directors – hair was cut – and an obligation to remain for a period of two years was exacted.[21]

In order to attract the 'better' class, the institution had to sever its association with the House of Refuge because the newly 'fallen' and victims of seduction would be afraid to enter an institution with a penal character. The new institution was to have a new management style and a new target clientele. Like Tait, Bryce was also impressed with the familialist approach, which he had observed in John Blackmore's Moonlight Mission in London. Bryce advocated Blackmore's 'Family Home System', which would replace a large institution with a number of smaller private homes. This would facilitate the classification of inmates in a manner impossible in a single institution. The homes would operate as small family units, each headed by a 'kind motherly woman of humble position in life'. He also recommended that the two-year residence requirement be abolished because it inevitably led to discontent. Bryce intended that the young women regard residence in the home as a privilege, rather than an obligation. Finally, he wanted to abolish the institutional dress and the harsh discipline which characterized the old regime:

> The sameness of dress too, in public institutions, gives an aspect of crime or pauperism. The uniformity is perhaps more pleasing to the eye than the ordinary mixture of attire, but neither this, nor the unbroken silence of the work-room are natural. Why should not every inmate retain the individuality, and speak and act with freedom enjoyed in a well regulated family? Reading of an instructive and entertaining kind would both occupy and inform the mind, and liberty of conversation would promote cheerfulness. Nor should music be forgotten. Together with sacred melodies, moral songs of a cheerful character might be employed with advantage. They would not only enliven the work-room, but imprint useful lessons on the memory.[22]

As well as Tait and Bryce, Miller, Logan, and Wardlaw had also complained that the number of penitentiaries was totally inadequate to meet the needs of the community and they demanded an increase in institutions for penitent women throughout Scotland.[23] Wardlaw was particularly critical of the state of the reform movement in Scotland, but in contrast to Bryce's élitism, Wardlaw criticized the House of Refuge because it only benefited three categories of women: adult women under 25, adolescent offenders, and indigent girls considered at 'risk' of becoming 'prostitutes'. Wardlaw argued that provision should be made for females of all ages, especially those over 25. Although these reformers were critical of the administration of these existing institutions they had not lost faith in the reformative potential of 'voluntary' incarceration.

In addition to disputes over whom the penitentiaries should cater for, and over their internal management, there were also critics who doubted their value entirely. One critic argued that they 'crush unaided labour'. He observed that public institutions supported by state funds or charitable donations could afford to cut the prices of the work done by inmates. He noted that the House of Refuge washed and dressed plain shirts for two pence, whereas the usual price charged by washer-women who worked from their homes was three pence each. 'Girls who do not know where their dinner is to come from, call at some of our warehouses soliciting work, it is denied, because these warehouses send their work to the House of Refuge for Females'. Consequently, these institutions forced down the price of female labour.[24]

Owenite socialists were also critical of female penitentiaries. They regarded them as decidedly inefficient in arresting the 'monster evil' of prostitution. It was useless, they remarked, to bolster up at an enormous expense of time and labour these institutions, mis-named charities, which only prolonged suffering by 'palliating its extremities and industriously diverting the attention of the public from investigating the causes of evil'.[25] The socialist critique of prostitution was integrated into its criticism of middle-class paternalism. An 1841 article on 'British Female Penitentiaries' stated that 'if grave and virtuous' and 'repentant gentlemen snatch from the vortex of prostitution one sorrowing victim, their sons are ready on the other side, to thrust in fresh ones'. Socialism was the only refuge: 'It is in Socialism alone that the conditions are to be found of the annihilation of this atrocious – this master vice of civilized life'.[26] They argued that the 'prostitutes' who entered institutions simply made room for others to take their place. 'Of every five daughters born per annum, one will turn into a prostitute; we shall be loath to increase this foul system by the further multiplication of asylums'.[27]

Somerville also criticized female penitentiaries because girls became too dependent on them. Through his midnight meetings Somerville merely tried to draw them out of their old haunts, and to put them under the charge of respectable individuals. He argued that the moment a girl 'falls' an invisible wall arose between herself and the rest of society, and he hoped that his scheme would help to break down the wall by helping women become independent. The attraction of the midnight meeting plan was that girls never became dependent because there was no charitable allowance or institution. All they received from the 'congregational plan' was employment in sewing or factory work, and after work was secured, lodgings were found with respectable families. They would not even give the girl money to redeem her possessions from the pawnbroker.[28]

On the question of midnight meetings, Acton argued that of all the philanthropic practices, these were the most 'useless' of the private measures adopted for eliminating 'public wrongs'. He complained that these public exhibitions and appeals designed to excite feelings were incapable of producing durable impressions. He explained that what midnight meetings seldom achieved, the medical inspections and hospital detentions under the C. D. Acts, guaranteed: namely, permanent reform.[29] The editor of the *Magdalen's Friend*, the 'watch-dog' journal of the philanthropic movement, was not as critical of midnight meetings as he was of Somerville. The editor argued that Somerville and his congregation simply did not know what they were doing. He was particularly perturbed by Somerville's claim that a period of penitence in an asylum was not necessary to return a girl to respectable society. The editor stated: 'Let him not suppose that his work is done if he can only snatch a girl from the streets and place her in a position of honest industry.' Society was entitled to extract its 'pound of flesh'. He argued that penitentiaries could not be done away with and a period of probation was necessary because society was entitled to some retribution. Further, on sanitary grounds, 'we should view with suspicion the sudden and indiscriminate re-absorption of the unhealthy element into the social community'. Furthermore, 'society must not open wide her arms to receive back her prodigals unless they give genuine token of penitence'.

> The effect of such treatment would disorganize society . . . technically speaking, a great gulf is supposed to separate the criminal offender from the sound proportion of the community. . . . We should be sorry to remove this landmark, or to see it carelessly infringed by the exercise of an unbounded clemency. The object of punishment is two-fold: the reformation of the criminal and satisfaction of the injured party, then no punitive system can be considered complete which does not embrace these two-fold attributes.[30]

While Tait, Miller, Wardlaw, and Logan each demanded that private charities make provision for more magdalene institutions, Acton argued that they were totally ineffective. He stated that the trouble with female asylums was that the directors knew nothing of the natural history, habits, and career structure of prostitution.[31] The central error which lay at the heart of the penitentiary system was the old idea, 'once a harlot always a harlot', which implied that every woman who entered an asylum was a 'woman snatched from an otherwise interminable life of sin'. On the contrary, Acton argued that sooner or later most women tired of the trade and through the natural course of events – marriage or wage labour – were reabsorbed into the general population. It was society's responsibility to assist them while they were in the trade and not after they had left it.[32]

Acton objected to the practices of asylums for three reasons. First, they were too limited in scope. Upper- and lower-class 'prostitutes' never entered them. As stated Acton believed that 'prostitutes' only followed the trade for a couple of years and most of them were perfectly capable of 'rescuing' themselves. Penitentiaries only collected 'paupers' and individuals who, for reasons of ill health and loss of personal attractiveness, had given up prostitution. Acton argued that these cases would be better off in a workhouse.[33] Second, the institutions had a low success rate. Acton stated that most women entered the asylum 'under the influence of some momentary impulse, and [were] liable to return as suddenly as they left it'.[34] He argued that philanthropists merely offered lodging to a 'promiscuous herd of vicious women on the off chance that some few may really reform and succeed in breaking off old habits'. Finally, there was the problem of the two-year period of detention. Acton argued that the seclusion of inmates did little to prepare them for the trials of the real world. In fact, they became less capable of coping with pressures than they had been when they entered the institution. He questioned whether one should spend so much time and money on individuals who would either escape from the asylum at the first opportunity or who would relapse immediately upon release.[35]

Acton stated that prostitution would never be suppressed by private, irregular, and unsystematic efforts. What was needed was a combined effort and regular machinery. He argued that 'prostitutes' had to be helped while in the trade, and not after. His plan proceeded on the principle that satisfactory reformation could not be accomplished by sudden change from one mode of existence to another, therefore, a change of lifestyle had to be gradual. True reformation demanded bringing 'prostitutes' into contact with virtuous men and women, who would encourage them to acquire habits of cleanliness, decency, and self-respect. 'The [revelation] that their mode of life is a fatal mistake, will thus arise gradually in their minds; and if this growing conviction had for its companion the knowledge that a change is possible',[36] permanent reformation would result. He argued that this could not be accomplished by voluntary association, nor by disjointed efforts, but by a system supported and enforced by authority.

Thus, although criticism of the female penitentiary system ranged widely, with the exception of the Owenites, critics were united in the belief that some institutional apparatus, whether voluntary or statutory, was necessary for the moral regeneration of the 'prostitute'. The solution endorsed by the most influential parties was to extend the size and scope of the penitentiary movement. The result was an increase in the number of penitentiaries after 1840 throughout the country.

THE NEW INSTITUTIONS

The initial motivation behind the female penitentiary movement was to divert young women from the prisons and poorhouse systems which were believed to aid their corruption. The most general criticism of the resulting institutions, however, was of their penal character. By the middle of the century their liberal and reformist programmes, designed to save women from the criminal justice system, had actually resulted in the expansion of the entire system, which began to include more women of a greater age range and type of offence. In order to examine this process in more depth it is necessary to take a brief look at the shifts in the activities and goals of the older institution and to discuss some of the new institutions that opened in Scotland during the last half of the century.

The Edinburgh Magdalene Asylum was the least progressive of the older institutions. It remained under the patronage of Queen Victoria, and throughout the period representatives on the board of directors were drawn largely from the clergy.[37] In contrast, the management practices of many of the new institutions which opened throughout Scotland by the middle of the nineteenth century reflect a new trend in rescue work. Many of the directors of these new institutions were also members of the local branches of the National Association for the Promotion of Social Sciences (S.S.A.). Annual meetings of the S.S.A. were held throughout the United Kingdom and were regarded as events of national importance. Though many Conservatives took part, it was primarily a Liberal forum, whose meetings also attracted radicals and socialists like Robert Owen.[38] The belief that held these diverse groups together was that for every social problem there was an optimal ameliorating measure which could be discovered by scientific investigation and by patient discussion between all interested parties.[39]

Between 1857 and 1886 the S.S.A. was an active agent of social and moral reform in Britain. In 1862 *The Times* described it as an 'outdoor Parliament', in which 'every man is his own representative, in which women are enfranchised, in which small minorities may find a voice for their crochets, and in which unappreciated philosophers of both sexes may meet together to talk over the welfare of the world'.[40] Historians have pointed out that, on the whole, the S.S.A. lacked a clear concept of the social system, an analysis of structural interactions between individuals or classes, or a theory of the social basis of the state.[41] Its analyses of social problems, therefore, were atheoretical and fragmented. Those who gathered 'moral statistics' viewed society as an atomized collection of individuals and tended to see social problems as rooted in individual weakness, although they were willing to recognize that certain social situations could tempt and exacerbate underlying moral frailty. According to Walkowitz, one consequence was that investigators often assumed a contradictory stance towards their working-class subjects and even towards their explanations. While they felt entirely removed and alienated from the class of subjects under examination, they were shocked at the abuses of industrialization and urbanization; 'prostitutes' symbolized the social casualties of these developments.[42] This ambivalence is manifested in their analyses by a tension between moralizing and environmentalism. Bearing in mind these limitations, it should be noted that the exhaustive and detailed information collected by the S.S.A. members reflects their acceptance of the standards set by the emerging social sciences,[43] which was an approach considered progressive in its time.

Some Scottish organizations associated with the S.S.A. were the local branches of the Society for the Protection of Young Females and Prevention of Juvenile Prostitution in Glasgow and Edinburgh, local branches of the British Ladies' Society for Promoting the Reformation of Female Prisoners, (founded by Elizabeth Fry in

1835), and the Reformatory and Refuge Union. These organizations were responsible for a great deal of rescue work in Scotland and opened a number of non-statutory penitentiaries. The Edinburgh Rescue Shelter was opened in 1841 by the Scottish Ladies' Association for Promoting the Reformation of the Most Destitute of Their Own Sex. This was a local branch of the British Ladies' Society. Its goal was to seek out and reform women recommended by prisons, lock hospitals, houses of refuge, and magdalene asylums.[44] In Edinburgh, these women visited three workhouses, the Royal Infirmary, the Magdalene Asylum, and the jail. The Glasgow branch visited the Bridewell. The Greenock branch, called the Ladies of the Jail Committee, visited the hospital three times a week and taught women's Bible classes at the paper, cotton, wool, and flax mills. In the early 1840s the Ladies' Committee in Perth were trying to drum up support for a women's shelter.[45] Some other homes in Edinburgh were the Industrial Home (1856) for women who had been on the streets. The Falconer Rescue Home for 'fallen' women which opened in 1860 and the St Andrew's House of Mercy, admitted 'fallen' girls and discharged prisoners if they were also former 'prostitutes'.

Rescue work in Glasgow reflected the more aggressive trend. By 1864 the directors of the Magdalene Institution had denounced Bryce's experiment with the 'family home system' as a total failure. These directors, unlike the directors of the old Magdalene Asylum, who were largely drawn from the clergy, were merchants, bankers, industrialists, and various professionals, many of whom were also members of the local branch of the National Association of Social Sciences. It was their interest in the social sciences which led them to develop some of the most progressive methods in moral reform in the United Kingdom.[46] Through careful analysis of the statistics of the first three years they concluded that Bryce's plan to attract a better class of 'prostitute', whom he believed existed to cater to upper-class gentlemen, was a fantasy. The statistics revealed that the women who solicited admission to the homes were no different to those in the House of Refuge, whom they regarded as women of the 'lowest order'. Contrary to their expectation that among their ranks there would be found 'prostitutes' who would be averse to entering a penal institution like the House of Refuge, being 'accustomed, in earlier and better days to the comforts and elegances of a well-appointed family circle', the directors concluded that 'such a class [did] not exist'.[47] Since the applicants were the same as those admitted previously, they concluded that their goals would be accomplished more effectively by adopting the ' "regime" and discipline' used in large institutions. The careful selection of statistics convinced them that prostitution was caused by the individual's inability to cope. A careful balance between religion and work was all that was needed to teach these women the social skills they lacked, and this could best be accomplished in a well managed institution. Thus, the era of the 'cult of sentimentality' came to an end, and the 'cult of the individual' was ushered in. In 1864 the detached homes were replaced by a new asylum on rural land in Lochburn, where inmates would be placed under a course of 'mild discipline and continuous education'.[48]

As stated, new methods of rescue work involved more than the mere provision of a refuge for penitent women and career training. The new Glasgow Magdalene Institution was to be no exception. From its all-male board of directors it appointed a Repressive Committee, which was intended to be the most important branch of the institution. The Committee was responsible for establishing an 'enlightened' public sentiment on the question of public morality. A Reclamation Committee was also established, which was responsible for the daily activities in the institution, including the moral education and industrial training of inmates, as well as the placement of those who successfully completed their training in employment. Finally, a Ladies' Committee was depended upon as tutors, home visitors, and fund-raisers.

By the mid-nineteenth century homes for 'fallen' women were no longer the only form of female refuge. In Glasgow, for example, the Night Asylum for the Houseless opened the Female House of Industry in 1841 for women classified as 'in danger of going astray'.[49] The Home for Deserted Mothers was established in 1873 to take pressure off the Magdalene Institution, but it restricted admission to women who had become pregnant by their first sexual experience ('first time fallen').[50] The Young Women's Christian Association opened a home for working-class women in 1874, but restricted it to women who could provide certification of character. They also opened a lunch room to give women employed in factories a place to go during the meal hour. The Ladies were concerned that in most cases employees were forced to leave the workroom during the meal hours, and 'when there was not sufficient time to return home, the young women were obliged to walk the streets, whatever the inclemency of the weather'.[51]

Two charities for older women were the House of Shelter for Females established in 1850[52] and the Prison Gate Mission, established in 1878.[53] These last two refuges provided shelter for felons, problem drinkers, and the unemployed over the age of 25. Each of these non-statutory female penitentiaries supplemented rather than replaced the older state institutions: prisons, poorhouses, and the insane asylum, and each evolved its own body of 'experts' who established monopolistic claims over a select population of clients.

Rescue work in Aberdeen was largely under the control of representatives of the S.S.A. and the Aberdeen Branch of the British Ladies' Society for Promoting the Reformation of Female Prisoners. These groups opened a female penitentiary in 1842, but due to the lack of employment for women in the home and the general reluctance of Aberdonians to hire former inmates as servants the institution remained small. Local mill owners were eager to hire the girls, but the directors were hesitant to send them because they could not be guaranteed 'respectable people to live with and watch over them', and it was feared that the other workers would be a 'bad influence'.[54] In addition to the activities in the penitentiary Aberdonians also supported local branches of the Association for the Promotion of Social Purity, the Aberdeen Association for Reclaiming Fallen Females, and the Aberdeenshire Association of Ladies for the Rescue of Fallen Women.

Although Dundee was noted for its absence of any real prostitution problem, owing to the jute industry and its opportunities for the employment of women, it too had its homes for 'fallen' women. The Dundee Lodging House Association opened a home in 1848 to provide protection for women who would otherwise be forced to find shelter in the cheap lodging-houses, which were described as the resort of thieves and 'the most dissolute and abandoned of [the] population'. The managers claimed that young women were frequently seduced in these hostels. The Superintendent of Police, Donald Mackay, was particularly concerned about the young mill girls. 'Not a few of these unfortunate women – are now the most abandoned street pests – who, a few years ago, on coming to town, were comparatively respectable – trace their ruin to having become inmates of a common lodging-house'.[55] The same year the Institution for the Reformation of Females opened a home for 'friendless, fallen and inebriate' women between 18 and 35.[56] In 1877 the Dundee and District Female Rescue Home was opened to accommodate forty women under the age of 20 who were classified as 'fallen', or in danger of going astray. Finally, in 1900 the Dundee Salvation Army Home opened for women of any age who had been on the streets.[57]

Similar homes were also opened in Greenock, Paisley, and Perth. The Greenock House of Refuge for 'fallen' women and inebriates between 15 and 30 opened in 1853. The Greenock Discharged Prisoners' Home, opened in 1873, preferred women under 33 who were either discharged prisoners or who 'had gone astray'. The Paisley Female Refuge admitted women of any age who had been on the streets. The Perth House of the Good Shepherd opened in 1900 for girls between 14 and 20 who had been seduced, but who had never been on the street.[58]

In sum, by the middle of the century a new generation of reformers emerged with new ideas about the moral regulation of 'fallen' women. The institutional practices of the other female penitentiaries that opened in Scotland by the end of the nineteenth century indicate that rescue work became more interventionist than it had been at the beginning of the century, and a greater percentage of the female working class became potential targets for moral reform.

The moral reform activities in Scotland provide a unique opportunity to examine the process whereby local state representatives and philanthropists established apparatuses designed for the social control and moral reform of women who defied middle-class standards of sexual and vocational propriety. The nineteenth-century public discourse on the prostitution 'problem' maintained a distinction between a 'magdalene' and a 'criminal', at least in the early stages of their career. They argued that repressive punitive control was inadequate; they did not want to criminalize 'magdalenes' or to incarcerate them as a form of punishment. Rather, they wanted to 'save' them, hence justifying and supporting an institution or apparatus to catch women before they were 'hardened in vice'. Magdalene homes were intended to catch young women and channel them into the appropriate regime of moral education and industrial training, and to save them from the courts and prisons, and thus prevent them from becoming inmates of state institutions. As a consequence the system as a whole expanded, which meant that

more females of a greater age range were incarcerated than previously. New categories of women were drawn into the system,
which began to include many who had previously escaped the notice
of the authorities. In effect, by the late nineteenth century the
process became more interventionist than it had been at the beginning of the century and a greater percentage of the female working-
class population became potential clients. Instead of reducing the
amount of stigmatization, labelling, and the overcrowding of prisons
and poorhouses, intervention now came earlier, and was more intensive, because it swept in more forms of deviance, through extension
to those not yet formally adjudicated.

Female penitentiaries served two social control functions directly:
sexual control and vocational control. Their activities reflect the
notion that a 'fallen' woman could regain her character, but this
required intensive resocialization and moral education. Through
moral education and industrial training the magdalene institutions
attempted to create an industrial labour force and competent domestic servants which responded to the need for a pool of cheap
female labour. It is necessary, however, to go beyond a simple
economic explanation of their activities. The social control mechanisms were also designed for the reform of inmates' sexual behaviour.
This entailed the socialization of inmates to conform to the middle-
class codes of class and gender. In this case, reformers hoped that
inmates would embrace middle-class values. Magdalene homes and
the female penitentiary movement were not apolitical institutions,
but deliberate agencies for remaking working-class culture.

In order to assess the impact of moral regulation on subjected
clientele it is necessary to admit that no simple cause and effect
relationship can be established. It appears, however, that a percentage went on to lead lives that met with the Institution's criteria for
success: marrying, or remaining with relatives, or in domestic service. Others became temperate and industrious factory workers
and self-employed tradeswomen, while others resisted the bourgeois
moral code offered by the institution either by ignoring it, refusing to
enter, or leaving before the institution classified them as 'reformed'.
Although these agencies never ceased to espouse the claim that
women entered the homes 'voluntarily', by the end of the century
they became increasingly willing to use the police to enforce their
moral code.

Part three

The Glasgow system: police repression or veiled regulation?

In the later decades of the nineteenth century, as in the 1840s, Scottish cities continued to be regarded by the public as 'crying scandal[s] of poverty, bad housing and ill-health'. Between 1841 and 1911 Glasgow's population grew from 275,000 to 784,000: nearly a three-fold increase. Over the same period the populations of Edinburgh and Leith more than doubled, growing from 164,000 to 401,000. Aberdeen grew from 65,000 to 165,000 and Dundee from 60,000 to 165,000.[1] By the middle of the century a conviction arose among various local councils, magistrates, social reformers, and philanthropists of the necessity for the state to develop mechanisms for policing these large urban populations. The intervention of central government in this regard was not unprecedented, as evident in mid-century factory legislation, public health, and poor law and prison reforms. Although the liberties and freedoms of individuals and local authorities were still paramount, it was increasingly apparent that in some areas *laissez-faire* was not enough and that the government must be responsible for social reforms and thus set minimum standards for the whole country. This advance in legislative regulation had many implications for criminal law. It led to the emergence of a code of new offences, thus affecting both the content of the law and the structure of the courts and penal system. It implied that the state had a responsibility for crime prevention, law enforcement, and the treatment of offenders. And the whole system required a well regulated police force to carry out its aims.[2]

The activities of the newly expanded urban police forces are of particular interest. By the middle of the century voluntary philanthropic initiatives were criticized for their ineffectiveness and many looked to the law and the police as the new agents of social control.[3] As stated elsewhere, many social and moral reformers were moved to action to alleviate human suffering, which was a result of living conditions in the urban slum; but, the populations of these districts were also regarded as a threat. As one observer wrote, the urban poor contained within it 'the pauper class' who were 'dangerous to the country, in every sense of the term'.[4] The expanded police forces in industrial districts, which were a side-effect of both social change and ruptured class relations,[5] focused their attention on the surveillance of public drunkenness, prostitution, gambling, vagrancy, and other 'unrespectable' manifestations of urban working-class culture.[6]

The police force was to be responsible for containing street disorder and averting the danger from the 'uncontrolled and unsocialized classes'.[7] It represented a significant extension of the moral and political authority of the state.[8] The constables' role was to act as a 'domestic missionary', translating and mediating bourgeois values in working-class communities, which historians describe as a radical effort to remake working-class culture and to root out the traditional social and sexual habits of the poor.[9]

Disciplined and efficient police forces, however, were slow to assemble and reform, and they had many problems. In 1836 in Aberdeen, Superintendent Alexander attempted to bribe a witness with strong drink.[10] In the late 1840s, a quarter of the Edinburgh police force was dismissed annually for misconduct and 63 per cent were recorded as drunk on duty.[11] The situation in Glasgow was similar, where patrolmen were reprimanded for frequenting brothels.[12] But reforms were eventually made, and the older voluntary methods and individualistic charities established earlier in the century, which had never experienced much success, gave way to more interventionist methods. Charities such as magdalene homes and lock hospitals began to depend on the police to enforce their moral code.

Increasingly, local governments used their legal powers to isolate specific groups as targets for police intervention. For example, in the hub of activity and legislation around the subject of public health, venereal disease, contagion, and prostitution, 'it was women who were defined as the human agents of infection, threatening national health and security and challenging the social order by their active and autonomous sexuality'.[13] Thus, at the heart of coercive policing were the working-class women labelled as 'prostitutes', who symbolized wider anxieties about public order and the moral habits of the 'unrespectable' poor. One mission of the police was to segregate them from the 'respectable' working-class community.[14] Moral reformers demanded that the police be granted the authority to curb soliciting and brothel-keeping and other undesirable activities associated with prostitution. For example, Miller argued that the ineffectiveness of the police in dealing with 'prostitutes' actually bred more prostitution:

> the slackness of our civic rule in permitting prostitution, brazen-faced and open-handed, to prowl upon the streets for prey . . . the prostitute, though such by habit and repute, and seen in the act of ensnaring the silly one, is left undisturbed in her vocation.[15]

With few exceptions, however, new legislation[16] was piecemeal and only randomly enforced by local burghs.

From the contemporary accounts there is little doubt that Glasgow and Edinburgh had some of the worst prostitution problems in the United Kingdom:

> Let anyone walk certain streets of London, Glasgow, or Edinburgh, of a night, and, without troubling his head with statistics, his eyes and ears will tell him at once what a multitudinous amazonian army the devil keeps in constant field service, for advancing his own ends. The stones seem alive with lust, and the very atmosphere is tainted.[17]

While parts of England and Ireland moved in the direction of state regulation under the Contagious Diseases Acts to control their prostitution problems, great innovations were made in Glasgow. Glasgow developed its own system of police repression, which later became the model for similar systems in Edinburgh, Manchester, Leeds, and other cities and towns in the United Kingdom. The development of the 'Glasgow system' allows us to examine the process whereby segments of the bourgeoisie attempted to control prostitution in the city. The analysis and assessment of their initiative should not, however, be made solely in terms which the reformers themselves used. It is not enough simply to consider whether the Glasgow system did or did not reduce prostitution – or at least its visibility – or whether it succeeded in its other aims of reforming 'wayward' girls. It is also necessary to examine this episode in the wider context of the policing of working-class communities and especially how this policing of morals reproduced ideologies of class and gender. This was accomplished through the identification and treatment of one dangerous character, 'the prostitute', whose behaviour violated codes of both sexuality and vocation.

Chapter seven

Fighting the 'multitudinous amazonian army'

In the early nineteenth century Glasgow had many large brothels. The reputation of some, like the notorious 'Triple Decker' which occupied three storeys, spread even to London. Recalling the Glasgow of his youth, Chief Constable McCall revealed that the streets had been thronged with 'prostitutes'. During the day and early evening, they sat in the brothel windows, 'in a kind of semi-nude state, just to draw the attention of men passing along the street'.[1]

> It used to be quite a common thing on fine summer afternoons for the keepers of such houses to bring out a squad, as it were, of women who were living in the house with them and parade the principal streets dressed up in their best clothes, and making a circuit around and back to their houses, so as to let it be known where they were to be had.[2]

The surgeon at the lock hospital recalled that at night the brothels were brilliantly lit up, and sounds of 'riot were to be heard at all hours'. He added that soliciting was so impudent and indiscreet that in many parts of the city pedestrians were driven off the pavement and forced to walk in the middle of the road.[3] Most people regarded the presence of these women as a nuisance to be endured. Therefore, prior to 1870 the police seldom interfered with brothels unless sent to investigate a crime or theft said to have been committed by the inhabitants.[4] Legislation granting municipal authorities the power to suppress brothels and soliciting was included in the Police Act of 1843, which was amended in 1862 and again in 1866. The Acts, however, remained a 'dead letter' until McCall was made Chief Constable in 1870.[5]

The development of the system for the policing and control of street soliciting and brothels used in Glasgow after 1870 can be largely attributed to the initiative of the directors of the Glasgow Magdalene Institution. The purpose of this chapter is to examine the operation of the Glasgow system. It is argued that from among the competing mid-century discourses on prostitution one account and one remedy became hegemonic, that of the Glasgow system, with its particular emphasis on the 'magdalene'. Its development was due to the coalition of moral entrepreneurs – doctors, business-men, and senior police officials – who were in a position not merely to investigate, agitate, and speculate, but to see their ideas embodied in the interlocking apparatuses of the police, Lock Hospi-tal, and Magdalene Institution.

These institutional responses were regarded as encompassing 'repressive law, municipal vigilance, and organized benevolence'.[6] The Lock Hospital continued to be a non-statutory charity for indigent women with venereal disease who were considered to be 'prostitutes'. The Magdalene Institution also continued to be a charity. Its official policy was to reclaim women who had been 'led astray' from the 'paths of virtue', to 'dry up sources of prostitution', and to repress the growth of the 'Great Social Vice' in the city.[7] The final component of the system was the Glasgow Police Act (1866), which provided the municipal police and magistrates with extensive new powers to imprison or fine 'prostitutes' and brothel-keepers and to enter private property or any establishment sus-pected of harbouring 'prostitutes'.

THE GLASGOW POLICE ACT: 'REPRESSIVE LAW'

The sections of the 1866 Police Act[8] that dealt with brothels allowed a constable, upon the sworn testimony of a private citizen, to apply to the magistrate for a warrant allowing him to enter the establish-ment at any time of day or night for a thirty-day period, and to arrest the proprietor if residents inside were found to be in the 'act of prostitution'. If charged, the proprietor was either fined £10 or sentenced to sixty days in prison. For a second offence the house was closed and the brothel-keeper faced sixty days in prison. This was more serious than a fine, which was no deterrent to the wealthy. This legislation, which was designed with women in mind because brothel-keeping was regarded primarily as a female profession, was meant to force them out of the trade by making it unprofitable.

McCall claimed that the threat of prison was 'rather a frightening thing for women of that sort'.[9]

The Act[10] was also directed at women on the streets. With regard to soliciting and street disorder it stated that 'every prostitute, or nightwalker loitering in any road or street, court, or common stair, or importuning passengers for the purpose of prostitution shall be liable to a fine of forty shillings or fourteen days imprisonment'.[11] This legislation did not require that a private citizen first file a complaint against a woman; the testimony of a constable before a magistrate was all that was necessary for conviction.[12] As indicated in chapter four, the only 'test of a prostitute' was that she was 'known to be going about the streets by the police, following no other occupation, and earning her livelihood in that way'.[13] The problem with this 'test' was that it could be applied to any woman, including the unemployed or a casual labourer found in the streets who could not give a satisfactory account of how she earned her living. The Chief Constable admitted that this legislation could be oppressive, but he dismissed the possibility of mistaken identity by claiming that there was no difficulty in finding out whether a woman was a 'prostitute'. He had a great deal of faith in his constables' ability to use their discretion and was satisfied that the constables who testified against a woman had known 'her for months, or for years, and ha[d] seen her out at all hours of the night apparently doing nothing to earn a livelihood'. 'You may well know a prostitute as you would know as sweep', the Chief Constable explained: 'a man with a black face may not be a sweep, but at the same time you would say he was a sweep.'[14] The strict enforcement of this legislation was meant to force these women either to find 'respectable' employment if they could, or to drive them out of the city or into the Magdalene Institution.

The effective administration of the Police Act depended on both repression and reform. The repressive measures involved the suppression of brothels and soliciting. This was accomplished through the intensive policing of working-class neighbourhoods where these activities were believed to exist. The authorities, however, did not stop with the suppression of prostitution *per se*. They were also concerned with reforming the women who were directly and indirectly affected by the Police Act, and to this end the Lock Hospital and Magdalene Institution eagerly assisted the police. The Lock Hospital performed the curative function and the Magdalene

Institution played the reformatory role and they depended on each other for the exchange of inmates. Before a woman was admitted to the Magdalene Institution she was expected to submit to a medical examination by the Institution's surgeon. If found to have venereal disease, she was sent to the Lock Hospital to be cured. Following this she returned to the Magdalene Institution for moral rehabilitation. The directors of the Lock Hospital were anxious to send 'cured' women to the Magdalene Institution, where they would receive moral and industrial education and therefore cease to be a burden on public charities or the state.

THE GLASGOW LOCK HOSPITAL: 'MUNICIPAL VIGILANCE'

Although the Lock Hospital had no legal power to detain patients against their will, it had the character of a reformatory or prison.[15] In 1870, the year the Police Act was first enforced, it adopted the policy that the hospital should have the right to detain all patients until cured. Patients were forced to sign a contract promising to abide by the hospital's rules and to remain until formally discharged by the surgeon. After a year the experiment in compulsory detention was abandoned because the women became frightened and refused to enter the hospital.[16] Subsequently, the directors discovered that the problem of early dismissals could be more easily solved by threatening not to readmit patients who demanded early release.[17] Moreover, after the enforcement of the Glasgow Police Act, the directors reported that it had become difficult to get the women to leave the hospital.[18] Between 1871 and 1881, only three women were discharged early: this was not because they demanded to leave but because they were dismissed for fighting. The apparent success of the Police Act, however, did not prevent the hospital from attempting to strengthen its ties with the police. In 1872 they presented a motion to the magistrates requesting that 'diseased prostitutes sent to prison for offences against the Police Act' be transferred to the hospital in cases where the wardens were satisfied that 'a prostitute prisoner against whom 14 days or any shorter term . . . has been awarded expresses her willingness to become an inmate of the Lock hospital during the term of imprisonment . . . that her sentence should be restricted and should be allowed to do so'.[19]

Alexander Patterson, surgeon at the hospital and vigilant supporter of the Glasgow system, attributed the hospital's success rate to more than just efficient police work by indicating the humane treatment patients received while in the hospital. Unlike many of his contemporaries, Patterson refused to allow medical students to use the hospital as a laboratory to observe venereal diseases because he found that women refused to enter the examination room if he was accompanied by strangers or groups of medical students. Contrary to popular opinion, he believed that 'prostitutes' never totally lost their sense of shame, and he argued that the compulsory examination of women under the C.D. Acts destroyed the last remnants of their modesty. Patterson claimed that the 'voluntary' system of care and cure used in Glasgow was morally superior to that provided by the C.D. Acts in so far as it rendered moral reclamation 'possible'.[20]

Patterson observed that lock patients avoided the label 'prostitute' for as long as possible; only one in ten women admitted to the hospital gave it as her occupation. He regarded this as a healthy sign because it meant they were 'ashamed of the calling': as long as a woman refused to recognize herself as a 'prostitute' there was hope of reforming her.[21] He appears to have overlooked the possibility that these women simply did not regard themselves as 'prostitutes' or their activities as prostitution. Furthermore, he believed that their chances of reformation decreased with age. Between 1870 and 1880 the average age of the patients was 18, the eldest being 22. There were nine 'school girls' between 7 and 14. The surgeon reported that the 7 year-old had 'contracted the disease herself'.[22] When possible, the hospital placed younger women in wards apart from the older, more 'hardened prostitutes' and provided religious instruction in an effort to reclaim them.[23]

After a woman 'voluntarily' entered the Lock Hospital she was examined with a vaginal speculum. This was similar to the way women were examined in areas where the C.D. Acts were enforced. In both cases this procedure was compulsory, although this was denied in Glasgow. The Lock Hospital did not admit women who would not submit to the examination, which Patterson admitted was a physically 'painful process', especially for young women who were 'newly fallen'. At times chloroform was necessary to make it endurable.[24] The surgeon maintained that it was impossible to do a proper scientific examination without using a speculum, although he admitted that he would not use it on a 'virgin', on the rare occasion that one entered the hospital.[25]

The cultural significance of the speculum and controversy around its use to inspect the cervix cannot be over-emphasized. The vaginal speculum was first developed in Paris to inspect 'prostitutes' in the state-run lock hospitals. When it was introduced to the British medical profession in the 1850s as a general gynaecological tool, many doctors revolted, reminding its proponents of its sordid origins. They stated that it would be better for British women if it were confined to those 'prostitutes' who had been institutionalized.[26] Speculum examinations were only recommended for 'prostitutes' and were considered a shocking 'immorality' when imposed on 'virtuous' women: 'the female who has been subjected to such treatment is not the same person in delicacy and purity that she was before'. The uterus, 'the heart of the female reproductive mysteries', had been violated. Medical journals reported cases of women whose minds had been 'poisoned by the experience' and many regarded the speculum examination as voyeuristic and degrading. It was regarded as 'instrumental rape' with a 'steel penis' by anti-C.D. Acts activists.[27] It is important, therefore, to bear in mind that the distinction between compulsory examinations under the C.D. Acts and supposed 'voluntary' examinations under the Glasgow system carried a great deal of cultural currency. This raises two points: first, neither the Lock Hospital nor the Magdalene Institution accepted women who refused to submit to this examination, and Patterson stated that 'prostitutes in Glasgow had nowhere else to go'.[28] Second, the majority of these women claimed that they were not 'prostitutes' even though they had no reason to conceal it.

Between 1870 and 1881 Glasgow's population rose from approximately 550,000 to 700,000, while the number of admissions to the Lock Hospital fell gradually from 598 in 1869 (the highest number of admissions in its history) to 349 in 1881.[29] The physicians attributed this 'remarkable feature' to the rigid enforcement of the Police Act. Patterson testified to the Select Committee that the year 1870 was the dividing line, because the Act led to a decrease in the number of brothels and 'prostitutes' and, therefore, of the amount of extra- and premarital sexual intercourse among the general population. This resulted in an overall decrease in the amount of venereal disease in the city. However, that the decrease in admissions to the hospital also coincided with a general recognition by the British medical community that venereal diseases were no longer as severe as they had been is evidenced by a decrease in deaths from syphilis and the length of stay in the hospital.[30] Although Patterson attributed this to the fact that women entered the hospital earlier because of the friendly and competent treatment they received there, he also acknowledged the influence of extraneous variables such as the decrease in the severity of the disease among men as well as women, and the general health and sanitary improvements in the city which had reduced the severity of other contagious diseases as well.

Patterson's impressions were based on over thirty years of familiarity with Glasgow street life. He affirmed without the slightest hesitation that the conditions had improved after the Police Act was enforced in 1870. He regarded police repression as the best means of diminishing sexual vice and disease and concluded that the success of the Glasgow system proved that legislation such as the C.D. Acts was unnecessary. A voluntary lock hospital, with abundant accommodation for the classification of patients, 'well-baited with every comfort and necessary appliance', was all that was necessary to induce women to stay in the hospital until cured. It was the opinion of supporters of the Glasgow system like himself that a voluntary system of care and cure was morally superior to the compulsory systems or state regulation like the C.D. Acts.[31]

Patterson argued that compulsory detention was not necessary in Glasgow because women knew that they would be admitted to the hospital without any difficulty. This spread by word of mouth throughout the city. Although he was not prepared to claim that all 'prostitutes' with venereal diseases came to the hospital, he believed that sooner or later most found their way there. He stated that the hospital had no trouble keeping patients until 'cured' since the Police Act had been introduced in 1870; in fact, he claimed that 'as a rule, we can get them to remain as long as we please'.[32] In the case of 'avowed prostitutes' some would 'stay all of their days with us, in fact they had to be sent away' (these were women between 18 and 22, remember). This was attributed to the extremity of their need and general poverty since 'they were more comfortable than they were at home'.[33] In sum, Patterson believed that the 'voluntary' system used in Glasgow was superior to the state regulation under the C.D. Acts, which destroyed the 'last remnant of modesty' and the last hope of reclaiming the women.[34] On the question of whether or not the C.D. Acts should be extended to Glasgow, he stated that 'they would not have it'.[35] 'People [are] too strongly opposed to any recognition of vice'.[36]

THE NEW MAGDALENE INSTITUTION: 'ORGANIZED BENEVOLENCE'

The development of the Glasgow system can, in part, be attributed to the directors of the new Glasgow Magdalene Institution's Repressive Committee, which began operating in 1860. As stated in chapter six, the new institution was founded by a group of Glasgow merchants, bankers, industrialists, and various professionals, many of whom were speakers at the Social Sciences Association's national conferences, which were held in Glasgow in 1860 and 1874. The goals of the new institution were not limited to the reformation of 'fallen' women, as is evidenced by the fact that the Repressive Committee was regarded as the most important branch of the institution. Between 1860 and 1890 its activities included lobbies for amendments to, and the strict enforcement of the Police Act, rallies against the C.D. Acts, campaigns against nude models in Scottish art schools, and the banning of the 'demoralizing' influences of working class theatres, public exhibitions, and, most notably, the Glasgow Fair.

The first victory in the Repressive Committee's battle against 'social evil' was its campaign to close Parry's Theatre. They described it as the 'lowest place in Glasgow'. For many years it had been regarded as a breeding ground of prostitution and crime and the 'hotbed' of obscenity. The theatre opened for three shows nightly, and a fourth on Saturday. It was capable of holding 700 people, and the audiences were generally composed of youths between 10 and 20 years of age. The extent of its 'evil influences' was said to be enormous. The Magdalene Institution admitted more than one girl who reported to have been first 'led astray' in Parry's Theatre.[37] In 1860 the Repressive Committee succeeded in having the theatre closed down. Actually, John Henderson, one of the Board of Directors, simply bought it and converted it into a place for Sunday prayer services and the 'innocent and useful recreation [of] the working classes'.[38] The practice of purchasing or leasing property containing offending establishments was a fairly common method of social reform in cases where magistrates were slow or hesitant to act.[39]

The Repressive Committee next turned its attention to another 'immorality' in the same neighbourhood: the Glasgow Fair. This was the annual 'saturnalia' held on Glasgow Green; the park at the foot of Saltmarket Street. The history of the Fair dated back to the twelfth century. Instituted by William the Lion, it was an annual event where merchants from the surrounding countryside sold their wares. By the nineteenth century, however, the Fair was mainly a social event which attracted travelling shows, circuses, and 'freak' and side shows from all over Europe.[40] It had five acting theatres, nine exhibitions, six peepshows, and two waxworks. Historians claim that by the 1860s the upper working class had become increasingly able to leave the city for its annual holiday, and the Fair became more stridently frequented by the 'lower' working class. The Glasgow roads to ruin at that time were summed up as 'dress, drink, and the Glasgow Fair'.[41]

The Repressive Committee argued that the Fair holiday had become a 'prolific source of evil', especially to young women. In 1859, for example, the Magdalene admitted four girls who attributed their 'fall' to these 'seasons of riot and debauchery'.[42] Eighteen months after the Institution opened the Repressive Committee began submitting regular petitions to have the Fair abolished. It claimed that the Fair had out-lived its usefulness and that the entertainment was demoralizing.[43] It was associated with 'crime and vice' and it attracted hundreds of 'prostitutes', who supplemented the notorious part-time 'prostitutes' who 'pl[ied] their horrible trade only at certain times'. And, finally, during the Fair the number of brothels in the neighbourhood multiplied, as did cases of seduction.[44] The Town Council, however, was reluctant to close the Fair down because it welcomed the revenue the entertainers paid for leasing the property.

As it became more and more evident that the Repressive Committee would be unable to sway the magistrates, they became more eager to take the law into their own hands. In 1863 they instigated an independent fact-finding mission in order to provide empirical grounds on which to demand a formal inquiry into the Fair's future. The Committee conducted a survey of the neighbourhoods in question. From street corners, doorways, and windows 'spies' from the Committee, who travelled in twos for protection, recorded the activities of brothels, singing saloons, penny-reels, and lodging-houses.[46] The Committee was extremely disturbed by what they observed at the exhibitions. Singing saloons and penny-reels, which were cheap dance halls, were reported to be the greatest sources of 'social evil'. Two reporters recorded their visit to the saloons as follows:

> We visited the Jupiter and Shakespeare Saloons. In the Jupiter there is a cellar where Penny-Reels are held, but it had such a forbidding appearance that we deemed it expedient to venture down to see them. . . . The performers were of the lowest class, and profane oaths were frequent. We also visited the Shakespeare, and think this the most dangerous because the most fascinating. We heard some comic songs which had a very immoral tendency being double entendre. . . . At 10.30 the place was half filled with persons of dissolute habits, chiefly prostitutes, with a sprinkling of young men.[47]

As for penny-reels:

> On July 16th, I found in close No. 46 Saltmarket, a place for Penny-Reels, filled with 30 women, chiefly bad girls, 10 boys about 16 years of age, and a blind fiddler. In No. 68 Saltmarket, I found in a Penny-Reel place 34 women, a few men, and two women with children in their arms. In No. 78 I found two Penny-Reel places, and in them about 50 young girls, 10 known prostitutes and a number of men. . . . It is reported that in connection with those Penny-Reels, are houses of accommodation let out by the half hour . . . for immoral purposes during the Fair.[48]

The performances at the other exhibitions were without exception reported to 'deprave the tastes and impair the moral feelings' of all who attended them. Audiences consisted of 'loose' women, mill-girls, boys, the 'lowest' of working people, and 'the occasional respectably attired person'. The following are accounts of the behaviours at the exhibits which the Committee found most objectionable.

> 7th July – Noticed a most unseemly exhibition outside on the stage of Brown's Royal Hiberian, a man dressed as a young woman, going through immoral antics – lifting her skirts, exposing what seemed bare legs: again as a young lady of fashion, with large crinoline; this scene was immoral in the extreme – some respectable people turned away from the sight, limbs exposed in

every variety of attitude, crinoline raised as high as the waist, altogether it was horrible.[49]

15th July – ... we saw a woman dancing upon a tight rope which ought not to have been allowed, as her person was exposed at times in a most unseemly manner; the audience was chiefly composed of boys and girls. We also saw three male performers acting immodestly toward three mill-girls whilst they were sitting together in a corner of the show.[50]

Tuesday, July 11 – ... saw at the 'Cirque Unique' a prostitute acting on the stage in the garb of a highlander. ... Saw a man dressed as a woman acting on the outer stage, and going through a very indecent performance. ... [I] was frequently solicited by women. It is scarcely possible to walk through Saltmarket without being laid hold of. Spoke to a policeman and he said that the number of prostitutes was greatly increased of late, and added that if something were not done soon to repress them, it would be dangerous to walk the streets at a late hour. At midnight, Saltmarket was ferment with prostitutes and thieves; their language was shocking. The police seemed to have little power over them. Left the survey in utter disgust.[51]

At the end of the three-week period their data was collated, and the observations of these gentlemen of 'undoubted character and integrity' yielded only one conclusion: that 'Glasgow Green at Fair time [was] just one huge brothel'. They noted that the area around the Green contained 119 brothels. During Fair week a district which normally housed 1,070 families contained forty-three public houses and forty-seven brothels; in other words, one public-house for every twenty-five people and a brothel for every twenty-three families.[52]

The motivation behind keeping careful track of the street names and addresses of the brothels was to publish the names in the local newspaper and to inform the landlords of what was being done with their property. In many cases the owners knew perfectly well the purpose for which the property was leased. In fact, brothel-keepers were reputed to be preferable tenants to 'respectable' working people because they paid their rent in advance and could be charged more. At one point the wife of a Government official in Glasgow let several furnished houses for 'second-class' brothels, and visited them personally to collect the rent. Another citizen who had been 'knighted for his public service and was highly regarded for his philanthropy' kept brothels and shebeens (unlicenced drinking establishments) all over the city.[53]

The Committee's report recommended that the city pay close attention to the very large number of girls and young women who worked as 'prostitutes' while employed part-time as mill-girls. They stated that the number of women working as seasonal and clandestine 'prostitutes' was exceedingly large, and filled the gaps created by those afflicted with venereal disease among the regular population. In addition they directed attention to the overall low moral state prevalent among working-class women and girls. They argued that when the moral tone of females was so low, it was logical that the morality of the males would follow. In order to elevate the moral tone of working-class females, they prescribed education and moral training; repressive measures alone, they argued, would be inadequate.[54]

As for the future of the Fair, the Committee did not succeed in swaying the Town Council until 1866, when licences for booths were restricted to the ground outside the railing of the Green. The Committee still insisted, however, that the Fair be abolished as a general holiday. They suggested that it would be far more 'rational, moral, and pleasure-giving' if employers arranged their employees' holidays at different times of the year.[55] In 1870, the Town Council discontinued the licences for the shows' altogether. This was heralded as a victory in the Committee's crusade to suppress the 'sources of evil'. They stated, hypocritically, that they had no desire to see the holidays of the working classes abridged, or their 'innocent amusements and recreations lessened'. In the end Glasgow Green ceased to be used for the Fair altogether, and what remained of it was moved to Vinegar Hill.[56]

By the 1870s the Magdalene Institution was running with great self-confidence and zeal. On 20 December 1869 the Committee marched into the Magistrates' Committee General Meeting and demanded that attention be paid to the 'great and growing' prevalence of solicitation and loitering by 'prostitutes' in the streets. After the directors left the meeting the matter was discussed, and it was resolved that the terms of the deputation would be 'met as far as practicable by a more stringent enforcement of the provisions of the Police Act'.[57] Four days later, Chief Constable Miller received notice from the magistrates directing him to 'put the law in force strictly in this respect and bring all offenders before the magistrates that the streets and thoroughfares may be kept clean'. The Chief Constable sent copies of this notice to all of his superintendents,[58] and McCall, who replaced Miller as Chief Constable some months later, ensured that these orders were carried out, and the Glasgow system was born. The fact that the orders of the Repressive Committee were responded to so promptly gives a clear indication of the influence this body possessed.

For the Magdalene Institution, the immediate result of the repressive policing of working-class neighbourhoods was a flood of applications from women who were harassed or forced off the streets by the police. In 1870 they had to increase the number of beds in the house at Lochburn to 120 and leased two flats on Renfrew Street to accommodate another twenty 'probationary' cases. In 1873, the adjoining flat was leased, which provided five additional places, plus a more convenient work-room.[59] In 1874 the Probationary home took over a 700-yard lot and a four-storey tenement on Stirling Road. The new location provided accommodation for another forty inmates. This rapid expansion was necessary to meet the increased demand for admission 'owing to the enforcement of the Police Act against soliciting and streetwalking'.[60]

The pressure on the institution was compounded by a spin-off from the wave of religious revivalism that hit Glasgow in the early 1870s. It was spearheaded by the renowned evangelists Moody and Sankey and other vigorous crusaders who campaigned to suppress vice and reform the 'fallen'. On two occasions in 1874 the Magdalene Institution was invaded in the middle of the night by hoards of 'fallen' women coming from a midnight revival meeting. Throughout that year the Magdalene was so pressed for space that it appealed to the public not to make any 'extraordinary efforts to reach the fallen, until some means [had] been taken to enlarge the probationary home'.[61]

During the 1870s and 1880s the Magdalene Institution continued to be filled to capacity. By 1875 it was dealing with 400 cases annually. In 1878, the directors revealed that after nineteen years of operation over 3,000 young women had been restored to lives of 'respectability'. By 1884, this figure exceeded 4,000,[62] and in 1905 they reported that 7,540 inmates had been received, although they did not go so far as to claim to have reclaimed them all.[63]

135

In conclusion, by 1870 a coalition of influential moral reformers was formed. This group dominated the discourse and succeeded in marginalizing other contenders. Through their control over key repressive, regulatory, and ideological apparatuses such as the police, Magdalene Institution, and Lock Hospital, their ideas were reproduced in the operation of the Glasgow system for the repression of prostitution. The Glasgow system did not stop with the suppression of prostitution *per se*. Reformers were also concerned with reforming the women who were directly and indirectly affected, and to this end the Lock Hospital and Magdalene Institution were depended upon.

Chapter eight

Police repression or veiled regulation?

It is possible to identify three approaches for controlling prostitution in the nineteenth century: *laissez-faire*, state regulation, and police repression. For the first half of the century the police appear to have been 'reluctant agents of moral reform'.[1] They adopted the *laissez-faire* approach to controlling prostitution and seldom interfered with brothels unless the inhabitants committed crimes or disturbed the peace. They also endeavoured to keep 'prostitutes' from making too great a nuisance of themselves by controlling street disorders and public drunkenness. Their actual effectiveness, however, is difficult to judge. For example in 1839 the Aberdeen police lacked the authority to respond to complaints about the 'indecent and blasphemous language used by the large numbers of profligate and dissolute females' who congregated in the Castle Street area, except by forcing them to 'move on', which was ineffective because they returned once the patrol had left.[2] In 1857 the police estimated that about 400 'prostitutes' and many brothels were in Aberdeen, but they were handicapped by the lack of statutory power to deal adequately with complaints.[3] Similarly, in 1849 the Glasgow police conducted a survey of brothels which revealed that there were 211, housing 538 'prostitutes'. The number found walking the streets was 500, but the police lacked the authority to put this information to use other than by making it available to philanthropists. By the middle of the century, *laissez-faire* policing came under attack and local state authorities were forced to respond to mounting public pressure which demanded that the police and magistrates be granted the authority to close brothels, suppress soliciting, and maintain order in the streets.

There is little historical evidence to indicate that prostitution or venereal disease was actually increasing, or why they became 'social problems' in the way they did, although historians agree that by the late nineteenth century factions of the bourgeoisie found them increasingly offensive and *laissez-faire* was denounced as ineffective in controlling the problem. For some the remedy lay in state regulation under the C.D. Acts. Others argued that state regulation 'cause[ed] the destruction of the moral fibre of the nation' by removing individual responsibility for behaviour.[4] Opponents of state regulation argued that the state should have the civic power 'to "repress" prostitution, not to "regulate" it'.[5] For some the best solution was the system of police repression adopted in Glasgow. They promoted it as a compromise between the *laissez-faire* and state regulation and argued that, unlike the C.D. Acts, the Glasgow system did not 'produce cynicism, corruption, and deep seated moral degradation'[6] in all social classes. Nor did it violate women's civil rights because, unlike state regulation, under the Glasgow system entry to the Lock Hospital and Magdalene Institution was totally voluntary. The purpose of this chapter is to look at the impact of the Glasgow system. Unlike the *laissez-faire* approach, which controlled only the criminal side-effects of prostitution, or state regulation, which controlled the medical consequences, police repression was designed to suppress the prostitution trade entirely. Therefore, it was not a compromise between the other two approaches, as its supporters claimed, but in effect the most extreme approach. In order to examine the Glasgow system it is necessary first to look briefly at the system of state regulation under the C.D. Acts.

THE CONTAGIOUS DISEASES ACTS

The Contagious Diseases (Women) Act was given Royal Assent by 21 July 1864.[7] It was intended to be an 'exceptional' piece of legislation designed for the military and navy in an effort to increase the efficiency of the armed forces by decreasing the cost of treating venereal diseases among the bachelor troops. In other words, the Act, which was enforced in Portsmouth, Plymouth, Woolwich, Chatham, Sheerness, Aldershot, Colchester, Shorncliffe, the Curragh, Cork, and Queenstown, was a special piece of legislation which provided for the registration or licencing of 'prostitutes' in these districts.

A special branch of the Metropolitan Police, entirely outside the jurisdiction of the local authorities and answerable only to the Admiralty and War Offices was established. Special plain-clothes constables were stationed in subjected districts and assigned the task of identifying the women and forcing their submission to a medical examination. The Act also provided for the establishment of state-run lock hospitals for the treatment of women with venereal disease. No provision was made for infected men, or their wives and families. The Act was directed only at the women, who were charged as 'common prostitutes'. This term, however, was never properly defined. Consequently the authorities had broad discretionary powers. According to the Act, any woman could be charged with prostitution upon the testimony of a police inspector, superintendent, or medical examiner before a magistrate. At the trial the burden was on the woman to prove that she was not a 'prostitute'. If a woman failed to prove her 'virtue' she was forced to undergo a vaginal examination by an army surgeon. If she was found to be infected, she was sentenced to three months detention and treatment in a lock hospital. Failure to comply with the conditions of the Act meant imprisonment for one month for the first offence and two months for every subsequent offence. The initial suggestion that the examination of enlisted men be included under the Act in order to discourage soliciting by both sexes was quickly ruled out because the Act was based on the premise that women and not men were responsible for the spread of disease and that while men would be degraded if subjected to genital examination, the women who satisfied male sexual urges were already so degraded that further indignities scarcely mattered.[8] Protection for men was supposed to be assured by the inspection of women. Hence, by not imposing periodic inspection upon male clientele, the architects of the Act obliterated from the start whatever effectiveness they might have had as a sanitary measure.[9]

The first C.D. Act passed through Parliament without debate at any reading in either House. Although originally intended to be restricted to the policing of 'prostitutes' in sixteen garrison towns and naval ports, a campaign for its extension quickly arose and the Act was amended in 1866. The amended Act, which included the town of Windsor, was a more comprehensive version of the first. Under the amended Act, known 'prostitutes' were forced to undergo an examination every three months, again on the evidence of one appointed official before a magistrate. Suspected women within a ten mile radius of the protected area could avoid a court appearance if they agreed to submit to a medical examination every three months. This draft of the Act proved equally ineffective because many women avoided the police simply by moving out of the area and commuting to town each night. The Act was amended for the final time in 1869 when a report by the Association for the Extension of the C.D. Acts revealed that the legislation was not succeeding. The resulting and most thorough piece of legislation extended the Act to six more towns: Canterbury, Dover, Gravesend, Maidstone, Winchester, and Southampton, making eighteen in all. The protected area was extended to a fifteen-mile radius of the towns, thus making commuting expensive and inconvenient. Other loop-holes were avoided by a clause which provided for a five-day compulsory incarceration of women before their examination, without trial or provision for release by habeas corpus.

The membership of the Association for Promoting the Extension of the C.D. Acts can be divided into three groups from the higher social strata: the military, the medical profession, and the civilian élite, including aristocrats, politicians, and intellectuals. The military had initiated the legislation to decrease the cost of treating diseased soldiers on the grounds that this would further the military interests of the nation by increasing the efficiency of the troops. Consequently, the military did not push for extension as long as the Acts continued to be enforced in the garrison towns. Therefore, it was really the medical profession and the civilian élite who were responsible for the C.D. Acts' change from a limited sanitary measure to a far-reaching piece of social legislation.[10]

The members of the medical profession who supported the Acts did so largely in the name of science. This reflects the implementation of the belief that strict scientific laws of social improvement were discoverable and applicable to the masses,[11] as discussed in chapter two. Although the C.D. Acts split the medical profession into two opposing camps, physicians like Acton, who supported them, argued on medical grounds that just as the state made provision for controlling other contagious diseases, it should also endeavour to control syphilis and other venereal diseases. Sanitary arguments like this were complemented by the civilian élite who had the power and political clout to get the Acts passed and extended. The civilian push for extension, however, was just as ideological as the military and medical spheres. For many 'regulationists', as these groups were called, the C.D. Acts were another phase of progressive legislation in Victorian public-health policy which reflected the new interventionist approach to social problems.[12] The mid-century sanitary movement perceived public order as synonymous with public health. The registration of 'prostitutes', however, was seen as more than just a vehicle for controlling venereal disease; it was also a system for controlling prostitution and a means of containing street disorder and intervening in the lives of the 'unrespectable' poor.[13] Finally, for those who supported the Acts because of the double standard, prostitution was regarded as an inevitable and necessary consequence of social life. The Acts were seen as central to the maintenance of the chastity and virginity of higher-class females. They therefore defended sexual access to working-class women as a 'time-honoured prerogative of gentlemen'.[14]

A campaign against the Acts had been under way since 1863. But, like the Acts themselves, it aroused little public attention until 1870. A coalition of middle-class Nonconformists, evangelical clergy, feminists, and radical working men united under the direction of Josephine Butler's Ladies' National Association and James Stansfeld's and Henry Wilson's National Association for the Repeal of the C.D. Acts. They came together to challenge the Acts as immoral and unconstitutional, and called for their full repeal.[15] The radical message of the repeal campaign was linked with an enlightened view of prostitution (not unlike Acton's). They argued that prostitution was an irregular and temporary livelihood for adult working-class women. But, unlike Acton and other supporters of the Acts, 'repealers', as they were called, argued that state regulation sentenced registered women to a 'life of sin' by publicly stigmatizing them and thus preventing them from leaving prostitution or finding alternative 'respectable' employment.

After an active twelve-year campaign the Acts were suspended in 1883 and full repeal came in 1886. The impact of the sixteen-year period of regulation on the lives of working-class females was considerable. Walkowitz argues that the Acts and repressive legislation such as the Industrial School Amendment Act (1885) and the Criminal Law Amendment Act (1885) which accompanied their repeal marked the end of prostitution as a temporary occupation or survival strategy for working-class women. The medical inspec-

141

tion of registered women left them emotionally scarred, and stigmatized them in ways that prohibited them from moving in and out of prostitution as the female labour market dictated. The clampdown on brothels drove women out of their working-class neighbourhoods and with them their traditional support networks, family ties, and integration into the local community. The consequences of the experiment in state regulation were the destruction of the social and economic autonomy of 'prostitutes', which forced them to stay on the streets longer, as pimps replaced the family as a source of protection and support. Finally, 'prostitutes' were labelled as deviants, criminals, and social outcasts.[16]

Thus Walkowitz argues that the C.D. Acts transformed the structure of prostitution in regulated towns. Her hypothesis raises interesting questions concerning the impact of the Acts on port and garrison towns and large industrial cities where they were not enforced. Finnegan's study of 'prostitutes' in York during the same period, for example, suggests that the lives of York's 'prostitutes' were largely unaffected by the Acts,[17] though she claims that, even before the Acts, drink, destitution, and disease took such a rapid toll of girls' lives that once they resorted to prostitution there was little likelihood of ever getting out. Other studies of the same period suggest that attacks on prostitution by moral reformers, evangelical philanthropists, and rescue workers before and after the introduction of the C.D. Acts were not without impact.[18] Moral reformers claimed success in suppressing street soliciting and brothels throughout Britain in areas where the Acts were not enforced.[19] One such city is Glasgow, where the C.D. Acts were not enforced, but where city officials claimed to have abolished street soliciting, closed all large brothels, and driven 'prostitutes' and brothel-keepers from the city by the year 1871. According to the Glasgow Police Chief Constable:

> You may now go along the streets without any interruption from women of that sort. Before such measures were adopted you could scarcely walk any distance without some woman putting herself in your way, or getting hold of you.[20]

Opponents of the C.D. Acts in Glasgow argued that state regulation was not necessary in the city because it had developed its own methods for controlling prostitution which had accomplished the same results without state regulation.

THE GLASGOW SYSTEM: 'THE MORAL CLEARANCE OF THE STREETS'

The system of moral policing and control introduced in Glasgow during the period in which the C.D. Acts were enforced provides an opportunity to examine the impact of repressive legislation on a community while at the same time exploring the relationship between ideological practices and institutions designed for social control. It raises interesting questions concerning the difference between police repression as an alternative to the state regulation of prostitution. The impact of the Glasgow system on brothels and 'prostitutes' can be seen in the evidence presented to the Select Committee on the Contagious Diseases Acts between 21 July 1881 and 27 June 1982.

Chief Constable McCall testified that the amendments to the Police Act in 1866 provided the municipal police force and magistrates with new and extensive powers to imprison or fine brothel-keepers and to enter private property or any establishment suspected of harbouring 'prostitutes'. The purpose was to force brothel-keepers out of the trade by making it unprofitable, and in this McCall appears to have succeeded. On the basis of his evidence and the criminal statistics it appears that the number of brothels in Glasgow was reduced between 1870 and 1879. When McCall first became Chief Constable the number of 'prostitutes' living in brothels was 559. By 1871 the number was reduced to 181, and by 1879 there were only thirty-seven.[21] The Criminal Returns for 1871 reported:

> In the city, during the year vigorous action was taken for the suppression of open female prostitution. A large majority of the unhappy women of the streets are thieves as well as prostitutes, and practise their blandishments merely as a decoy and cloak for purposes of robbery. The moral clearance of the streets has considerably diminished the number of thefts from the person; but more important even than the preservation of property, it has also, I trust, by removing seductive temptations, saved the youthful and thoughtless of both sexes from straying from the paths of virtue, and been much improved by the comparative absence of loose females. Brothels also have been subjected to strict surveillance. Wherever private complainers appeared before the magistrates with a complaint against such houses, warrants

have been issued, and the keepers of them prosecuted, if men and women have been found in them for improper purposes.[22]

McCall also reported that there were 204 brothels in Glasgow in 1870 when he was appointed Chief Constable. By the end of the first year, however, his administration had reduced the number to seventy-nine 'low class' brothels. By 1879 there were only twenty-two 'known' brothels, which he described as 'miserable hovels'[23] and the 'very lowest class'.[24]

The Magdalenes

The Glasgow police only collected data on the 'prostitutes' living in brothels, so there is no evidence that the total number of 'prostitutes' in the city actually decreased. But both McCall and Patterson testified to a change in the appearance of women on the streets. Patterson observed that by 1882 their dress and manners were no longer distinguishable from that of other working-class women.

> You cannot tell them now from other females that pass along the streets, so far as dress goes. Formerly they used to dress in a manner conspicuous; and it was a common thing to see the mistress of the house with a troop of four or five females marching in Indian file along the streets in their gaudiest array. That is never seen now.[25]

McCall, on the other hand, claimed that Glasgow's 'prostitutes' had become 'miserable creatures', many of whom could not even afford shoes:

> They are not the kind of women that were in Glasgow at the time that those brothels were in full operation; they were better dressed, what you might call respectable women; now they are most miserable creatures, going about the streets barefooted in many cases.[26]

Patterson and McCall were obviously not observing the same women. Patterson's observation that 'prostitutes' no longer wore clothing which distinguished them from other women implies that their soliciting became more discreet;[27] while McCall's statement indicates that the frequent fines or prison sentences under the Police Act either deterred women from casual or part-time soliciting, or that the frequent fines, harassment, stigmatization, and prison sentences may have served to harden the core of professional 'prostitutes'[28] at the other end of the spectrum.

McCall claimed that the number of 'prostitutes' in Glasgow had decreased in the same ratio as brothels. In order to clear the streets of 'prostitutes', the police endeavoured to make the trade 'so hard and unprofitable' that women were 'glad to take refuge' in the Magdalene Institution. The conditions of the system – frequent fines, harassment, and imprisonment – gave women three choices: leave the city, find 'respectable' employment, or enter the Institution. Any of these would have been recognized as testifying to the success of the Glasgow system. The increase in admission to the Magdalene Institution[29] suggests that many women considered it as the best of the alternatives available. The Magdalene Institution focused their attention on women who might respond positively to their programmes for the least amount of cost, and, therefore, did not accept many professional 'prostitutes'.[30] In other words, from among the women driven from the streets of Glasgow by the repressive regime of the city police, only a fraction could reasonably expect to find shelter in the Magdalene Institution, which, incidentally, was the only charity in the city willing to admit this segment of the female working class.

The other evidence McCall offered on this question was the declining 'illegitimacy' rate, decreases in admissions to the Lock Hospital, the decline in thefts reported in brothels, and the increased number of thefts committed by 'prostitutes' on the street, and the increase in admissions to the Magdalene Institution. McCall admitted that statistical evidence in the reduction of brothels did not prove that 'vice' was less frequent; he testified, however, that on the basis of the number of rooms and the amount of rent for these houses, it was clear that the introduction of rigorous policing meant that brothels were no longer luxurious or elaborate, but 'miserable places', of very low description. Apparently in 1882 no 'person pretending to be a respectable man' would have set foot in a brothel where the rent was only £9 a year.[31] Further, the appearance of Glasgow's 'prostitutes' after 1870 indicates that they were not growing rich off the decrease in competition. On the question of clandestine prostitution he stated that there was no evidence that the Police Act had indirectly increased 'illicit sexual behaviour'. Contrary to those who felt that the suppression of bro-

145

thels would lead to the 'debauching' of 'respectable' women and increase illegitimacy, between 1869 and 1879 the illegitimacy rate decreased from 9.7 per cent to 8.1 per cent.[32] To further his point, he demonstrated that the number of crimes committed by 'prostitutes' in brothels and on the streets had also been reduced. McCall claimed that the removal of 'prostitutes' and 'seductive temptation' made the streets of Glasgow safe for the 'youthful and thoughtless and also intoxicated and foolish adults'.[33] He did not believe that young men deliberately went to brothels. Instead, he argued that it was an 'impulse' triggered by contact with women in the streets, 'and being caressed by them in a kind of way, and seduced to go to their places'. In short, 'taking away the temptation in the streets from the men lessen[ed] their desire to use prostitutes.'[34]

The system's critics

Like the C.D. Acts, the Glasgow system was not without its critics. The system's critics were either supporters of state regulation, who wanted to see it extended to the rest of the United Kingdom, or repealers, like many members of the men's and women's Association for the repeal of the C.D. Acts who pointed out that police repression contained the same problems as state regulation. For the latter the Glasgow system was just another form of 'veiled regulation'.[35]

The critics argued that the Glasgow police were armed with the power to arrest any woman suspected of prostitution or soliciting; a complaint against the woman by a private citizen was not necessary, and the definition of a 'prostitute' used by McCall was ambiguous to say the least. The bottom line was that the police in Glasgow had large discretionary powers and the repeated arrests and fines simply stigmatized women in the same way that registering women in Plymouth and Southampton did.[36] Furthermore, the evidence provided by McCall and Patterson suggested that the activities of the police, Lock Hospital, and Magdalene Institution hardened the 'hard core of the professional prostitutes, to whom frequent fines became in effect like licence-renewals'.[37]

One of the most outspoken critics of the Glasgow system was anti-C.D. Acts activist and women's rights advocate Dr Elizabeth Blackwell, who argued that considering the relationship between the Magdalene Institution and the police it was playing with words to call entry into the Institution 'voluntary':

> women are virtually compelled to enter these 'homes', [magdalene institutions] and that their managers recognize the fact that the police fill them. . . . The police are armed with power to put down 'solicitation'. In other words they have the power to denounce any poor woman as a prostitute, and punish her as such. For the rest of her life she is virtually registered as a harlot, and any place she lives may be denounced as a brothel. An outcast from the sympathies of 'respectable' people, the finger of scorn pointed at her in all directions, hunted about from place to place, and virtually at the mercy of the men who have set society against her, she at last knocks at the door of a 'home' [magdalene institution] she is here met by the demands that she submit her body to the investigation of the surgeon, and, as an alternative to this, the door is slammed in her face.[38]

On the question of the 'compulsory' medical examination, it is clear that the 5,000 women who entered the Institution between 1860 and 1890 would have been subjected to the same form of examination so violently objected to by opponents of the C.D. Acts. Clearly, women in Glasgow had basically the same amount of choice as women in regulated areas: they could resist the police by paying fines, going to prison, or leaving town. But these were high prices to pay. It should be noted that the regulationists, repealers, and feminists who opposed the Glasgow system were not as critical of the Lock Hospital and Magdalene Institution as they were of their willingness to work with the police. Blackwell stated that the Glasgow Magdalene Institution had 'excellent intentions and did some good'. She only preferred that they work independently of the police.

> In no other way can they do all the good which is possible. As it is the examination on which they insist as a condition of entry, though insisted for far more praiseworthy objects than that authorised by the Acts, is objectionable on the very same grounds.[39]

It should be added that Blackwell regarded the medical examination which the Magdalene Institution insisted upon as a 'violation of a woman's right over her own person'.

Obviously the supporters of the Glasgow system were not among

those who regarded prostitution as a necessary or inevitable consequence of social life, but their support for the Police Act indicates
that they recognized it as an 'existing fact'.[40] Many regulationists
and feminists argued that the women, driven out of the area by the
police, were practising the trade elsewhere because the system did
nothing to attack the causes of female prostitution and it reinforced
the double standard by only punishing women.

In addition to the contemporary criticisms of the Glasgow system
certain problems with the evidence presented to the Select Committee should be identified. To begin with, although the statistics were
selected from a variety of sources, such as the criminal statistics,
the Registrar General, and the annual reports of various charities,
they were intended to present as favourable a case for the Glasgow
system as possible. More seriously, there is a problem stemming
from the authorities' confidence that suppressing prostitution was
simply a matter of policing the women identified as 'prostitutes'.
As we have seen, 'improper' behaviour, garish dress, the unemployed, and unwed mothers were all associated with women being
labelled as 'prostitutes'. Thus, when McCall claims to have
decreased the number of 'prostitutes' we must question whether he
was actually describing 'prostitutes' before or after 1870.

Similarly, it should be pointed out that 'illegitimacy' rates are
poor indicators of the decrease in clandestine prostitution or illicit
sexual activity particularly after 1870, because the popularity of
formal marriages increased in Scotland. T. C. Smout argues that
during this period marriage itself became a more important institution for couples intending to have children.[41] The decline in
admissions to the Lock Hospital[42] also reflected the decline in the
virility of the disease, which increased the likelihood of individuals
contracting the disease without their knowledge[43] as well as the
wider availability of home remedies and 'quack' cures, such as
sandalwood or Dr Cullen's 'Scarlet Pills' advertised in the *Glasgow
Chronicle*. Cullen's pills were advertised as the most infallible anti-
venereal remedy ever discovered and sufferers were assured that
they could 'cure themselves with safety and secrecy'.[44] On the question of crime statistics the decline in the number of thefts committed
in brothels is no indication of the true crime rate. The police cited
a long history of individuals' reluctance to report the thefts which
occurred in brothels. Under the new moral code social pressure
would have made it more difficult for 'reputable' gentlemen to

admit to having been victimized and go to the police. Further, the increase in the number of thefts by 'prostitutes' on the street raises familiar questions concerning the true identity of the thief. It has been demonstrated that 'prostitute' was a convenient label to apply to women, like thieves and pick-pockets, who defied the feminine ideal. Finally the increase in admissions to the Magdalene Institution should also be viewed with suspicion because it could just as easily reflect the fact that the years 1878–9 and 1884–6 were times of depressed trade in Glasgow.[45] As demonstrated, the occupations given by inmates in the Institution were those most vulnerable to the trade cycles.

It is also necessary to question whether women truly entered the Institution 'voluntarily' or were driven from the streets by the police. If the latter is true, then entrance into the Institution cannot be said to have been 'voluntary' in every case. Further, if a woman expected to be admitted to the Lock Hospital or the Magdalene Institution she had to submit to a medical examination, in the same way she would have been examined in areas where the C.D. Acts were enforced. Considering the cultural significance of the speculum, this was no small request. As stated previously, the speculum was recommended only for 'hardened prostitutes', and it was considered a shocking 'immorality' when imposed on 'virtuous' women; although women in the Magdalene Institution did not fit the Victorian definition of 'virtuous', they were not necessarily 'hardened prostitutes', which was why critics objected to their compulsory medical inspection.

In conclusion, it is necessary to evaluate the impact of the Glasgow system on the community. It is clear that between 1870 and 1880 the policing practices in Glasgow reduced the total number of brothels and forced women to be more discreet. But it is doubtful that the system had any permanent effect on prostitution in Glasgow. The Chief Constable accepted that the majority of women had simply left the area and had not given up the trade. For example the police reports indicate that many 'prostitutes' moved to the west end of the city.[46] Similarly, in 1880 when repressive police measures modelled on the Glasgow system were adopted in Edinburgh the number of brothels in Glasgow jumped from twenty-two to sixty, indicating that many women left Edinburgh.[47] The brothel system also appears to have been reorganized geographically to some extent. McCall stated that by 1880 Glasgow brothels had been restricted to the poorest neighbourhoods in the city where residents may have protected the girls and resisted the police by refusing to complain or co-operate with them in their investigations.[48] Other evidence suggests that many women were deterred from resorting to occasional prostitution as a means of supplementing their incomes, while those who were not deterred became more secretive as women were forced to leave the security and companionship of the brothels and to adopt a less conspicuous manner of soliciting. Consequently many residents observed changes in the street conditions.

As to the future of the Glasgow system, the Lock Hospital and the Magdalene Institution had always supported legislation intended to control prostitution in the United Kingdom. They endorsed the Criminal Law Amendment Act (1885) designed for the protection of women and girls, which raised the age of consent of girls from 13 to 16 years of age, which the Magdalene Institution would have preferred to see at 18 years of age.[49] This reflected the perceived threat of the 'white-slave trade' and fear of child prostitution evident in the late nineteenth century. In 1911, representatives from the Glasgow police, the Lock Hospital and the Magdalene Institution attended a conference dealing with the extension and better enforcement of the following pieces of legislation: the Education (Scotland) Act (1908); the Cleansing of Persons Act (1897); the Children Act (1908); the Aliens Act (1905); and other repressive legislation designed for the suppression of juvenile prostitution.[50]

After 1896 applications to the Magdalene Institution began to fall, which was attributed to the opening of other institutions with similar objectives. The Directors were slightly hostile toward the new 'competition'.[51] Although the number of inmates declined, the Repressive and Reclamation Committees maintained an active interest in new pieces of legislation and kept a keen eye on other institutions around town. They were influential in seeing that 'unsuitable' applicants found their way into more suitable institutions, and, thereby, struggled to maintain a monopoly over the inmates most likely to benefit from their programme. In 1898, they supported the Habitual Inebriates Bill for Scotland, which had the power to institutionalize inebriates after a third conviction. They hoped that it would take some of the pressure off their institution.[52] By the end of the century many of the original Board of Directors had died and a new generation of reformers and professional social workers began to take their places. The annual reports retained their old muck-raking tone, which often meant revelling in old victories and nostalgia, as they struggled to keep alive the 'moral panic' around prostitution and the 'dangerous sexualities' of the urban proletariat.

On the question of whether the Glasgow system had any permanent effect on soliciting by 'prostitutes' or on women's behaviour in general, apart from the evidence provided by McCall and Patterson, which is contradictory to say the least, a recent study of the female casual labour market suggests that a considerable amount of casual or temporary prostitution continued to exist. J.H. Treble argues that between 1890 and 1914 arrests for soliciting continued to rise during seasonal trade depressions.[53] Furthermore, although the Glasgow Magdalene Institution reported a change between 1860 and 1890 in the age of first sexual experience, education, and occupation of inmates, these are variables which may have affected the female population in general and did not imply any change in the inmates' social and economic situation.[54] The directors continued to describe inmates as having been brought up in poverty with little or no education. In 1906 they were described as the most 'hapless and helpless of their sex: orphan girls, motherless girls, ill-used stepdaughters, and girls of weak intellect'.[55]

In contrast to the first half of the nineteenth century when soliciting was largely unrestrained, with repressive policing the 'prostitute' became more discreet, 'indicating her object by a stealthy glance or mumbled word. Hoping for a nibble she retires into a side street waiting to be approached by her supposed quarry'.[56] Public houses were used less for that purpose because publicans feared the loss of their licences. Women were forced to use parks, cabs, closes, and other less conspicuous locations in order to escape molestation by the police.[57] Finally, at the other end of the spectrum, the fines and prison sentences may have had a stigmatizing effect on women, which prevented them from moving in and out of prostitution. Other evidence for this might be found in the increased number of 'unsuitable' applications to the Magdalene Institution in the 1890s. Finally, in 1911 the new Chief Constable admitted that repression and punishment failed because they did not deter the 'hardened offender'.[58]

CONCLUSION

In studying discourses about sexuality Mort argues that at certain times the law can come to dominate the field, not in a strictly 'repressive' sense, but by 'seeking out and redefining forms of dangerous or 'deviant' sexuality.[59] The case of the Glasgow system has provided a unique opportunity to examine this argument. It has been demonstrated that 'prostitutes' were, in part, the product of discourses about them; discourses with the aim of establishing knowledge of their characters and careers. There were competing knowledges in play, but in Glasgow in the 1870s one came to dominance because of the strategic positions occupied by the discursants: a select group of city professionals and philanthropists who were in a position to operationalize their definitions of the situation.[60] The Glasgow system and state regulation had many features in common. More particularly, the Glasgow system has to be understood both as repressive and reformatory in its aims. However its significance is best appreciated not simply as one local initiative to control prostitution, but as part of a longer and more general process by which dangerous sexualities are identified and disciplined.

In the early twentieth century attention turned toward juvenile prostitution in Glasgow and the seduction of young girls in Italian ice-cream parlours and Temperance Hotels.[61] In 1910, there were twenty-five cases of 'girls reported as defiled': twenty had venereal disease, two were pregnant, and three had been raped.[62] The ice-cream parlours, which attracted many young girls and men, were notorious and many were said to double as brothels. An inquiry singled out Brazilian soldiers as guilty of seducing young girls in exchange for chocolate, sweets, trumpery scarves, and cheap jewellery.[63] Juvenile 'prostitutes' were also said to frequent taxi-stands in Hope Street, where drivers allowed them to use their cabs when they picked up a man. In order to suppress this behaviour the inquiry pressed for more prosecutions under the Criminal Law Amendment Act described above, which had harsher penalties than the Police Act.[64] In 1913 the Magdalene Institution spoke favourably of the Mental Deficiency Bill, which was due to come into operation later that year. They hoped that it would help to secure the safety of many of the young women who were frequently admitted to the Magdalene Institution whom they judged to be 'hardly responsible for their actions'.[65] This indicates a change in the description of the 'prostitutes', who were putting pressure on the institution for admission. The concern about the large number of 'feeble-minded' applicants implies a shift in the discourse, which suddenly included another cause of prostitution. It illustrates a shift away from defining 'prostitutes' as morally deficient towards an analysis of them as mentally or psychologically deficient and anticipates the mid-twentieth century Freudian definition of 'prostitutes' in psychoanalytic terms as psychopaths and nymphomaniacs. Conversely, the change in the characteristics of applicants may also indicate a change in the social profile of Glasgow's poor and desperate women, which began to include a greater number of women who were not seen as suitable cases for the Magdalene. In either case it suggests that, as always, the directors intended to control the quality of inmates admitted to the Institution.

Conclusion:
Prostitutes, Magdalenes, and wayward girls
Dangerous sexualities of working-class women[1]

Throughout the nineteenth century segments of the Scottish bourgeoisie responded to what they called the 'Great Social Evil' – the prostitution problem – by exerting pressure through a number of material practices and key institutions, both statutory and non-statutory, which targeted and attempted to control and reform the 'dangerous' urban proletariate. The resulting social control apparatuses constitute what Foucault calls 'technologies of power': in this case, institutions for the surveillance, sexual and vocational control, and moral reform of a segment of the female working-class population (chiefly women whose dress, behaviour, or vocation, rather than their criminal records, led to their being labelled as 'prostitutes'). It is significant, therefore, that in the debate around the causes of prostitution it was mainly working-class women who were scrutinized and stigmatized. For a brief period the directors of the Glasgow Magdalene attempted to reach a 'better' class of girl, whom they believed catered to upper-class men, but they abandoned this after a notable lack of success. Similarly, there was no suggestion that 'prostitutes' might ever be male. There was no functional equivalent of a magdalene asylum for working-class men. When men were arrested for the same petty offences and for vagrancy which indirectly led women to penitentiaries, they were either fined or sentenced to short prison terms, just as women had been before penitentiaries were established.[2] If philanthropy was in fact an effort to remake working-class culture, then reformers saw the fastest path to reformation in working-class women.

As we have seen, the 'prostitute' meant different things to different people at the time. For Acton they were generally the healthiest

155

women of their class, who might only make a living from prostitution for a few years before leaving to take up respectable employment on a cushion of their savings.[3] Others claimed that prostitution
was not a temporary stage, and that the most common 'termination
of the career [was] early death'.[4] For the Owenites she was a victim
of seduction by upper-class rakes. Others blamed the socialists;
Logan, for example, charged that socialist foremen seduced their
female factory labourers. Others maintained that the presence of
young women in the streets was itself a temptation to otherwise
virtuous men.[5] There were arguments, too, over the proper course
to be taken. These ranged from the C.D. Acts to the private initiatives of virtuous citizens willing to lodge and befriend 'prostitutes',
advocated by Somerville.[6] The Owenites argued that socialism was
the only refuge for 'prostitution's sorrowing victims'.[7]

In Glasgow, one account and one remedy came to prevail, that
of the Glasgow system, with its particular focus on the 'magdalene'.
Its success was due to the coalition of doctors, businessmen, and
senior police officers which was established by 1870. These men
were in a position not merely to investigate, agitate, and speculate,
but to see their approach embodied in the interlocking apparatuses
of the police, Lock Hospital, and Magdalene Institution. Public
attention and initiative was thus overwhelmingly directed at one
section of the urban population alone: the working-class woman.
In order to understand the histories of social-control apparatuses
in the nineteenth century we must recognize that it was a gendered
process. Thus an adequate explanation of it must incorporate this
dual focus, on class as well as gender. In order to understand this
process some context is necessary. Two possible approaches are the
context of histories of the prison and histories of sexualities.

CLASS: THE PROLETARIANIZATION OF WORKING-CLASS WOMEN

The key features of the history of crime and deviancy apparatuses
in western industrial societies have been identified as a shift from
publicly punishing the body to reforming the mind and character
of the offender. This has been attempted through the increase in
state involvement and the increase in differentiation of deviants,
who were segregated into separate institutions for their punishment
or cure, each with a separate body of experts investigating and

treating them. Over this, the institution of the modern prison casts its shadow and successive reform movements have had little impact on either its dominance or logic.[8] Until recently few of the histories and interpretations have mentioned women as subjects of the new corporal regimes. It has been observed that prisons and penitentiaries developed and operated with particular views about the nature, causes, and appropriate treatment of deviance. This deviance was gendered. As Rafter points out women were more likely to be sent to a penitentiary for minor public order offences than men.[9] In a contemporary survey, Carol Smart concludes that in contradiction to the view that female offenders are more leniently treated than male offenders, adolescent girls are more likely to be institutionalized for sexual misbehaviour than boys.[10] Furthermore, the founding of magdalene homes institutionalized the double standard by only punishing women. They also became an informal branch of the criminal justice system. Although non-statutory, they had the socially sanctioned authority to incarcerate women for years for sexual misdemeanours. The pattern for this double standard was established in the nineteenth-century penitentiaries and institutions, in their use not simply to punish or even reform the inmates, but to protect them from themselves or undesirable influences.[11]

Obviously, not all female offenders or 'deviants' were subject to this particular paternalist logic. But, as a justification for statutory or 'voluntary' incarceration it was marked by distinct paternalist ideology, which constructs as its objects men and women whose lowly station in life, frailty, ignorance, or sinfulness marked them as the dependents of those blessed with property, rationality, and Christian conscience. The discourse of paternalism was not only deployed in penitentiaries; it informed the church, landowners, industrialists, the legislature, and popular fiction.[12] But, as a justification for incarceration it was only selectively employed. Though it could encompass children, the 'insane', or others who were seen as in need of protection, women emerged as particularly appropriate candidates for its exercise on 'sane' adults. There was no corresponding class of men whose status and behaviour was targeted in this way, and this was primarily because women seemed so 'naturally' to appear as paternalism's objects, based as it was on the rhetoric of the family, and the sex-specific roles of 'sturdy oak and clinging vine'.

To some extent, fear and loathing of a dangerous female sexuality can be identified as suffusing the discourses on prostitution. This coincided with a fascination to investigate and expose its 'causes' in order to eradicate them. In order to understand why the 'prostitute' was not criminalized and abandoned to her fate in a common prison or bridewell, it must be acknowledged that a great many philanthropists were motivated by an honest and benevolent desire to help these women, however much we might now recoil from their moralizing force. This is why the directors of the Girls' House of Refuge wanted to distinguish and separate her from the common felon. Furthermore, behind the protecting impulses, several contradictory accounts of the (potential) moral virtues of women can be identified. Moral reformers believed that without their intervention only horrible fates awaited the unwary young woman of the urban streets. And from these they would save her, though this might mean first persuading her that she needed to be saved.

Another aspect of the incarceration of women at this time concerns the regime to which they were subjected in penitentiaries such as a magdalene asylum. Broadly, there are two interpretations of what penitentiaries were attempting to do to the inmates (apart from simply segregating them). Departing from Foucault's account, which sees discipline as an end in itself, D. Melossi and M. Pavarini argue that prisons were machines 'for the production of proletarians by the enforced training of prisoners in factory discipline'.[13] This explanation focuses on capital's need for a disciplined labour force. A more helpful approach is found in Ignatieff's emphasis on the bourgeoisie's need to legitimize its rule by persuading the poor in general and prisoners in particular 'to accept the benevolent intention behind institutional deprivations' and convince them of 'the moral legitimacy of the law and its custodians'.[14] Neither account, though, recognizes that 'the language of class formation was gendered'.[15] This book has demonstrated that Scottish philanthropists were not just concerned to produce 'proletarians', even proletarians reconciled to their status, but 'female' proletarians who were to take up quite distinctive positions in the class and gender order. The model offered to women, through which they were to come to accept their dependent status, was that of the Christian family.

Thus, the accounts of the histories of social-control apparatuses generally fail to acknowledge that both the offences and the regimes that were developed in the nineteenth century discriminated between men and women, and to that extent it could be said to be as involved as any other institutional apparatus in the social and ideological reproduction of sexual difference. One other feature of the system which is also worth remarking on is best understood by looking at what may be called Cohen's paradox.

GENDER: THE FEMALE PENITENTIARY MOVEMENT

In *Visions of Social Control*, Stanley Cohen discusses the community control movement of the 1970s. He uses the concept of 'destructuring' to describe the process whereby interest groups in the community attempted to decrease the size, scope, and intensity of the formal deviancy control systems. Cohen identifies a paradox whereby, as a result of destructuring in the 1970s, the entire criminal justice system expanded. There is evidence of a similar paradox at work in the female penitentiary movement as it developed throughout Britain in the mid-nineteenth century. The reformist programme designed to save women from the criminal justice system resulted in the expansion of the entire control system, which began to include more women of a greater age range and type of offence. The purpose of these non-statutory penitentiaries was not to incarcerate 'hardened prostitutes' or female felons, but part of the population not previously reached, namely those variously defined as 'prostitutes', 'magdalenes', and 'fallen' women. The process therefore became more interventionist than it was at the beginning of the century as a greater percentage of the female working-class population became potential clients. Instead of reducing the amount of stigmatization, labelling, and the overcrowding in prisons, intervention came earlier and was more intensive, as it swept in more forms of deviance through extension to women not yet formally adjudicated. Finally, each new institution supplemented rather than replaced existing institutions and each evolved 'experts' who established monopolistic claims over a select population of clients.

This process is seen most clearly in the Glasgow Magdalene between 1815 and 1864. By examining the changes in its management and policies it is possible to see how it changed its definitions of which women were 'prostitutes' and how it functioned as a diversion agency. Four distinct phases can be located in the asylum after it opened. To begin with, its primary goal was to provide 'fallen' women with an alternative to the streets, prisons, and poorhouse. The contradiction was that it did not accept 'hard-core prostitutes', only the newly 'fallen' and victims of seduction. In other words, their idea of a 'prostitute' was not a pre-existing woman who was readily identifiable by a criminal record; rather, they developed their own definition of a 'prostitute'. In this case she was defined as a 'magdalene': the 'unhappy daughter' of a poor but honest working man, sentimentally modelled on the popular perception of Mary Magdalene.

The second phase is marked by the association of the 'magdalene' with the 'criminal' in the Girls' House of Refuge. The movement to divert children from the adult prison system initiated by the Juvenile Department led to the directors of the magdalene division temporary losing control over the institution, which lasted until the Youthful Offenders Act took control of the admissions and the directors of the asylum refused to tolerate the mixing of juvenile offenders with 'magdalenes'. In the third phase the 'magdalene' was rescued from association with criminality by Bryce, who was determined that these categories be separated. For as long as Bryce managed the institution the 'magdalene' was once again the senti-mental 'victim' for whom reform meant cheerful conversation, sacred melodies, and moral songs. In contrast, the last phase prod-uced a new discourse. Although the pendulum never swung back so far as to recommend a return to head-shaving and solitary con-finement, the 'prostitute' ceased to be defined as a helpless 'victim'. After 1864, either through her employment in the 'public' sphere or lack of education, she was perceived as a threatening social problem which could only be controlled by a regime of discipline and hard work.

This illustrates the process whereby decarceration results in the expansion of the entire social-control system. The magdalene asyl-ums were intended to divert women from the prison and poorhouse systems. In turn the House of Refuge was intended to divert young offenders from the adult prison system while the re-incorporation of the new magdalene institution was a second attempt to divert criminals and juvenile delinquents away from the 'magdalenes'. But the merging of the asylum and the refuge released a whole new set of problems, owing to the increase in the total number of inmates and the fact that many were of a classification not intended for that institution. In other words, the 'wrong' populations were getting in and desirables were being kept out. This resulted in power struggles between the directors and between institutions, with each wanting to select only those clients most likely to benefit from their programme and to divert those who would be liabilities into other institutions. The conflict led to the separation of the institutions. The new institution, the Magdalene Institution, differed from the House of Refuge because it selected a class of 'soft delinquents' who had committed less serious offences and had less serious criminal records. Moreover, the Institution also admitted clients who had not committed any offences at all. The Magdalene, therefore, supplemented rather than replaced the House of Refuge. Far from diverting clients away, it diverted them into a control system. It might be argued, as it was by those who opposed the extension of the C.D. Acts, that the Glasgow system was different; it was not part of the statutory control system (and was preferable because of it). But looking at it from the outside we can only be struck by the formalization and intensification of 'the disciplinary society', which is intended not so much 'to eliminate offences, but rather to distinguish them, to distribute them, to use them'.[16]

Similarly, the Glasgow Magdalene and other Scottish institutions were highly selective in their admission policies: all new applicants were subject to an interview, a medical examination, and a probationary period, which progressively eliminated 'unsuitable' cases. The statistics they published, therefore, cannot be generally applied to the Scottish 'prostitute' population. What the statistical information indicates more clearly is the selection process as it operated in these institutions. The selection process was a function of the directors' perception of the causes of prostitution (poor education, broken homes, early sexual experience, and employment in the public sphere) and their model of reformation which required newly 'fallen' young women who would respond quickly to their programme for a minimum cost. The directors were not, therefore, selecting from a pre-existing population of 'prostitutes' in the city, but rather creating candidates for their programme which, in turn, was informed by one very particular view of the prostitution problem and the remedies for it. What can begin as a liberal, reformist policy designed to reduce the numbers of inmates in penal institutions by intervening at an early stage in what are projected as progressively deviant and criminal careers, can end up by extending and not diminishing the whole control apparatus.

The 'magdalene', however, was not just a product of agencies designed to save her; she had a far wider currency in popular discourses of the time. Nead, for example, discusses the portrayal of 'magdalenes' in Victorian painting and prints, arguing that their meaning is constructed in terms of guilt and memories of lost innocence. She explains that the threat the 'magdalene' might embody 'could be deflected by defining the prostitute as a victim and in terms of a mythology of her tragic life and death',[17] whereby she is 'constituted instead as an object of pity and compassion'.[18] Implicit, of course, in the evocative term 'magdalene' is the Christian figure of Mary Magdalene who was redeemed. This image gives a particularity to the deviant sexuality of the 'prostitute': if, now, she behaved as a woman 'with half the woman gone'[19] as Acton put it, she was not completely immune to feelings of guilt and remorse, and could be saved. And the sooner her career was interrupted, the less hardened she was in the ways of vice, the better her chances of salvation. What makes the operation of Glasgow's and other cities' magdalene homes significant is that through their activities the 'magdalene' was reproduced and not merely as the stock figure of sentimental poems, paintings, or moral homilies. Further, because of their prominent status the directors who ran these homes were in a position to impose their interpretation of the causes, consequences, and cures for prostitution on the community. In Foucault's words, they established a whole technology of control for keeping that body and sexuality under surveillance.[20] Thus moral reform exemplifies the value of Foucault's suggestion that sexuality was not just condemned, 'but managed, inserted into systems of utility, regulated for the greater good of all, and made to function according to an optimum'.[21]

The figure of the 'prostitute' was not only a sexuality, but also a vocational status. The discourses on prostitution appear to divide the population up on other grounds by singling out specific objectionable sexual characteristics and especially 'feminine' gender behaviours,[22] but they also contained a class component. Although apparently non-class-based characters emerge, these were mobilized in class-specific ways. The course of moral training which 'magdalenes' underwent exemplifies their class-specific and engendered status. Not only was character to be reformed, but the girls were provided with useful skills to sell to enable them to support themselves by 'honest' labour. The character and skills they were to acquire, however, were those thought particularly appropriate for young working-class women, and different from those of either working-class men or middle-class women. Apart from the socialists, Tait was the only philanthropist who ever suggested that the girls might be trained for better paid jobs. While the other reformers acknowledged that poor wages caused prostitution and that the employment they received in the homes would never free them from their vulnerable position in the labour market, they comforted themselves with the thought that the moral training would neutralize and fortify inmates against evil influences and temptations. Reform therefore definitely meant an acceptance of women's dependent status as much as learning the habits of modesty, sobriety, and industriousness. The 'fresh start' the girls were offered was, ideally, an opportunity to serve their superiors, whether commercial, industrial, or domestic employers, or relatives and husbands.

In conclusion, this account of prostitution in Scotland emphasizes that 'prostitutes' were the product of discourses about them, discourses with the aim of establishing knowledge of their characters and career. Female penitentiaries served two social-control functions directly: sexual control and vocational control.[23] Their activities reflect the notion that a 'fallen' woman could regain her character, but this required intensive resocialization and moral education. Through moral education and industrial training magdalene asylums attempted to create an industrial labour force and competent domestic servants which responded to the need for a pool of cheap female labour benefiting both the asylum and the community. It is necessary, however, to go beyond a simple economic explanation of their activities. The social control strategies were also designed for the reform of inmates' sexual behaviour. This entailed the socialization of inmates to conform to the middle-class codes of class and gender. In this case reformers hoped that inmates would embrace middle-class values such as family, cleanliness, chastity, domesticity, and appropriate feminine gender roles.[24] Their desire to protect working-class girls was part of a larger programme to control their sexual and vocational behaviour, which reflects the desire to impose a middle-class social code on working-class women.[25]

In the case of Glasgow, it might be objected that the importance of the Glasgow system has been overstated since it only succeeded in reaching, let alone 'reforming', several thousand young women out of a total adult female population of 58,400 in 1891.[26] It was, however, only one (although the longest lived and best known at

163

the time) of many initiatives in the city which were designed to control and/or reform wayward women. Though ostensibly voluntary, it had many features in common with the system of regulation in operation in English towns as described by Walkowitz. Police repression apparently drove many women from the streets, without even the rudimentary defence of a law court. Reception in the Magdalene Institution was dependent upon a medical examination and, once admitted, inmates lost freedom of dress, association, movement, and recreation, and were subjected to an intensive regime designed to remake wanton and troublesome real subjects into the ideal subjects of penitent 'Magdalenes'. The Glasgow system was very much in line with a host in interventionist mid-Victorian projects, indicative of certain sectors of the bourgeois' zeal to reform others.

The other dimensions to this process which must be emphasized are the issues of gender and class. The 'prostitute' was a gendered status, and both the deployment of the discourses which produced these characters and the apparatuses which administered them have to be understood in the context of gender and class inequality. It was, after all, an assumed female sexuality which was scrutinized and reformed, principally by middle-class men. Feminist and radical opponents of the C.D. Acts did attempt to reverse the terms in which the question of prostitution was discussed, presenting 'prostitutes' instead as 'victims of male pollution . . . who had been invaded by men's bodies, men's laws and by that "steel penis" the speculum'.[27] But as Walkowitz comments, 'this attack on male dominance and male vice did not involve a positive assertion of female sexuality' but remained 'couched within the terms of a "separate sphere" ideology'.[28] Further, the problematic female characters at issue in this debate were applied overwhelmingly to working-class women. Assumptions were made, and solutions proposed, which were not just about women's sexuality in general, but more specifically about working-class women, both their sexuality and their vocational status. This discourse therefore reproduced engendered sexualities and engendered class identities. Without this double focus on gender and class any understanding of this episode, whether it is put in the framework of a history of sexuality or a history of the disciplinary society, remains only a partial account.

Although the history of the Glasgow Magdalene Institution in the twentieth century is not part of this book, its recent history and the circumstances surrounding its closure are of interest. Even today, where institutions for teenage girls are state-run, the same concern for physical and mental or 'moral welfare' persists.[29] The general perception of the dangers and temptations which face young working-class girls supported the Magdalene Institution well into the twentieth century. By the 1950s 'wayward' girls (juvenile offenders and girls in 'moral danger') were placed in the Lochburn home by their parents or probation officers. They were incarcerated for two years and received the same mix of basic education, moral training, and laundry work. The twentieth-century inmates were perceived as being in need of a special regime which would remedy personality problems or social maladjustment, thus protecting them from the same sorts of risks (alcohol, low entertainment, poverty, broken homes, low wages, and bad company) which faced the earliest inmates.

On 17 September 1958 the *Glasgow Herald* reported a 'Mass Escape from Glasgow Home'. The article stated that twenty-six girls aged between 15 and 19 had broken out of the Lochburn home by climbing a ladder and dropping from the wall. The city police instructed citizens to be on the look-out for the missing girls, who were wearing blue frocks and white aprons.[30] The following day the headlines read '18 More Girls Climb out of the Glasgow Home'. During this incident notes 'alleging ill-treatment' were thrown from the windows to waiting reporters. One note reported that the girls were held as 'prisoners' and some had been 'battered black and blue', while others had buckets of cold water thrown at them or were forced to take cold baths.[31] Two days later there was another 'breakout' and William Hannan M.P. assured the public that the Institution would be looked into by the Secretary of State for Scotland. The Magdalene Institution was closed down some months later.[32]

This book has emphasized women's capacity for agency by focusing on indicators of women's choice either in the form of acceptance or resistance to the moral code offered by the magdalene asylums. The nineteenth-century discourse on prostitution and the incarceration of 'wayward' girls today must be treated as a process rather than an automatic consequence of bourgeois economic domination. The problem of the engineering of consent within the framework of agency must also be considered. This is the process whereby some women accepted the definition of themselves as 'magdalenes' and chose to reform along bourgeois lines, whereas others resisted the bourgeois moral code and its sanctions on their behaviour. As we have seen there has been resistance, although unorganized and unarticulated, from all of those recalcitrant, saucy, and ungrateful girls who refused to submit to the asylums' efforts. Although the construction of gender-specific discourses mark us today, let us not, in the end, attribute more power to this discourse than it merits. Opposition comes now, as then, from all the 'wayward' girls whose struggles evidence their resistance to a bourgeois (and patriarchal) moral code even when they are caught up in its technologies of power.

Notes

ABBREVIATIONS

EMA Edinburgh Magdalene Asylum
GMA Glasgow Magdalene Asylum
GMI Glasgow Magdalene Institution
Select Committee Reports of the Select Committee on the Contagious
Diseases Acts.

INTRODUCTION: THE DEPLOYMENT OF 'DANGEROUS'
FEMALE SEXUALITIES

1   T. C. Smout, *A Century of the Scottish People, 1830–1950*, (London: Collins,
    1986, p. 292). The recent publication of the *Scottish Women's Bibliography*
    (Open University Press, 1988) demonstrates that Smout's observation
    is no longer accurate.
2   'Technologies of power': a concept developed by Foucault to describe
    agencies and institutions such as jurisprudence, legal medicine, and
    agencies of social control for the surveillance of dangerous or endang-
    ered populations. In the case of my research it refers to apparatuses
    (female penitentiaries and the 'Glasgow system') for the regulation,
    surveillance, sexual and vocational control, and moral reform of a
    segment of the female working-class population who defied middle-
    class notions of feminine respectability.
3   F. Prochaska, *Women and Philanthropy in England* (Oxford: Oxford Uni-
    versity Press, 1980); O. Banks, *Faces of Feminism: A Study of Feminism
    as a Social Movement*, (Oxford: Martin Robertson, 1981); E. Bristow,
    Vice and Vigilance: Purity Movements in Britain Since 1700, (London: Gill
    & MacMillan, 1977). Harrison suggests that 'moral' reformers can be
    distinguished from 'social' reformers on the basis of their views of the
    ideal role of the state. See: B. Harrison, 'State Intervention and Moral
    Reform in Nineteenth Century England' in P. Hollis (ed.) *Pressure from
    Without in Early Victorian England* (London: Edward Arnold, 1974).

167

4 J. Evans, 'The Iron Cage of Visibility', *Ten–8: International Photography Magazine* (1988), no. 28, p. 40.
5 'Colonization': a concept as used by Foucault and by J. Weeks in *Sex, Politics and Society: The Regulation of Sexuality since 1800* (New York: Longman, 1981). Systematic campaigns for the 'moralization' of the poor.
6 For criticism of early studies of Victorian sexual behaviour such as: V. C. Pearl, *The Girl with the Swansdown Seat* (New York: Bobbs-Merill, 1955); K. Chesney, *The Victorian Underworld* (London: 1970); Pearsall, *The Worm in the Bud* (New York: 1969), see: B. Harrison, 'Underneath the Victorians', *Victorian Studies*, vol. 10 (1966–7), pp. 239–62; and E. M. Sigsworth and T. J. Wyke, 'A Study of Victorian Prostitution and Venereal Disease' in M. Vicinus (ed.) *Suffer and Be Still* (London: Methuen, 1972), pp. 77–99.
7 T. C. Smout, 'Aspects of Sexual Behaviour in Nineteenth Century Scotland', in P. Laslett, K. Oosterveen, and R. Smith (eds) *Bastardy and its Comparative History* (London: Edward Arnold, 1980), p. 192.
8 J. Walkowitz, *Prostitution and Victorian Society*, (Cambridge, Cambridge University Press, 1980); p. vii.
9 K. Thomas, 'The Double Standard', *Journal of the History of Ideas*, vol. 20 (1959), p. 215.
10 P. T. Cominos, 'Late-Victorian Sexual Respectability and the Social System', *International Review of Social History*, vol. 8 (1963), p. 230.
11 Thomas, op. cit., p. 207. Studies which use this particular construct to explain the necessity of prostitution in the nineteenth century are problematic for a number of reasons. First, while the double standard may provide a useful cultural interpretation, as a methodological approach in a study of Victorian prostitution it is too simplistic. See: Walkowitz, op. cit., p. 3. F. Finnegan, *Poverty and Prostitution* (Cambridge, Cambridge University Press, 1979) claims that historians who use this model generally rely on secondary sources, and the observations and biases of authorities such as William Acton, the Victorian venereologist, or Sigmund Freud are reproduced as if they were fact. Second, the conclusions drawn are chiefly concerned with middle-class male sexuality, as distinct from working-class male or female sexuality. Third, the ideology that two categories of women: 'pure' and 'impure', and that two standards of sexual behaviour existed in the nineteenth century is uncritically accepted. Fourth, the model is non-dialectical. The only class relations analysed are those between middle-class men and working-class women. Finally, it ignores the problem of how prostitution became 'problematized' in the nineteenth century.
12 Finnegan, op. cit., p. 137.
13 J. Walkowitz and D. Walkowitz, ' "We are not Beasts of the Field": Prostitution and the Poor in Plymouth and Southampton under the Contagious Diseases Acts' in M. Hartman and L. Banner (eds) *Clio's Consciousness Raised* (London: Harper and Row, 1974), p. 192.
14 Walkowitz, op. cit., p. 9.
15 Walkowitz's work is only one example.

16 M. Foucault, *The History of Sexuality. Volume I: An Introduction*, trans. R. Hurley (New York: Random House, 1980), p. 43.
17 Walkowitz, op. cit., p. 4.
18 E. Hellerstein, L. Hume, and K. Offen, *Victorian Women: A Documentary Account of Women's Lives* (London: Harvester, 1981), p. 289.
19 L. Gordon and E. Dubois, 'Seeking Ecstacy on the Battlefield: Danger and Pleasure in Nineteenth Century Feminist Sexual Thought', *Feminist Studies*, vol. 9 (1983), p. 44.
20 L. Nead, 'The Magdalene in Modern Times: The Mythology of the Fallen Woman in Pre-Raphaelite Painting' in R. Betterton (ed.) *Looking at Images of Femininity in the Visual Arts and Media* (London: Pandora Press, 1987), p. 66.
21 S. Cohen, *Visions of Social Control: Crime, Punishment and Classification* (Cambridge: Polity Press, 1985), p. 10.
22 See: P. Dews, 'Power and Subjectivity in Foucault', *New Left Review*, no. 144 (1984); B. Smart, *Michel Foucault* (London: Tavistock, 1985); V. Beechey and J. Donald (eds), *Subjectivity and Social Relations* (Milton Keynes: Open University Press, 1985); J. Weeks, 'Foucault for Historians, *History Workshop*, no. 14 (1982), pp. 106–119.
23 Sigsworth and Wyke, op. cit., p. 77.
24 Weeks, op. cit., p. 21.
25 Foucault, op. cit., p. 17.
26 C. Weedon, *Feminist Practice and Post-Structuralist Theory* (Basil Blackwell, 1987), p. 35.
27 N. Wood, 'Foucault on the History of Sexuality: An Introduction', in V. Beechey and J. Donald, op. cit., p. 162.
28 Weeks, op. cit., p. 7.
29 Wood, op. cit., p. 162.
30 Weeks, op. cit., p. 21.
31 Foucault, op. cit., p. 43.
32 O. Checkland, *Philanthropy in Victorian Scotland: Social Welfare and the Voluntary Principle* (Edinburgh: John Donald, 1980), p. 233.
33 Foucault, op. cit., p. 5.
34 Weeks, op. cit., p. 22.
35 Foucault, op. cit., p. 17.
36 ibid., p. 34.
37 ibid., p. 24.
38 M. Foucault, *Discipline and Punish: The Birth of the Prison*, trans. A. Sheridan (Harmondsworth: Penguin, 1979), p. 194.
39 Weedon, op. cit., p. 26.
40 J. Smail, 'New Languages for Labour and Capital: The Transformation of Discourse in the Early Years of the Industrial Revolution', *Social History*, vol. 12, no. 1 (1987), pp. 51–2.
41 D. MacDonell, *Theories of Discourse* (London: Basil Blackwell, 1986), p. 2.
42 ibid., p.101; Foucault, 1980, op. cit., p. 12.
43 Foucault, 1980, op. cit., p. 101.
44 ibid., p. 96.

45 Mary Ryan argues that if we are willing to recognize women as full agents in history we must also face the fact that they have participated in the creation and reproduction of the oppression of women of classes and cultures other than their own. See: M. Ryan, 'The Power of Women's Networks', in M. Ryan, J. Newton, and J. Walkowitz (eds) *Sex and Class in Women's History* (London: Routledge & Kegan Paul, 1983), p. 67. Women oppressing other women is not a part of this study, though I recognize that work in this area is badly needed. To my knowledge there are no surviving records from the Glasgow Magdalene Institution's Ladies' Committee. The Scottish Ladies' Association for Repeal of the C.D. Acts was very active at the national level. Many prominent members were also on the Ladies' Committee of the Edinburgh Magdalene Asylum. Unfortunately they are only referred to in passing in recent studies of the C.D. Acts.

PART ONE: THE BIRTH OF SOCIAL MEDICINE AND THE STATE

1 T. Ferguson, *The Dawn of Scottish Social Welfare* (London: Thomas Nelson & Sons, 1948), p. 97.

2 V. Bullough and B. Bullough, *Women and Prostitution: A Social History* (New York: Prometheus, 1987), p. 233.

3 F. Mort, *Dangerous Sexualities: Medico-Moral Politics in England* (London: Routledge & Kegan Paul, 1987), pp. 24, 25.

4 M. Foucault, *The History of Sexuality. Volume 1: An Introduction*, trans. R. Hurley (New York: Random House, 1980), p. 40.

5 Mort, op. cit., p. 24.

1 'HARLOTS, WITCHES AND BAR-MAIDS':

1 R. S. Morton, *Venereal Disease* (2nd ed., Harmondsworth: Penguin, 1972), p. 21.

2 J. Y. Simpson, *Antiquarian Notices of Syphilis in Scotland in the Fifteenth and Sixteenth Centuries*, (Edinburgh: Edmonston & Douglas, 1875), p. 3.

3 Morton, op. cit., p. 25.

4 Simpson, op. cit., p. 4.

5 T. Ferguson, *The Dawn of Scottish Social Welfare* (London: Thomas Nelson & Sons, 1948), p. 97.

6 D. Newman, 'The History and Prevention of Venereal Disease', *The Glasgow Medical Journal*, vol. 81 (1914), p. 92.

7 R. S. Morton, 'Some Aspects of the Early History of Syphilis in Scotland', *British Journal of Venereal Disease*, vol. 38 (1962), p. 176; Newman, op. cit., p. 92; Ferguson, op. cit., p. 108.

8 Annals from the extracts of the Kirk Session, quoted in A. Duncan, *Memorials of the Faculty of Physicians and Surgeons of Glasgow* (Glasgow: Maclehose, 1896), p. 14.

9 Simpson, op. cit., p. 23.

10 Ferguson, op. cit., p. 109; Newman, op. cit., p. 92.

11 Syphilis was referred to by several names in medieval Scotland: gor, gore, grandgore, grangore, grantgore, glengore (possibly from the French word meaning 'large sore'), the French seikness, the Spanish seiknes, the seiknes of Napillis, pokis, rognole. Morton, 1962, op. cit., p. 175; J. Cleland, *Dissolute Characters in Former and Present Times in the City of Glasgow* (Glasgow: 1840), p. 1.

12 Simpson, op. cit., p. 25.

13 Newman, op. cit., p. 93.

14 Morton, 1972, op. cit., p. 117.

15 Ferguson, op. cit., p. 109; Simpson, op. cit., p. 39.

16 Simpson, op. cit., p. 10.

17 K. M. Boyd, *Scottish Church Attitudes to Sex, Marriage and the Family, 1850–1914* (Edinburgh: John Donald, 1980), p. 176.

18 W. Tait, *Magdalenism: An Inquiry into the Extent, Causes and Consequences of Prostitution in Edinburgh* (Edinburgh: P. Richard, 1840), p. 220.

19 'Her medical history and that of her husbands has been well documented by medical historians', Morton, 1962, op. cit., p. 179; M. H. A. Davison, 'The Maladies of Queen Mary of Scotland and Her Husbands', *Reports and Proceedings of the Scottish Society of the History of Medicine*, vol. 28 (1955–6), p. 20.

20 Ferguson, op. cit., p. 109; Morton, 1962, op. cit., p. 178.

21 Cleland, 1840, op. cit., p. 1.

22 J. D. Comrie, *History of Scottish Medicine*, vol. 2 (London: Bailliere, Tindale & Cox, 1932), p. 201; Morton, 1962, op. cit., p. 177; Simpson, op. cit., p. 12.

23 Quoted in Boyd, op. cit., p. 176.

24 The Acts of the City of Edinburgh, Edinburgh, 1742. British Museum Library.

25 Tait, op. cit., p. 229.

26 ibid., p. 232.

27 J. Cameron, *Prisons and Punishment in Scotland: From the Middle Ages to the Present* (Edinburgh: Canongate, 1983), p. 10.

28 ibid., p. 6.

29 ibid., p. 10.

30 ibid., pp. 18, 19.

31 Tait, op. cit., p. 232.

32 Boyd, op. cit., p. 177.

33 Quoted in Tait, op. cit., p. 230.

34 ibid., p. 231.

35 M. Foucault, *The History of Sexuality. Volume I: An Introduction*, trans. R. Hurley (New York: Random House, 1980), p. 40.

36 Duncan, op. cit., p. 14.

37 I. B. Cowan, 'Church and Society' in J. Brown (ed.) *Scottish Society in the Fifteenth Century*, (London, Edward Arnold, 1977), p. 132.

38 Duncan, op. cit., p. 15.

39 J. H. F. Brotherston, 'Observations on the Early Public Health Move-

ment in Scotland', *London School of Hygiene and Tropical Medicine Memoir*, vol. 8 (London: H. K. Lewis, 1952), p. 21.

40 G. M. Cullen, 'Concerning Sibbens and the Scottish Yaws', *Caledonian Medical Journal*, vol. 8 (1909–10), pp. 347–9.

41 Brotherston, op. cit., p. 21.

42 ibid., p. 22.

43 Cullen, op. cit., pp. 347–9.

44 Foucault, op. cit., p. 120.

45 ibid., p. 121.

46 ibid., p. 126.

47 ibid., pp. 126, 127.

48 M. Foucault, *Discipline and Punish: The Birth of the Prison*, trans. A. Sheridan (Harmondsworth: Penguin, 1979), p. 18; O. Checkland, *Philanthropy in Victorian Scotland* (Edinburgh: John Donald, 1980), p. 233.

2 A MEDICAL MODEL OF IMMORALITY

1 O. Checkland, *Philanthropy in Victorian Scotland: Social Welfare and the Voluntary Principle* (Edinburgh: John Donald, 1980), p. 199; J. Walkowitz, *Prostitution and Victorian Society* (Cambridge: Cambridge University Press, 1980), p. 59; D. Newman 'The History and Prevention of Venereal Disease', *The Glasgow Medical Journal*, vol. 81 (1914), p. 92.

2 W. Acton, *Prostitution Considered in its Moral, Social and Sanitary Aspects in London and other Large Cities and Garrison Towns* (2nd edn, London: John Churchill, 1869), p. 78.

3 Walkowitz, op. cit., p. 59.

4 The existence of lock hospitals shows a long-standing acceptance of a medical problem, but the nineteenth century brought with it an increasing concern about 'moral' problems. Checkland, op. cit., pp. 194–6; Walkowitz, op. cit., p. 59.

5 F. Mort, *Dangerous Sexualities: Medico-Moral Politics in England since 1830* (London: Routledge & Kegan Paul, 1987), p. 23.

6 Walkowitz, op. cit., p. 59.

7 For a full development of this argument see: G. Steadman-Jones, 'The Threat of Outcast London', in M. Fitzgerald *et al.*, *Crime and Society: Readings in History and Theory* (London: Routledge & Kegan Paul, 1986), pp. 173–88; Mort, op. cit., p. 81.

8 Mort, op. cit., p. 81.

9 J. Weeks, *Sex, Politics and Society: The Regulation of Sexuality since 1800* (New York: Longman, 1981), p. 25.

10 Buchan quoted in J. H. F. Brotherston, 'Observations on the Early Public Health Movement in Scotland', *London School of Hygiene and Tropical Medicine Memoir*, vol. 8 (1952), pp. 9–21.

11 Mort, op. cit., p. 27.

12 W. Buchan, quoted in Brotherston, op. cit., p. 20.

13 Mort, op. cit., p. 27.

14 I.B. Cowan, 'Church and Society', in J. Brown (ed.) *Scottish Society in the Fifteenth Century* (London: Edward Arnold, 1977), p. 133.
15 Brotherston, op. cit., p. 24.
16 Walkowitz, op. cit., p. 58.
17 Checkland, op. cit., p. 194.
18 *Glasgow Courier* (14 February 1805).
19 ibid.
20 Mort, op. cit., p. 29.
21 *Glasgow Courier* (14 February 1805).
22 ibid. (16 February 1805).
23 ibid. (2 March 1805).
24 Brotherston, op. cit., p. 42.
25 *Glasgow Courier* (2 March 1805).
26 ibid., 11 February 1805.
27 M. Foucault, *The History of Sexuality. Volume 1: An Introduction*, trans. R. Hurley (New York: Random House, 1980), p. 26.
28 *Glasgow Courier* (11 February 1805).
29 ibid.
30 ibid. (16 February 1805).
31 ibid. (11 February 1805).
32 ibid. (16 February 1805).
33 ibid. (11 February 1805).
34 ibid. (14 February 1805).
35 O. Checkland, op. cit., p. 199.
36 *Glasgow Medical Journal*, vol. 30 (1888), p. 48.
37 Checkland, op. cit., p. 195.
38 The remainder were in the hospital when the report was published. Glasgow Lock Hospital, *Annual Report* (1806).
39 A. Patterson, 'Statistics of the Glasgow Lock Hospital since its Foundation in 1805: With Remarks on the Contagious Diseases Acts, and on Syphilis', *Glasgow Medical Journal*, vol. 6 (1882), p. 405.
40 W. Tait, *Magdalenism: An Inquiry into the Extent, Causes and Consequences of Prostitution in Edinburgh* (Edinburgh: P. Richards, 1840), p. 115.
41 R. S. Morton, *Venereal Disease* (2nd edn, Harmondsworth: Penguin, 1974), p. 23.
42 J. Ferrier, *The Greenock Infirmary, 1806–1968* (Greenock: Greenock and District Board of Management, 1968), p. 29.
43 Patterson, op. cit., p. 414; Morton, op cit., p. 30.
44 A. G. Miller, 'Four and a Half Years Experience in the Lock Wards of the Edinburgh Royal Infirmary', *Edinburgh Medical Journal*, vol. 28 (1882), p. 400; *Glasgow Medical Journal*, (1888), vol. 30, p. 48.
45 Checkland, op. cit., p. 195.
46 A. L. Turner, *Story of a Great Hospital: The Royal Infirmary of Edinburgh, 1729–1929* (Edinburgh: Mercat Press, 1979), p. 98.
47 A. Duncan, '*Letter to Sir William Fettes, (affording demonstrative evidence, that much greater benefit will arise to those who have at once to struggle both with poverty and disease, from improving the Royal Infirmary by the establishment of a lock hospital and an hospital for incurables than by beginning a new rival*

infirmary which may be productive of many evils), (Edinburgh: P. Neill, 1825), p. 11.

48 Checkland, op. cit., p. 195.

49 F. Cadell, *The Contagious Diseases Acts* (Edinburgh: The Scottish National Association for the Abolution of the State Regulation of Vice and Promotion of Social Purity, 1881), p. 6. In his article A. G. Miller reveals that when the lock ward was moved to the new building 'my case-books were removed for me, and I have never seen them since. I understand that a number of the case-books were sold for waste paper, and fear that mine have suffered this horrible fate. . . . It is also unfortunate that owing to the regulation of the Royal Infirmary, none but females are admitted to the Lock wards', op. cit., p. 386.

50 Turner, op. cit., p. 273.

51 Morton, op. cit., p. 32.

52 Glasgow Lock Hospital, *Annual Report*, 1810.

3 FAMILIARITY WITH THE ILLICIT

1 R. S. Morton, *Venereal Disease*, (2nd edn, Harmondsworth: Penguin, 1974), p. 31.

2 M. Foucault, *The History of Sexuality. Volume 1: An Introduction*, trans. R. Hurley (New York: Random House, 1980), p. 33.

3 ibid., p.3.

4 See J. Y. Simpson, *Antiquarian Notices of Syphilis in Scotland in the Fifteenth and Sixteenth Centuries* (Edinburgh: Edmonston & Douglas, 1875), p. 13.

5 Quoted in I. Muirhead, 'Churchman and the Problems of Prostitution in Nineteenth Century Scotland', *Records of the Scottish Church History Society*, vol. 18 (1974), p. 223.

6 E. C. Mossner, *The Life of David Hume*, (London: Thomas Nelson & Sons, 1954), p. 243.

7 Muirhead, op. cit., p. 224.

8 J. Walkowitz, *Prostitution and Victorian Society* (Cambridge: Cambridge University Press, 1980), pp. 26–8.

9 W. Tait, *Magdalenism: An Inquiry into the Extent, Causes and Consequences of Prostitution in Edinburgh* (Edinburgh, P. Richards, 1840); W. Logan, *An Exposure from Personal Observation of Female Prostitution in London, Leeds, and Rochdale and Especially Glasgow, with Remarks on the Cause, Extent, Results and Remedy of the Evil* (Glasgow, 1843); Walkowitz, op. cit., p. 25.

10 Walkowitz, op. cit., pp. 26–8.

11 For a recent example see F. Finnegan, *Poverty and Prostitution: A Study of Prostitution in York* (Cambridge: Cambridge University Press, 1979).

12 Walkowitz, op. cit., pp. 20–9, 31.

13 Tait, op. cit., p. 4.

14 Logan, op. cit., p. 32.

15 ibid., p. 23.

16 ibid., p. 22.
17 Tait, op. cit., p. 4.
18 ibid., p. 49.
19 ibid.
20 ibid., p. 68.
21 ibid., p. 61.
22 ibid., pp. 56, 57.
23 *Ranger's Impartial List of the Ladies of Pleasure in Edinburgh, with a Preface by a Celebrated Wit* (1775) (London: Paul Harris, 1987).
24 *A Complete List of All the Sporting Ladies: who are to be in Glasgow during the Fair, with their names, characters, and where they were to be found; together with an account of their different prices.* Muirhead, op. cit., dates this broadside at 1820. Glasgow University Library, Mu 1x11(8).
25 For one of the few articles dealing with this interesting subject see E. King, 'Popular Culture in Glasgow', in R. A. Cage (ed.) *The Working Class in Glasgow, 1750–1914* (London: Croom Helm, 1987), p. 148.
26 *A Complete List of the Bonny Ladies who are Assembled in Edinburgh during Race Week, with their names and character and the places from whence they come and where they are to be found together with an account of their different prices* (1828), British Museum Library.
27 Tait, op. cit., p. 3.
28 *A full and particular account of the Extravagant Adventures of a young inexperienced farmer from the country, on Wednesday last, who fell in with a dandy young lady, that took him to the famed Battery, in Canongate [Edinburgh] with the funny conversation that took place on that occasion* (September 1828), British Museum Library.
29 Glasgow University Library, Mu 22x3(171).
30 King, op. cit., pp. 148, 149.
31 *Execution of Mrs Mckinnon, who was executed at Edinburgh on Wednesday morning the 16th April, 1823, in the presence of 3,000 spectators, for the murder of Mr Wm. Howat, and her body given for dissection with an account of her dress, behaviour and dying declaration on the scaffold* (Edinburgh: 1832) Glasgow University Library, Mu 1x11.
32 *A warning to all young lovers, being the last dying speech and confession of Ann Smith* (n.d.), Glasgow University Library, Mu 1x11.
33 *An Affecting Account of a young woman, a servant girl in the Grassmarket of Edinburgh, who put an end to her life, for the sake of a young man, who deceived her* (1823), Glasgow University Library, Mu 1x11.
34 *A beautiful young Lady who was brought to bed of a son on the night of her marriage*, Glasgow University Library, Mu 22x3. The Glasgow broadsides in this collection were printed by John Muir of Glasgow and related to local affairs 1810–30.
35 Foucault, op. cit., p.33.
36 M. Foucault, *Discipline and Punish: The Birth of the Prison*, trans. A. Sheridan (Harmondsworth: Penquin, 1979), pp. 7, 8.
37 S. Cohen, *Visions of Social Control: Crime, Punishment and Classification* (Cambridge: Polity Press, 1985), p.26.

PART TWO: PHILANTHROPY, PIETY, AND THE STATE

1 T. C. Smout, *A Century of the Scottish People, 1830–1950* (London: Collins, 1986), p. 22.
2 C. A. Oakley, *Second City*, New edn (London: Blackie, 1967), p. 50.
3 F. Engels, *The Conditions of the Working Class in England*, trans. W. O. Henderson and W. H. Chaloner (Oxford: Basil Blackwell, 1958), pp. 41, 45.
4 Dr Alison quoted in Engels, op. cit., p. 76.
5 ibid., p. 45.
6 ibid., p. 46.
7 G. Steadman-Jones, 'The Threat of Outcast London', in M. Fitzgerald *et al.* (eds) *Crime and Society: Readings in History and Theory* (London: Routledge & Kegan Paul, 1986), p. 174.
8 Smout, op. cit., p. 40.
9 These anxieties re-emerged with the socialist movements of the later century. See: Steadman-Jones, op. cit.

4 AN INVITATION TO DISCOURSE

1 M. Ignatieff, *A Just Measure of Pain* (London: Macmillan, 1978), p. 208.
2 G. A. MacKay, *Practice of the Scottish Poor Law* (Edinburgh; William Green & Sons, 1907), p. 49; R. A. Cage, *The Working Class in Glasgow, 1740–1914* (London: Croom Helm, 1987), p. 82; A. Paterson, 'The Poor Law in Nineteenth Century Scotland', in D. Fraser (ed.) *The New Poor Law in the Nineteenth Century* (London: Macmillan, 1976), p. 187.
3 S. Cohen, *Visions of Social Control: Crime, Punishment and Classification* (London: Polity Press, 1986).
4 V. Bullough and B. Bullough, *Women and Prostitution: A Social History* (New York: Prometheus, 1987).
5 E. Bristow, *Vice and Vigilance: Purity Movements in Britain since 1700* (London: Gill & Macmillan, 1977), p. 64.
6 Anon., A Scotchwoman, *Hospital Prisons: A Warning from Scotland*, (Nottingham: Stevenson, Bailey and Smith, 1870).
7 Bristow, op. cit., p. 67.
8 Quoted in Steadman-Jones, 'The Threat of Outcast London', in M. Fitzgerald *et al.* (eds) *Crime and Society: Readings in History and Theory* (London: Routledge & Kegan Paul, 1986), p. 177.
9 M. Foucault, *The History of Sexuality. Volume 1: An Introduction*, trans. R. Hurley (New York: Random House, 1980), p. 24.
10 Glasgow Society for the Encouragement of Penance, *Annual Report* (1815).
11 Glasgow Lock Hospital, *Annual Report* (1810).
12 S. Mechie, *The Church and Scottish Social Development, 1780–1870* (Westport, Conn.: Greenwood Press, 1975), p. 42.

13 S. MacGill, *Discourses and Essays on Subjects of Public Interest* (Edinburgh: Waugh and Innes, 1819), p. 127.

14. ibid., pp. 128, 130.

15. ibid., p. 130.

16. ibid.

17 Wet-nursing was regarded as a suitable occupation by Acton, Miller, and Tait for newly 'fallen' women. It was perceived as a way of performing penance.

18 K. M. Boyd, *Scottish Church Attitudes to Sex, Marriage and the Family, 1850–1914* (Edinburgh: John Donald, 1980), p. 83.

19 A. C. C. List, *The Two Phases of Social Evil* (Edinburgh: Ogle and Murray, 1859), p. 18. The second 'evil' was alcohol!

20 O. Checkland, *Philanthropy in Victorian Scotland: Social Welfare and the Voluntary Principle* (Edinburgh: John Donald, 1980), p. 232.

21 GMI, *Annual Report* (1866).

22 L. Nead, 'The Magdalene in Modern Times: The Mythology of the Fallen Woman in Pre-Raphaelite Painting', in R. Betterton (ed.) *Looking at Images of Femininity in the Visual Arts and Media* (London: Pandora Press, 1987), p. 68.

23 A. Thomas, *On the Licentiousness of Scotland and the Remedial Measures Which Ought to be Adopted* (London: J. Nisbet, 1861), p. 3.

24 T. C. Smout, *A Century of the Scottish People, 1830–1950* (London: Fontana, 1986), p. 186.

25 Checkland, op. cit., pp. 30–3.

26 R. Wardlaw, *Lectures on Female Prostitution: Its Nature, Extent, Effects, Guilt, Causes and Remedy* (Glasgow: J. Maclehose, 1842), p. 1.

27 W. Logan, *The Great Social Evil: Its Causes, Extent, Results and Remedies* (London: Hodder and Stoughton 1871), p. 127.

28 W. Logan, *An Exposure from Personal Observation of Female Prostitution in London, Leeds, Rochdale, and Especially Glasgow, with Remarks on the Cause, Extent, Results and Remedy of the Evil* (Glasgow, 1843), p. 11.

29 *Glasgow Herald* (6 July 1860) p. 4; In 1871 along with 99 other Scottish clergy, Somerville announced his opposition to the C. D. Acts; *Shield* (17 June 1871), p. 189.

30 I. Muirhead, 'Churchmen and the Problems of Prostitution in Nineteenth Century Scotland', *Records of the Scottish Church History Society*, vol. 18 (1974), p. 233.

31 F. K. Prochaska, *Women and Philanthropy in Nineteenth Century England* (Oxford: Oxford University Press, 1980), p. 195.

32 *Glasgow Herald* (6 July 1860), p. 4.

33 Muirhead, op. cit., p. 233.

34 Checkland, op. cit., p. 232.

35 J. Weeks, *Sex, Politics and Society: The Regulation of Sexuality since 1800* (New York: Longman, 1981), p. 32.

36 For other examples of this process see J. Walkowitz, *Prostitution and Victorian Society* (Cambridge: Cambridge University Press, 1980); N. Rafter, 'Chastizing the Unchaste: Social Control Functions of a Women's Reformatory', in S. Cohen and A. Skull (eds) *Social Control*

and the State (Oxford: Martin Robertson, 1983), pp. 228–311; B. Brenzel, 'Domestication as Reform: A Study of the Socialization of Wayward Girls, 1856–1905', *Harvard Educational Review*, vol. 50 (1980), pp. 196–213; F. Finnegan, *Poverty and Prostitution: A Study of Prostitution in York* (Cambridge: Cambridge University Press, 1979).

37   In 1874 the authorities considered extending the C. D. Acts to the military camp at Maryhill (two miles northwest of Glasgow) *Report* (Society for the Prevention of the Extension of the C. D. Acts to Maryhill, 1874).

38   H. Ware, 'Prostitution and the State: The Recruitment, Regulation and Role of Prostitution in the Nineteenth and Twentieth Century', unpublished Ph.D. thesis (University of London, 1969), p. 14.

39   W. Tait, *Magdalenism: An Inquiry into the Extent, Causes and Consequences of Prostitution in Edinburgh* (Edinburgh: P. Richards, 1840), p. 26.

40   Ware, op. cit., p. 16.

41   Tait, op. cit., p. 176; Walkowitz, op. cit., pp. 33, 34.

42   J. Miller, *Prostitution Considered in Relation to its Causes and Cures* (Edinburgh: Sutherland and Knox, 1859), p. 19.

43   Tait, op. cit., p. 202.

44   Walkowitz, op. cit., pp. 33, 34.

45   Tait, op. cit., p. 124; W. Acton, *Prostitution Considered in its Moral, Social and Sanitary Aspects in London and other Large Cities and Garrison Towns* (2nd edn London: John Churchill, 1869), pp. 288–9.

46   List, op. cit., p. 9.

47   Tait, op. cit., p. 117.

48   ibid.; Walkowitz, op. cit., pp. 33, 34.

49   Tait, op. cit., p. 64.

50   K. Nield (ed.), Introduction, *Prostitution in the Victorian Age: Debates on the Issues from Nineteenth Century Critical Journals* (Westmead, England: Gregg International, 1973).

51   Walkowitz, op. cit., p. 44.

52   Acton, op. cit., p. 249.

53   ibid., p. 236.

54   Walkowitz, op. cit., p. 43.

55   Miller, op. cit., p. 24; Nield, op. cit.

56   Miller, op. cit., p. 19.

57   Walkowitz, op. cit., p. 41.

58   Nield, op. cit.

59   Walkowitz, op. cit., p. 35.

60   S. Pollard and J. Salt (eds), *Robert Owen: Prophet of the Poor* (London: Macmillan, 1971), p. viii.

61   Boyd, op. cit. p. 183.

62   A. L. Morton, *The Life and Ideas of Robert Owen* (London: Lawrence & Wishart, 1962), p. 21.

63   E. Yeo, 'Robert Owen and Radical Culture', in Pollard and Salt, op. cit., p. 85.

64   Morton, op. cit., p. 31.

65   Robert Owen, quoted in Morton, op. cit., p. 161.

66 ibid.; J. F. C. Harrison, 'A New View of Mr Owen', in Pollard and Salt, op. cit., p. ix.

67 Checkland, op. cit., p. 233.

68 R. Wilson, *Prostitution Suppressible: And Resistance to the Contagious Diseases (Women) Act, A Duty* (London: S. W. Partridge, 1871), p. 155.

69 *Shield* (2 June 1877), p. 152.

70 Miller, op. cit., p. 30.

71 Logan, 1843, op. cit., p. 41.

72 Wardlaw, op. cit., p. 124.

73 ibid., p. 159.

74 *New Moral World*, vol. 16 (15 October 1841), p. 127; *New Moral World*, vol. 22. (27 November 1841), p. 170; *New Moral World*, vol. 25 (19 December 1841), pp. 394, 395.

75 Logan (1843), op. cit., p. 13.

76 Wardlaw, op. cit., p. 9.

77 *New Moral World*, vol. 16 (15 October 1841), p. 127.

78 J. Bertram (editor, *North Briton*), *Glimpses of the Social Evil in Edinburgh and Elsewhere* (Edinburgh: Charles Harvey, 1864), p. 12.

79 ibid., p. 13.

80 Walkowitz, op. cit., p. 38.

81 The Owenites were also guilty of this: 'Who, from being unaccompanied by gentlemen may be supposed to be women of unchaste character'. *New Moral World*, vol. 22 (27 November 1841), p. 170.

82 Ware, op. cit., p. 83.

83 M. Sumner, 'Prostitution and Images of Women', unpublished M. Sc. dissertation (University of Wales, 1980), p. 112.

84 *Select Committee* (4 July 1881), p. 373.

85 A. Patterson, 'Statistics of the Glasgow Lock Hospital since its Foundation in 1805: With Remarks on the Contagious Diseases Acts, and on Syphilis', *Glasgow Medical Journal*, vol. 6 (1882), p. 408.

86 *Select Committee* (4 April 1882), p. 123.

87 ibid., p. 118.

88 Sumner, op. cit., p. 154.

89 GMI, *Report on the Glasgow Fair* (1863), p. 9.

90 ibid, p. 7.

91 J. Myles, *Chapter in the Life of a Dundee Factory Boy: An Autobiography* (Edinburgh, 1850), p. 20.

92 Tait, op. cit., p. 176.

93 Sumner, op. cit., p. 182.

94 E. Gordon, 'Women, Trade Unionism and Industrial Militancy, 1850–1890', in Glasgow Women's Studies Collective, *Uncharted Lives: Extractions from Scottish Women's Experiences, 1850–1982* (Glasgow: Pressgang, 1983), pp. 52–73; E. King, *The Scottish Women's Suffrage Movement* (Glasgow: Glasgow Museums and Art Galleries, 1978), pp. 15–17.

95 J. D. Young, *Women and Popular Struggles: A History of Scottish and English Working Class Women, 1500–1984* (Edinburgh: Mainstream, 1985), p. 86.

96 In the nineteenth century domestic service was regarded as the only form of paid employment that did not break with the 'essential' feminine role. Sumner, op. cit., p. 179.

97 E. Hellerstein, *et al.*, *Victorian Women: A Documentary Account of Women's Lives* (Brighton: Harvester, 1981), p. 273; Scott and Tilly argue that working-class women were 'expected' to support themselves, see L. W. Scott and L. A. Tilly, 'Women's Work and the Family in the Nineteenth Century', *Comparative Studies in Social History*, vol. 17 (1975), pp. 36–64.

98 Wardlaw, op. cit., p. 101.

99 Ware, op. cit., p. 117.

100 Tait, op. cit., p. 210.

101 Logan (1871), op. cit., p. 53.

102 Acton, op. cit., p. 80; Miller, op. cit., p. 7; Wardlaw, op. cit., p. 117.

103 Sumner, op. cit., p. 154; The Glasgow Magdalene Institution reported: 'The fact is that women of education and intelligence have never yet applied for admission to our Institution; and it is comforting to think that few such are to be found among the class who require to seek such a home. This again reveals the baseness and the grossness of those men who find in our rude, ill-mannered, and miserably educated street-girls the companions of their pleasure . . . The bold, coarse women who, for a few short months flaunt themselves on our streets in satin and velvet of the extremest dyes, are . . . not educated even to the extent that our poorest charity school children are. GMI, *Annual Report* (1866).

104 Miller, op. cit., p. 15.

105 Sumner, op. cit., p. 113.

5 THE DOMESTICATION OF 'FALLEN' WOMEN

1 W. Tait, *Magdalenism: An Inquiry into the Extent, Causes and Consequences of Prostitution in Edinburgh* (Edinburgh: P. Richards, 1840), pp. 242, 243.

2 *Magdalen's Friend*, vol. 6 (1860); Reformatory and Refuge Union, *The Classified List of Child-Saving Institutions* (1912).

3 EMA, *Annual Report* (1802).

4 EMA, *Ladies' Committee Minute Book* (23 November 1798).

5 This appears to be the first name of the organization in support of the Glasgow Magdalene Asylum (Glasgow Society for the Encouragement of Penitents, 1814, 1815, 1816, 1819, 1820, 1821, 1822).

6 S. MacGill, *Discourses and Essays on Subjects of Public Interest* (Edinburgh: Waugh and Innes, 1819).

7 Glasgow Society for the Encouragement of Penitents, *Annual Report* (1815).

8 MacGill, op. cit., pp. 139, 141. The institution supplemented its income by holding public worship in which clergymen from various denominations were invited to preach. A popular speaker could draw

a large congregation, who must have found it somewhat unusual to attend service with thirty or forty 'prostitutes', GMA, *Annual Report* (1822). In the early 1800s the Edinburgh Magdalene Asylum published its own Psalms book.

9 GMI, *Annual Report* (1913).
10 Other institutions modelled after the Edinburgh asylum were the Female Penitentiary (1807) in London and the Liverpool Asylum (1809). EMA, *Annual Report* (1827–29).
11 F. Finnegan, *Poverty and Prostitution: A Study of Prostitution in York* (Cambridge: Cambridge University Press, 1979), p. 169.
12 GMA, *Annual Report* (1822).
13 EMA, *Annual Report* (1827–72).
14 N. Rafter, 'Chastizing the Unchaste: The Social Control Functions of a Women's Reformatory', in S. Cohen and A. Skull (eds) *Social Control and the State* (Oxford: Martin Robertson, 1983), p. 290.
15 EMA, *Sub-Committee Minute Book* (21 January 1797; 22 April 1799; 29 April 1803; 23 March 1808; 23 October 1809).
16 ibid., (August 1800; 5 April 1809; 17 January 1810).
17 EMA, *Monthly Report on Women's Conduct* (1800–07).
18 EMA, *Sub-Committee Minute Book* (4 July 1810).
19 EMA, *Annual Report* (1868).
20 Tait, op. cit., p. 253.
21 EMA, *Bye-Laws and Regulations of the Society for Support of the Magdalene Asylum* (1814), p. xvii.
22 GMA, *Annual Report* (1820).
23 See: J. Walkowitz, *Prostitution and Victorian Society* (Cambridge: Cambridge University Press, 1980), p. 220.
24 J. Cleland, *Annals of Glasgow, Comprising an Account of the Public Buildings, Charities and the Rise and Progress of the City* (Glasgow: J. Hedderwick, 1816).
25 See: Rafter, op. cit., p. 320.
26 Glasgow Society for the Encouragement of Penitents, *Annual Report* (1815).
27 EMA, *Monthly Report on Women's Conduct* (1800–7).
28 GMI, *Annual Report* (1868).
29 EMA, *Ladies' Committee Minute Book* (31 December 1800).
30 GMA, *Annual Report* (1820).
31 EMA, *Sub-Committee Minute Book* (12 May 1835).
32 EMA, *Ladies' Committee Minute Book* (January 1826).
33 EMA, *Monthly Report on Women's Conduct* (1800–7).
34 EMA, *Sub-Committee Minute Book* (15 April 1799).
35 EMA, *Annual Report* (1835).
36 Cleland, op. cit.
37 GMA, *Annual Report* (1820).
38 EMA, *Sub-Committee Minute Book* (17 January 1810).
39 ibid. (28 June 1802).
40 EMA, *Monthly Report on Women's Conduct* (1800–7); Bridewells were correctional institutions for the punishment of vagrants and petty

offenders by a term of hard labour. See: J. Cameron, *Prisons and Punishment in Scotland* (Edinburgh: Canongate, 1983), p. 59.

41 EMA, *Sub-Committee Minute Book* (3 October 1811).

42 EMA, *Bye-Laws and Regulations of the Society for Support of the Magdalene Asylum* (1814).

43 Walkowitz, op. cit.; Finnegan, op. cit.; Rafter, op. cit.; B. Brenzel, 'Domestication as Reform: A Study of the Socialization of Wayward Girls', *Harvard Educational Review*, vol. 50 (1980), pp. 196–213.

44 The asylum built its own chapel in 1805. EMA, *Annual Report* (1827–9).

45 EMA, *Sub-Committee Minute Book* (15 April 1799; 20 May 1799).

46 ibid. (21, 28 June 1802).

47 EMA, *Ladies' Committee Minute Book* (10 April 1821).

48 EMA, *Sub-Committee Minute Book* (16 March 1835).

49 ibid. (20 May 1835).

50 ibid. (2 May 1836).

51 MacGill, op. cit., p. 139.

52 See: Rafter, op. cit., p. 299.

53 EMA, *Ladies' Committee Minute Book* (28 October 1825).

54 EMA, *Monthly Report on Women's Conduct* (1800–7).

55 EMA, *Sub-Committee Minute Book* (2 January 1821).

56 ibid. (23 March 1801).

57 EMA, *Bye-Laws and Regulations of the Society for the Support of the Magdalene Asylum* (1814).

58 F. K. Prochaska, *Women and Philanthropy in Nineteenth Century England* (Oxford: Oxford University Press, 1980), p. 156.

59 M. Ignatieff, *A Just Measure of Pain* (London: Macmillan, 1978), p. 213.

60 Finnegan, op. cit., p. 211.

61 ibid., pp. 174, 209.

62 GMI, *Annual Report* (1877).

63 ibid. (1873, 1876).

64 See: Rafter, op. cit., pp. 296, 307.

65 GMI, *Annual Report* (1872).

66 M. Sumner, 'Prostitution and Images of Women', unpublished M.Sc. dissertation (University of Wales, 1980), p. 166.

67 GMI, *Annual Report* (1881).

68 See: Rafter, op. cit., p. 299.

69 GMI, *Interim Report* (1859).

70 ibid.

71 See: Brenzel, op. cit., p. 205.

72 EMA, *Annual Report* (1880).

73 EMA, *Sub-Committee Minute Book* (4 March 1799).

74 ibid. (7 May 1798).

75 ibid. (2 July 1835).

76 See: S. Bowles and H. Gintis, *Schooling in Capitalist America* (New York: Basic Books, 1977).

77 See: Walkowitz, op. cit., p. 221.

78 EMA, *Sub-Committee Minute Book* (12 May 1835).

79 ibid.

80 ibid.

81 ibid. (6 December, 1809).

82 E. Bristow, *Vice and Vigilance: Purity Movements in Britain since 1700* (London: Gill & Macmillan, 1977), p. 66.

83 EMA, *Sub-Committee Minute Book* (23 June 1801).

84 EMA, *Bye-Laws and Regulations of the Society for Support of the Magdalene Asylum* (1814).

85 EMA, *Sub-Committee Minute Book* (15 September 1801).

86 ibid. (4 August 1801).

87 ibid. (6 September 1814).

88 ibid. (30 June 1823).

89 EMA, *Annual Report* (1843).

90 EMA, *Sub-Committee Minute Book* (11 January 1833).

91 ibid. (12 March 1833).

92 ibid. (19 March 1833).

93 ibid. (1 March 1852).

94 ibid. (9 January 1854).

95 ibid. (26 January 1854).

96 EMA, *Annual Report* (1877).

97 EMA, *Sub-Committee Minute Book* (2 January 1821).

98 ibid. (4 September 1821).

99 GMI, *Annual Report* (1867).

100 See: Bristow, op. cit., p. 71.

101 See: Walkowitz, op. cit., p. 221.

102 GMI, *Annual Report* (1877).

103 GMI, *Annual Reports* (1879, 1886); R. A. Cage, 'The Nature and Extent of Poor Relief', in R. A. Cage (ed.) *The Working Class in Glasgow, 1750–1914* (London: Croom Helm, 1987), pp. 76–97. The pattern of women resorting to casual prostitution during slumps in trade continued into the twentieth century. See: J. H. Treble, 'The Characteristics of the Female Unskilled Labour Market in Glasgow, 1891–1914', *Scottish Economic and Social History*, vol. 6 (1986), pp. 33–46.

104 GMI, *Annual Report*, (1886).

105 ibid. (1887).

106 ibid. (1909).

107 See: Bristow, op. cit., p. 71.

108 See: Brenzel, op. cit., p. 205.

109 GMI, *Annual Report* (1863).

110 See: Finnegan, op. cit., p. 20.

111 GMI, *Annual Report* (1877).

112 EMA, *Sub-Committe Minute Book* (30 November 1803).

113 GMI, *Annual Report* (1864).

114 EMA, *Annual Report* (1856).

115 GMI, *Annual Report* (1866).

116 EMA, *Annual Report* (1867).

117 ibid. (1866).

118 GMI, *Annual Report* (1864).

119 ibid. (1865).

120 ibid. (1874).

121 EMA, *Sub-Committee Minute Book* (6 March 1821).

122 ibid. (5 June 1848).

123 GMI, *Annual Report* (1878).

124 N. Wood, 'Prostitution and Feminism in Nineteenth-Century Britain', *M/F: A Feminist Journal*, vol. 7 (1982), p.75.

125 EMA, *Sub-Committee Minute Book* (6 June 1809).

126 ibid. (21 January 1799).

127 GMI, *Annual Report* (1868).

128 ibid. (1878).

129 J. Weeks, *Sex, Politics and Society: The Regulation of Sexuality Since 1800* (New York: Longman, 1981), p. 61.

130 J. Walkowitz and D. Walkowitz, ' "We are not Beasts of the Field": Prostitution and the Poor in Plymouth and Southampton under the Contagious Diseases Acts', in M. Hartman and L. Banner (eds) *Clio's Consciousness Raised* (London: Harper and Row, 1974), p. 193.

131 T. C. Smout, 'Aspects of Sexual Behaviour in Nineteenth Century Scotland', in P. Laslett *et al.* (eds) *Bastardy and its Comparative History* (London: Edward Arnold, 1980), p. 296.

132 See: Rafter, op. cit., pp. 303, 307.

133 Ignatieff, op. cit.

6 FRIENDLESS, FALLEN, AND INEBRIATE WOMEN

1 K. M. Boyd, *Scottish Church Attitudes To Sex, Marriage and the Family, 1850–1914* (Edinburgh: John Donald, 1980), pp. 180, 181.

2 EMA, *Annual Report* (1841).

3 W. Tait, *Magdalenism: An Inquiry into the Extent, Causes and Consequences of Prostitution in Edinburgh* (Edinburgh: P. Richards, 1840), pp. 261, 262.

4 Ibid., p. 252.

5 W. Logan, *An Exposure from Personal Observation of Female Prostitution in London, Leeds Rochdale, and Especially Glasgow, with Remarks on the Cause, Extents, Results and Remedy of the Evil* (Glasgow, 1843), p. 43.

6 Tait, op. cit., p. 255.

7 ibid., p. 157.

8 D. Gorham, *The Victorian Girl and the Feminine Ideal* (Bloomington: Indiana University Press, 1982), p. 19.

9 EMA, *Annual Report* (1874).

10 ibid. (1877).

11 ibid. (1878).

12 *Report* (Glasgow Girls' Reformatory or Juvenile Department of the Female House of Refuge 1860).

13 J. D. Bryce, *The Glasgow Magdalene Asylum, its Past and Present: With Relative Facts and Suggestions* (Glasgow: David Bryce, 1859), p. 4.

14 J. Sliman, 'Food, Labour, and Rest for Reformatories for Girls', *Prison and Reformatory Gazette* (1 February 1857), p. 37.

15 *Report* (Glasgow Girls' Reformatory or Juvenile Department of the Female House of Refuge 1860).

16 For a fuller discussion see: L. Mahood, The 'Magdalene's Friend': The Control of Prostitutes in Glasgow: 1840–1890. Unpublished M. Litt. dissertation (University of Glasgow, 1987), Chapter 4.

17 Bryce, op. cit., p. 8.

18 ibid.

19 ibid., p. 18.

20 See: W. Wilson, *The Origins and Development of the Glasgow Magdalene Institution* (Glasgow, 1905), Strathclyde Regional Archives.

21 Bryce, op. cit., p. 10.

22 ibid., p. 8.

23 Logan, op. cit., p. 4; R. Wardlaw, *Lectures on Female Prostitution: Its Nature, Extent, Effects, Guilt, Causes and Remedy* (Glasgow: J. Maclehose, 1842).

24 Anon. (A Sabbath School Teacher), *The Moral Statistics of Glasgow in 1863, Practically Applied* (Glasgow: Porteous & Hislop, 1864), p. 18.

25 *New Moral World*, vol. 7 (February 1841), p. 97.

26 *New Moral World*, quoted in Walkowitz, *Prostitution and Victorian Society* (Cambridge: Cambridge University Press, 1980), p. 35.

27 *New Moral World*, vol. 7 (February 1841), p. 98.

28 *Glasgow Herald* (6 July 1860), *Magdalen's Friend* (5 August 1860), p. 130.

29 W. Acton, *Prostitution Considered in its Moral, Social and Sanitary Aspects in London and other Large Cities and Garrison Towns*, 2nd ed. (London: John Churchill, 1869), p. 266.

30 *Magdalen's Friend* (5 August 1860), p. 131.

31 Acton, op. cit., p. 266.

32 ibid., p. 270.

33 ibid., p. 269.

34 ibid., p. 268.

35 ibid.

36 ibid., p. 269.

37 EMA, *Annual Report* (1842).

38 L. Goldman, ' A Peculiarity of the English? The Social Science Association and the Absence of Sociology in Nineteenth Century Britain', *Past and Present*, vol. 114 (1987), p. 137.

39 P. Abrams, *The Origins of British Sociology, 1834–1914* (Chicago: Chicago University Press, 1968), p. 44.

40 Quoted in Goldman, op. cit., p. 137.

41 ibid., p. 170.

42 Walkowitz, op. cit., p. 37.

43 I. Muirhead, 'Churchmen and the Problems of Prostitution in Nine-

teenth Century Scotland', *Records of the Scottish Church History Society*, vol. 18 (1974), p. 229.

44 Female Shelter in Connection with the Scottish Ladies' Association for Promoting the Reformation of the Most Destitute of Their Sex in Prisons and Other Institutions, 9th *Annual Report* (Aberdeen, 1850).

45 British Ladies' Society for the Reformation of Female Prisoners, *Annual Report* (1842).

46 *Magdalen's Friend*, vol. 5 (1864), pp. 210, 211.

47 GMI, *Annual Report* (1862).

48 ibid. (1862, 1864).

49 Glasgow Night Asylum for the Houseless, Female House of Industry, *Annual Report* (1869).

50 Glasgow Home for Deserted Mothers, *Annual Report* (1879, 1881).

51 Glasgow Young Women's Christian Association, *Annual Report* (1874).

52 Glasgow House of Shelter for Females, Annual Reports published in the *Glasgow Herald* (1863, 1865, 1869, 1871).

53 The Prison Gate Mission was established around 1878 by two ladies. It was unique because it recognized that many women were so accustomed to a 'wild and careless' life that they could not cope with restraints found in the House of Shelter. Therefore, women were free to come and go as they pleased, although it was hoped that they would remain until they had saved a little money or found employment.

54 Aberdeen Female Penitentiary, 3rd *Annual Report* (1844).

55 Dundee Lodging House Association, *Annual Report* (1848).

56 Report of 'The Home', and Institution for the Reformation of Females, *Annual Report* (1848). I would like to thank Maureen Docherty, Department of Modern History, University of Dundee, for providing me with the Dundee references.

57 Reformatory and Refuge Union, *The Classified List of Child-Saving Institutions* (1912).

58 ibid.

PART THREE: THE GLASGOW SYSTEM

1 T. C. Smout, *A Century of the Scottish People, 1830–1950* (London: Collins, 1986, pp. 40, 41.

2 L. Radzinowicz, 'Towards a National Standard of Police', in M. Fitzgerald *et al.* (eds) *Crime and Society: Readings in History and Theory* (London: Routledge & Kegan Paul, 1986), p. 71.

3 O. Checkland, *Philanthropy in Victorian Scotland: Social Work and the Voluntary Principle* (Edinburgh: John Donald, 1980), p. 241.

4 Smout, op. cit., p. 46.

5 R. D. Storch, 'The Plague of Blue Locusts', in M. Fitzgerald *et al.*, op. cit., p. 87.

6 ibid., p. 86.

7 Smout, op. cit., pp. 46, 48.

8 Storch, op. cit., p. 86.

9   ibid.
10   F. Wyness, *The Diced Cap: The Story of the Aberdeen Police* (Aberdeen: Corporation of the City of Aberdeen, 1972), p. 30.
11   Smout, op. cit., p. 48.
12   Glasgow Chief Constables' Letter Book (16 August 1869), Strathclyde Regional Archives.
13   F. Mort, *Dangerous Sexualities: Medico-Moral Politics in England since 1870* (London: Routledge & Kegan Paul, 1987), p. 76.
14   ibid.
15   J. Miller, *Prostitution Considered in Relation to its Causes and Cure* (Edinburgh: Sutherland and Knox, 1859), p. 11.
16   Granted under the General Police and Improvement (Scotland) Act of 1862 by local burghs.
17   Miller, op. cit., p. 5.

7 FIGHTING 'THE MULTITUDINOUS AMAZONIAN ARMY'

1   *Select Committee* (21 July, 1881), p. 371.
2   ibid., p. 372.
3   A. Patterson, *An Exposure of the Contagious Diseases Acts, and of Government Lock Hospitals* (Glasgow: Alex MacDougall, 1883), p. 2.
4   *Select Committee* (21 July 1881), p. 375.
5   Anon., *The Glasgow System for the Repression of Vice* (London: 1881), p. 3.
6   ibid., p. 4.
7   GMI, *Annual Report* (1862).
8   Sec. 88, 136, 137, and 142, *Select Committee* (21 July 1881), p. 380.
9   ibid., p. 381.
10   Sec. 136, Clause 142, *Select Committee* (21 July 1881), pp. 370, 371.
11   *Select Committee* (21 July 1881), p. 372.
12   ibid., p. 373.
13   ibid.
14   ibid., p. 381.
15   O. Checkland, *Philanthropy in Victorian Scotland, Social Welfare and the Voluntary Principle* (Edinburgh: John Donald, 1980), p. 195.
16   A. Patterson, 'Statistics of the Glasgow Lock Hospital since its Foundations in 1805: With Remarks on the Contagious Diseases Acts, and on Syphilis', *Glasgow Medical Journal*, vol. 6 (1882), p. 407.
17   *Select Committee* (4 April 1882), p. 119.
18   ibid., p. 125.
19   Glasgow Magistrates' Committee Minute Book (11, 25 January 1872).
20   *Select Committee* (4 April 1882), p. 120.
21   ibid., p. 119.
22   Patterson, op. cit., p. 408.
23   *Select Committee* (4 April 1882), p. 122.
24   ibid.

THE MAGDALENES

25 Where the hymen had not been broken. *Select Committee* (4 April 1882), p. 125.
26 J. Walkowitz, *Prostitution and Victorian Society* (Cambridge: Cambridge University Press, 1980), p. 56.
27 ibid.
28 *Select Committee* (4 April 1882), p. 128.
29 The statistics for the years in between were as follows: 1870:534; 1871:394; 1872:369; 1873:405; 1874:436; 1875:402; 1876:424; 1877:422; 1878:426; 1879:343; 1880:385. McCall reported:

[Venereal diseases] have become a milder type, altogether less fatal, and more amenable to treatment than formerly, while at the same time, its frequency has become greatly diminished, and its sad effects, formerly to be seen upon the young and innocent, even among the better classes of the people, are not now so often made the subject of medical observation. Ibid. (21 July 1881), p. 378.

30 There were only 12 deaths (from all causes) between 1861 and 1881 compared with 33 deaths between 1841 and 1860. The average length of stay was reduced to 27 nights in 1881 from 68 nights in 1811; Patterson, op. cit., p. 406.
31 ibid., pp. 126–8.
32 *Select Committee* (4 April 1882), p. 118.
33 ibid., p. 126.
34 ibid., p. 120.
35 ibid., p. 125.
36 ibid., p. 212.
37 GMI, *Annual Report* (1861).
38 GMI, *Annual Report* (1860); I. Muirhead, 'Churchmen and the Problems of Prostitution in Nineteenth Century Scotland', *Records of the Scottish Church History Society*, vol. 18 (1974), p. 230.
39 A. A. MacLaren, *Religion and Social Class: The Disruption Years in Aberdeen* (London: Routledge & Kegan Paul, 1974), p. 150.
40 E. King, 'Popular Culture in Glasgow', in R. A. Cage (ed.) *The Working Class in Glasgow, 1750–1914* (London: Croom Helm, 1987), p. 158.
41 C. A. Oakley, *Second City*, (2nd edn, London: Blackie, 1967), p. 103; W. Logan, *The Great Social Evil: Its Causes, Extent, Results, and Remedies* (London: Hodder and Stoughton, 1871).
42 GMI, *Interim Report* (1859); Ibid. *Annual Report* (1860).
43 ibid., 1863.
44 ibid.
45 Muirhead, op. cit., p. 230.
46 GMI, *Report on Glasgow Fair* (1863), pp. 1–3.
47 ibid., p. 3.
48 ibid.
49 ibid., p. 5.
50 ibid.
51 ibid., p. 6.

188

52 ibid., p. 12.
53 Muirhead, op. cit., p. 239.
54 GMI, *Report on Glasgow Fair* (1863), p. 12.
55 GMI, *Annual Report* (1866).
56 W. Wilson, *The Origins and Development of the Glasgow Magdalene Institution* (Glasgow: 1905).
57 Glasgow Magistrates' Committee Minute Book (20 December 1869).
58 City of Glasgow Police Chief Constables' Letter Book (24 December 1869).
59 GMI, *Annual Report* (1873).
60 ibid., (1874).
61 ibid.
62 ibid., (1884).
63 ibid., (1905).

8 POLICE REPRESSION OR VEILED REGULATION?

1 J. Walkowitz, *Prostitution and Victorian Society* (Cambridge, Cambridge University Press, 1980), p. 42.
2 F. Wyness, *The Diced Cap: The Story of the Aberdeen Police* (Aberdeen, Corporation of the City of Aberdeen, 1972), p. 30.
3 ibid., p. 43.
4 Anon., *The Glasgow System for the Repression of Vice* (London: 1881).
5 J. Miller, *Prostitution Considered in Relation to its Causes and Cures* (Edinburgh: Sutherland and Knox, 1859), p. 28.
6 Anon., *The Glasgow System for the Repression of Vice* (1881).
7 Walkowitz, op. cit.; F. B. Smith, 'Ethics and Disease in the Late Nineteenth Century: The Contagious Diseases Acts'. *Historical Studies*, vol. 15 (1971), pp. 118–35; Jean L'Esperance, 'The Work of the Ladies' National Association for the Repeal of the Contagious Diseases Acts', *Bulletin of the Society for the Study of Labour History*, vol. 26 (1973), pp. 13–16; E. M. Sigsworth and T. J. Wyke, 'A Study of Victorian Prostitution and Venereal Disease', in M. Vicinus (ed.) *Suffer and Be Still* (London: Methuen, 1972), pp. 77–99. P. McHugh, *Prostitution and Victorian Social Reform* (Beckenham: Croom Helm, 1980).
8 McHugh, op. cit., p. 17.
9 Walkowitz, op. cit., p. 3.
10 ibid., p. 80.
11 Smith, op. cit., p. 119.
12 W. Acton, *Prostitution Considered in its Moral, Social and Sanitary Aspects in London and other Large Cities and Garrison Towns*, 2nd edn (London: John Churchill, 1869), p. 237.
13 Walkowitz, op. cit., p. 80.
14 J. Walkowitz, 'Male Vice and Feminist Virtue: Feminism and the Politics of Prostitution in Nineteenth Century Britain', *History Workshop Journal* (1982), vol. 13, p. 84.
15 ibid., p. 80; Scottish Branches were also formed in the early 1870s.

For an account of the early days of the campaign and the involvement of Scottish repealers see: Scott, B., *A State Iniquity: Its Rise, Extension and Overthrow* (London: Routledge & Kegan Paul, 1984).

16 J. Walkowitz and D. Walkowitz, ' "We are not Beasts of the Field": Prostitution and the Poor in Plymouth and Southampton under the Contagious Diseases Acts' in M. Hartman and L. Banner (eds) *Clio's Consciousness Raised* (London: Harper and Row, 1974), p. 220.

17 F. Finnegan, *Poverty and Prostitution: A Study of Prostitution in York* (Cambridge: Cambridge University Press, 1979).

18 B. Harrison, 'Underneath the Victorians', *Victorian Studies*, vol. 10 (1966–7), pp. 239–62; F. K. Prochaska, *Women and Philanthropy in Nineteenth Century England* (Oxford: Oxford University Press, 1980) pp. 144, 155–61; O. Banks, *Faces of Feminism: A Study of Feminism as a Social Movement* (Oxford: Martin Robertson, 1981) pp. 15–17.

19 E. Bristow, *Vice and Vigilance: Purity Movements in Britain since 1700* (London: Gill & Macmillan, 1977), p. 56.

20 *Select Committee* (21 July 1881), p. 375.

21 ibid.

22 ibid., p. 372.

23 ibid., p. 373.

24 ibid. In 1870 there were 204 brothels with an aggregate rent of £1,965; whereas by 1879 there were twenty-two brothels with an aggregate rent of £208.

25 ibid. (4 April 1882), p. 117.

26 ibid. (21 July 1881), p. 382.

27 A. Flexner, *Prostitution in Europe* (London: Grant Richards, 1914), p. 230.

28 K. Boyd, *Scottish Church Attitudes to Sex, Marriage and the Family: 1850–1914* (Edinburgh: John Donald, 1980), p. 205.

29 Admissions to the Magdalene Institution were as follows: 1870:104; 1871:189; 1872:147; 1873:146; 1874:218; 1875:173; 1876:242; 1877:251; 1878:276; 1879:244; 1880:244; 1881:209.

30 See: N. Rafter, 'Chastizing the Unchaste. Social Control Functions of a Woman's Reformatory', in S. Cohen and A. Skull (eds) *Social Control and the State* (Oxford: Martin Robertson, 1983), p. 293.

31 *Select Committee* (21 July 1881), p. 383.

32 ibid., p. 374.

33 ibid., p. 375.

34 ibid.

35 *Shield* (5 January 1884), p. 8.

36 ibid. (6 September 1884), p. 150.

37 Boyd, op. cit., p. 205.

38 *Shield* (6 September 1884), p. 150.

39 ibid.

40 A. Patterson, *An Exposure of the Contagious Diseases Acts, and of Government Lock Hospitals* (Glasgow: Alex MacDougall, 1883), p. 10.

41 T. C. Smout, 'Scottish Marriage, Regular and Irregular', in R. B.

Outhwaite (ed.) *Marriage and Society: Studies in the Social History of Marriage* (London: Europa, 1981), p. 277.

42   Admission decreased from 534 in 1870 to 349 in 1881; see Patterson, op. cit., p. 406.

43   E. Shorter, *A History of Women's Bodies* (New York: Basic Books, 1982), p. 265.

44   A. Fessler, 'Advertisements in the Treatment of Venereal Disease and the Social History of Venereal Disease', *British Journal of Venereal Disease*, vol. 25 (1949), pp. 84–7; I. Muirhead, 'Churchmen and the Problems of Prostitution in Nineteenth Century Scotland', *Records of the Scottish Church History Society*, vol. 18 (1974), p. 228; *Glasgow Chronicle* (22 October 1830).

45   R. A. Cage, *The Working Class in Glasgow, 1750–1914* (London: Croom Helm, 1987), pp. 76–97; GMI, *Annual Report* (1879, 1886). It should be noted that the number of admissions annually was always a function of the space available.

46   *Select Committee* (21 July 1881), p. 386.

47   ibid.

48   ibid., p. 384. 'I am less likely to get complainers in a low locality where the people are not much better or higher than the brothel-keepers themselves.'

49   GMI, *Annual Report* (1885).

50   Glasgow Parish Council, *Sexual Immorality and Prostitution in Glasgow* (1911), p. 53.

51   *Glasgow Herald* (7 December 1896), p. 9; *North British Daily Mail* (11 December 1899), p. 3.

52   *Glasgow Herald* (12 December 1898), p. 11.

53   J. H. Treble, 'The Characteristics of the Female Unskilled Labour Market in Glasgow and the Formation of the Female Casual Labour Market in Glasgow 1891–1914', *Scottish Economic and Social History*, vol. 6 (1986), pp. 33–46.

54   See: Walkowitz (1980), op. cit., p. 18.

55   GMI, *Annual Report* (1906).

56   Flexner, op. cit., p. 318.

57   ibid.

58   Boyd, op. cit., p. 205.

59   F. Mort, *Dangerous Sexualities: Medico-Moral Politics in England since 1830* (London: Routledge & Kegan Paul 1987), p. 149.

60   ibid., p. 46.

61   Glasgow Parish Council, op. cit., p. 4.

62   ibid., 'Appendix 1. Appendum: Report on Memorandum re: Social Evil in the City' (1911).

63   ibid., p. 10.

64   ibid.

65   GMI, *Annual Report* (1913).

CONCLUSION: PROSTITUTES, MAGDALENES, AND WAYWARD GIRLS

1 This chapter draws heavily on B. Littlewood and L. Mahood, 'Prostitutes, Magdalenes and Wayward Girls: Dangerous Sexualities of Working-Class Women in Victorian Scotland', *Gender and Class* (London: Basil Blackwell, forthcoming).
2 N. Rafter, 'Chastizing the Unchaste: Social Control Functions of a Woman's Reformatory', in S. Cohen and A. Skull (eds) *Social Control and the State* (Oxford: Martin Robertson, 1983), p. 291.
3 W. Acton, *Prostitution Considered in its Moral, Social and Sanitary Aspects in London and other Large Cities and Garrison Towns* (2nd edn, London: John Churchill, 1869), p. 39.
4 R. Wardlaw, *Lectures on Female Prostitution: Its Nature, Extent, Effects, Guilt, Causes and Remedy* (Glasgow: J. Maclehose, 1842), p. 37.
5 W. Tait, *Magdalenism: An Inquiry into the Extent, Causes and Consequences of Prostitution in Edinburgh* (Edinburgh: P. Richards, 1840), p. 176.
6 *Glasgow Herald* (6 July 1860).
7 *New Moral World*, quoted in J. Walkowitz, *Prostitution and Victorian Society* (Cambridge: Cambridge University Press, 1980), p. 35.
8 For an example of this process see: S. Cohen, *Visions of Social Control: Crime, Punishment and Classification* (Cambridge: Polity Press, 1985).
9 Rafter, op. cit., p. 292.
10 C. Smart, *Women, Crime and Criminology: A Feminist Critique* (London: Routledge & Kegan Paul, 1976), p. 132.
11 Rafter, op. cit., p. 291.
12 D. Roberts, *Paternalism in Early Victorian England* (London: Croom Helm, 1979).
13 D. Melossi and M. Pavarini, *The Prison and the Factory: Origins of the Penitentiary System*, trans. G. Cousins (London: Macmillan, 1981), p. 144.
14 M. Ignatieff, 'State, Civil Society and Total Institutions: A Critique of Recent Social Histories of Punishment', in S. Cohen and A. Skull, op. cit., pp. 87, 88.
15 L. Davidoff and C. Hall, *Family Fortunes: Men and Women of the English Middle Class, 1780–1850* (London: Hutchinson, 1987), p. 450.
16 M. Foucault, *Discipline and Punish: The Birth of the Prison*, trans. A. Sheridan (Harmondsworth: Penguin, 1979), p. 272.
17 L. Nead, 'The Magdalene in Modern Times: The Mythology of the Fallen Woman in Pre-Raphaelite Painting', in R. Betterton (ed.) *Looking at Images of Femininity in the Visual Arts and Media* (London: Pandora Press, 1987), p. 91.
18 ibid., p. 89.
19 Acton, op. cit., p. 166.
20 M. Foucault, *The History of Sexuality. Volume 1: An Introduction*, trans. R. Hurley (New York: Random House, 1980), p. 126.
21 ibid., p. 24.

22 F. Mort, *Dangerous Sexualities: Medico-Moral Politics since 1830* (London: Routledge & Kegan Paul, 1987), p. 47.
23 Rafter, op. cit., p. 291.
24 B. Brenzel, 'Domestication as Reform: A Study of the Socialization of Wayward Girls, 1856–1905', *Harvard Educational Review*, vol. 50 (1980), p. 209; Nead, op. cit., p. 80.
25 Walkowitz (1980), op. cit., p. 24.
26 R. A. Cage, 'The Nature and Extent of Poor Relief', in R. A. Cage (ed.) *The Working Class in Glasgow, 1750–1914* (London: Croom Helm, 1987), p. 87.
27 Walkowitz (1980), op. cit., p. 13.
28 ibid., pp. 13, 14.
29 P. Littlewood, *Care Appropriate to their Needs?* (Scottish Central Research Unit Papers, Scottish Office, Edinburgh: 1987).
30 *Glasgow Herald* (17 September 1958), p. 7.
31 ibid.
32 ibid. (19 September 1958), p. 9; the Edinburgh Magdalene Asylum was also supported throughout the first half of the twentieth century until it went bankrupt in 1950. 'Springwell House, formerly the Magdalene Asylum . . . was closed on 11th November, 1950. The property has been bought by the Town Council and the girls who remained in the House at the close were all placed in situations', *Report of the Society for the Support of Springwell House* (Edinburgh: 1950–1).

Bibliography

PRIMARY SOURCES

Newspapers and Periodicals

Edinburgh Medical Journal
Glasgow Chronicle
Glasgow Courier
Glasgow Herald
Glasgow Medical Journal
Magdalen's Friend and Females' Homes Intelligencer
New Moral World
Transactions of the *National Association for the Promotion of Social Science*
North British Daily Mail
North Briton
Reformatory and Refuge Journal/Prison and Reformatory Gazette
Shield

Annual Reports

Aberdeenshire Association of Ladies for the Rescue of Fallen Women
Aberdeen Female Penitentiary
Aberdeen Association for Reclaiming Fallen Females
British Ladies' Association of the Rescue of Fallen Females
British Ladies' Society for the Reformation of Females
Dundee Lodging House Association
Edinburgh Magdalene Asylum
Edinburgh Society for the Protection of Young Females and Prevention of
   Juvenile Prostitution
Glasgow Home for Deserted Mothers
Glasgow House of Shelter for Females
Glasgow Magdalene Asylum

Glasgow Magdalene Institution
Glasgow Lock Hospital
Glasgow Society for Encouragement of Penitents
Glasgow House of Shelter
Glasgow Young Women's Christian Association
Reformatory and Refuge Union
Scottish Ladies' Association for Promoting the Reformation of the Most
    Destitute of their Own Sex

Public Documents

City of Glasgow Police, Chief Constables' Letter Book, Glasgow, (E4/2/.10),
    2863–1869.
Glasgow Parish Council, Minutes of Joint Conference on Immoral Houses
    and Venereal Disease, 3 February 1911.
Glasgow Magistrates' Committee Minute Book, Glasgow, 1862–1868,
    1868–1876, 1876–1881, 1881–1886.
Reports from the Select Committee on the Contagious Diseases Acts,
    1866–1869, PP 1881 (351), viii, 193; PP 1882 (340), ix, 1.

Sources Published Before 1900

Acton, W. (1857, 2nd edn 1869) *Prostitution Considered in its Moral, Social and
    Sanitary Aspects in London and other Large Cities and Garrison Towns*, London:
    John Churchill.
Anon. (A Police Constable) (1860) *Profligacy and Prostitution of Females in the
    City of Glasgow, with an Interesting Letter from a Reclaimed Young Lady.*
Anon. (1881) *The Glasgow System for the Repression of Vice.*
Anon. (A Sabbath School Teacher) (1864) *The Moral Statistics of Glasgow
    in 1863, Practically Applied*, Glasgow: Porteous and Hislop.
Anon. (A Scotchwoman) (1870) *Hospital Prisons: A Warning from Scotland*,
    Nottingham: Stevenson, Bailey and Smith, 1870.
Bertram, J. (editor, *North Briton*) (1864) *Glimpses of the Social Evil in Edinburgh
    and Elsewhere*, Edinburgh: Charles Harvey.
Bryce, J. D. (1859) *The Glasgow Magdalene Asylum, its Past and Present: With
    Relative Facts and Suggestions*, Glasgow: David Bryce.
Cadell, F. (1881) *The Contagious Diseases Acts*, Edinburgh: The Scottish
    National Association for the Abolution of the State Regulation of Vice
    and Promotion of Social Purity.
Cleland, J. (1816) *Annals of Glasgow, Comprising an Account of the Public
    Buildings, Charities and the Rise and Progress of the City*, Glasgow: J.
    Hedderwick.
Cleland, J. (1840) *Dissolute Characters in Former and Present Times in the City
    of Glasgow*, Glasgow.
Duncan, A. (1825) *Letter to Sir William Fettes*, Edinburgh: P. Neill.
Duncan, A. (1896) *Memorials of the Faculty of Physicians and Surgeons of
    Glasgow*, Glasgow: J. Maclehose.

Ker, J. (1872) *The Nation's Attitude Toward Prevailing Vice*, Dundee.

List, A. C. C. (1859) *The Two Phases of the Social Evil*, Edinburgh: Ogle and Murray.

Logan, W. (1843) *An Exposure from Personal Observation of Female Prostitution in London, Leeds, Rochdale, and Especially Glasgow, with Remarks on the Causes, Extent, Results and Remedy of the Evil*, Glasgow.

Logan, W. (1849) *The Moral Statistics of Glasgow*, Glasgow: Scottish Temperance League.

Logan, W. (1871) *The Great Social Evil: Its Causes, Extent, Results and Remedies*, London: Hodder and Stoughton.

MacGill, S. (1819) *Discourses and Essays on Subjects of Public Interest*, Edinburgh: Waugh and Innes.

Miller, A. G. (1882) 'Four and a Half Years' Experience in the Lock Wards of the Edinburgh Royal Infirmary', *Edinburgh Medical Journal*, vol. 28, pp. 384–403.

Miller, J. (1859) *Prostitution Considered in Relation to its Causes and Cures*, Edinburgh: Sutherland and Knox.

Myles, J. (1850) *Chapters in the Life of a Dundee Factory Boy: An Autobiography*, Edinburgh: J. Myles Pub.

Patterson, A. (1882) 'Statistics of the Glasgow Lock Hospital since its Foundations in 1805: With Remarks on the Contagious Diseases Acts, and on Syphilis', *Glasgow Medical Journal*, vol. 6, pp. 401–18.

Patterson, A. (1883) *An Exposure of the Contagious Diseases Acts, and of Government Lock Hospitals*, Glasgow: Alex MacDougall.

Scott, B. (1894) *A State of Iniquity: Its Rise, Extension and Overthrow*, London: Routledge & Kegan Paul.

Simpson, J. Y. (1875) *Antiquarian Notices of Syphilis in Scotland in the Fifteenth and Sixteenth Centuries*, Edinburgh: Edmonston & Douglas.

Sliman, J. (1 February 1857) 'Food, Labour and Rest for Reformatories for Girls', *Prison and Reformatory Gazette*, pp. 36–8.

Tait, W. (1840) *Magdalenism: An Inquiry into the Extent, Causes and Consequences of Prostitution in Edinburgh*, Edinburgh: P. Richards.

Thomas, A. (1861) *On the Licentiousness of Scotland and the Remedial Measures Which Ought to be Adopted*, London: J. Nisbet.

Wardlaw, R. (1842) *Lectures on Female Prostitution: Its Nature, Extent, Effects, Guilt, Causes and Remedy*, Glasgow: J. Maclehose.

Wilson, R. (1871) *Prostitution Suppressible: And Resistance to the Contagious Diseases (Women) Act, A Duty*, London: S. W. Partridge.

SECONDARY SOURCES

Unpublished Works

Mahood, L. (1987) 'The Magdalene's Friend': The Control of Prostitutes in Glasgow: 1840–1890', M. Litt. (Sociology), University of Glasgow.

Sumner, M. (1980) 'Prostitution and Images of Women', M.Sc. (Economics), University of Wales.

Ware, H. (1969) 'Prostitution and the State: The Recruitment, Regulation, and Role of Prostitution in the Nineteenth and Twentieth Century', Ph.D. (History), University of London.

Sources Published After 1900

Abrams, P. (1968) *The Origins of British Sociology, 1834–1914*, Chicago: University of Chicago Press.

Banks, O. (1981) *Faces of Feminism: A Study of Feminism as a Social Movement*, Oxford: Martin Robertson.

Bowles, S. and Gintis, H. (1977) *Schooling in Capitalist America*, New York: Basic Books.

Boyd, K. M. (1980) *Scottish Church Attitudes to Sex, Marriage and the Family: 1850–1914*, Edinburgh: John Donald.

Brenzel, B. (1980) 'Domestication as Reform: A Study of the Socialization of Wayward Girls, 1856–1905', *Harvard Educational Review*, vol. 50, pp. 196–213.

Bristow, E. (1977) *Vice and Vigilance: Purity Movements in Britain since 1700*, London: Gill and Macmillian.

Brotherston, J. H. F. (1952) 'Observations on the Early Public Health Movement in Scotland', *London School of Hygiene and Tropical Medicine Memoir*, vol. 8.

Bullough, V. and Bullough, B. (1987) *Women and Prostitution: A Social History*, New York: Prometheus.

Butt, J. 'Housing' (1987) in R. A. Cage (ed.) *The Working Class in Glasgow, 1750–1914*, London: Croom Helm.

Cage, R. A. (1987) (ed.) *The Working Class in Glasgow, 1840–1914*, London: Croom Helm.

Cage, R. A. (1987) 'The Nature and Extent of Poor Relief' in R. A. Cage (ed.) *The Working Class in Glasgow, 1750–1914*, London: Croom Helm.

Cameron, J. (1983) *Prisons and Punishment in Scotland: From the Middle Ages to the Present*, Edinburgh, Canongate.

Checkland, O. (1980) *Philanthropy in Victorian Scotland: Social Welfare and the Voluntary Principle*, Edinburgh: John Donald.

Cohen, S. (1985) *Visions of Social Control: Crime, Punishment and Classification*, Cambridge: Polity Press.

Cominos, P. T. (1963) 'Late Victorian Sexual Respectability and the Social System', *International Review of Social History*, vol. 8, pp. 18–48, 216–50.

Comrie, J. D. (1932) *History of Scottish Medicine*, vol. 2, London: Bailliere, Tindale, & Cox.

Cowan, I. B. (1977) 'Church and Society', in J. Brown (ed.) *Scottish Society in the Fifteenth Century*, London: Edward Arnold.

Cullen, G. M. (1909–11) 'Concerning Sibbens and the Scottish Yaws', *Caledonian Medical Journal*, vol. 8, pp. 336–57.

Davidoff, L. (1984) 'Mastered for Life: Servant and Wife in Victorian and Edwardian England', *Journal of Social History*, vol. 7, pp. 406–28.

Davidoff, L. and Hall, C. (1987) *Family Fortunes: Men and Women of the English Middle Class, 1780–1850*, London: Hutchinson.

Davidson, M. H. A. (1956) 'The Maladies of Mary Queen of Scots and her husbands', *Proceedings*, Scottish Society for the History of Medicine, Gordon Wilson, Edinburgh, p. 20–33

Donzelot, J. (1979) *The Policing of Families*, trans. R. Hurley, London: Hutchinson.

Drummond, A. and Bulloch, J. (1975) *The Church in Victorian Scotland, 1843–1914*, Edinburgh: St Andrew's Press.

Engels, F. (1958) *The Conditions of the Working Class in England*, trans. W. O. Henderson and W. H. Chaloner, Oxford: Basil Blackwell.

Evans, J. (1988) 'The Iron Cage Visibility', *Ten–8: International Photography Magazine*, no. 28, pp. 40–51.

Ferguson, T. (1948) *The Dawn of Scottish Social Welfare*, London: Thomas Nelson.

Ferrier, J. (1968) *The Greenock Infirmary, 1806–1968*, Greenock: Greenock and District Hospital Board of Management.

Fessler, A. (1949) 'Advertisements in the Treatment of Venereal Disease and the Social History of Venereal Disease', *British Journal of Venereal Disease*, vol. 25, pp. 83–8.

Finnegan, F. (1979) *Poverty and Prostitution: A Study of Prostitution in York*, Cambridge: Cambridge University Press.

Flexner, A. (1914) *Prostitution in Europe*, London: Grant Richards.

Foucault, M. (1979) *Discipline and Punish: The Birth of the Prison*, trans. A. Sheridan, Harmondsworth: Penguin.

Foucault, M. (1980) *The History of Sexuality. Volume 1: An Introduction*, trans. R. Hurley, New York: Random House.

Goldman, L. (1987) 'A Peculiarity of the English? The Social Science Association and the Absence of Sociology in Nineteenth Century Britain', *Past and Present*, vol. 114, p. 133–71.

Gordon, E. (1983) 'Women, Trade Unionism and Industrial Militancy, 1850–1890', in Glasgow Women's Studies Collective, *Uncharted Lives: Extracts from Scottish Women's Experiences, 1850–1982*, Glasgow: Pressgang, pp. 52–73.

Gorham, D. (1982) *The Victorian Girl and the Feminine Ideal*, Bloomington: Indiana University Press.

Glasgow Women's Studies Collective (1983) *Uncharted Lives: Extracts from Scottish Women's Experiences, 1850–1982*, Glasgow: Pressgang.

Harrison, B. (1966–7) 'Underneath the Victorians', *Victorian Studies*, vol. 10, pp. 239–62.

Harrison, B. (1974) 'State Intervention and Moral Reform in Nineteenth Century England', in P. Hollis (ed.) *Pressure from Without in Early Victorian England*, London: Edward Arnold.

Harrison, J. F. C. (1971) 'A New View of Mr Owen', in S. Pollard and J. Salt (eds) *Robert Owen: Prophet of the Poor*, London: Macmillan.

Hellerstein, E., Hume, L., and Offen, K. (1981) *Victorian Women: A Documentary Account of Women's Lives*, Brighton: Harvester.

Ignatieff, M. (1978) *A Just Measure of Pain*, London: Macmillan.

Ignatieff, M. (1983) 'State, Civil Society and Total Institutions: A Critique of Recent Social Histories of Punishment', in S. Cohen and A. Skull (eds) *Social Control and the State*, Oxford: Martin Robertson.

King, E. (1978) *The Scottish Women's Suffrage Movement*, Glasgow: Glasgow Museums and Art Galleries.

King, E. (1987) 'Popular Culture in Glasgow', in R. A. Cage (ed.) *The Working Class in Glasgow, 1750–1914*, London: Croom Helm.

L'Esperience, J. (1973) 'The Work of the Ladies' National Association for Repeal of the Contagious Diseases Act', *Bulletin of the Society for the Study of Labour History*, vol. 26, pp. 13–16.

Littlewood, P. (1987) *Care Appropriate to their Needs?* Edinburgh, Scottish Central Research Unit Papers.

Littlewood, B. and Mahood, L. 'Prostitutes, Magdalenes and Wayward Girls: The Dangerous Sexualities of Working-Class Women in Victorian Scotland', *Gender and History*, (forthcoming).

MacDonell, D. (1986) *Theories of Discourse*, London: Basil Blackwell.

McHugh, P. (1980) *Prostitution and Victorian Social Reform*, Beckenham: Croom Helm.

MacKay, G. A. (1907) *Practice of the Scottish Poor Law*, Edinburgh: William Green & Sons.

MacLaren, A. A. (1974) *Religion and Social Class: The Disruption Years in Aberdeen*, London: Routledge & Kegan Paul.

Mechie, S. (1975) *The Church and Scottish Development, 1780–1870*, Westport, Conn., Greenwood Press.

Melossi, D. and Pavarini, M. (1981) *The Prison and the Factory: Origins of the Penitentiary System*, trans. G. Cousins, London: Macmillan.

Mort, F. (1987) *Dangerous Sexualities: Medico-Moral Politics in England since 1830*, London: Routledge & Kegan Paul.

Morton, A. L. (1962) *The Life and Ideas of Robert Owen*, London: Lawrence & Wishart.

Morton, R. S. (1962) 'Some Aspects of the Early History of Syphilis in Nineteenth Century Scotland', *British Journal of Venereal Disease*, vol. 38, pp. 175–80.

Morton, R. S. (1974) *Venereal Disease*, 2nd edn, Harmondsworth: Penguin.

Mossner, E. C. (1954) *The Life of David Hume*, London: Thomas Nelson and Sons.

Muirhead, I. (1974) 'Churchmen and the Problems of Prostitution in Nineteenth Century Scotland', *Records of the Scottish Church History Society*, vol. 18, pp. 223–47.

Nead, L. (1987) 'The Magdalene in Modern Times: The Mythology of the Fallen Woman in Pre-Raphaelite Painting', in R. Betterton (ed.) *Looking at Images of Femininity in the Visual Arts and Media*, London: Pandora Press.

Newman, D. (1914) 'The History and Prevention of Venereal Disease', *The Glasgow Medical Journal*, vol. 81, pp. 88–100.

Nield, K. (ed.) (1973) *Prostitution in the Victorian Age: Debates on the Issues from Nineteenth Century Critical Journals*, Westmead, England: Gregg International.

Oakley, C. A. (1967) *Second City*, 2nd edn London: Blackie.

Paterson, A. (1976) 'The Poor Law in Nineteenth Century Scotland' in D. Fraser (ed.) *The New Poor Law in the Nineteenth Century*, London: Macmillan.

Pollard, S. and Salt, J. (eds) (1971) *Robert Owen: Prophet of the Poor*, London: Macmillan.

Prochaska, F. K. (1980) *Women and Philanthropy in Nineteenth Century England*, Oxford: Oxford University Press.

Radzinowicz, L. (1986) 'Towards a National Standard of Police', in M. Fitzgerald, G. McLennan, and J. Pawson (eds) *Crime and Society: Readings in History and Theory*, London: Routledge & Kegan Paul, pp. 60–89.

Rafter, N. (1983) 'Chastizing the Unchaste: Social Control Functions of a Women's Reformatory', in S. Cohen and A. Skull (eds) *Social Control and the State*, Oxford: Martin Robertson.

Ramelson, M. (1964) 'The Fight Against the Contagious Diseases Acts', *Marxism Today*, vol. 8, pp. 177–84.

Roberts, D. (1979) *Paternalism in Early Victorian England*, London: Croom Helm.

Ryan, M. P. (1983) 'The Power of Women's Networks', in M. P. Ryan, J. L. Newton, and J. Walkowitz (eds) *Sex and Class in Women's History*, London: Routledge & Kegan Paul.

Scott, L. W. and Tilly, L. A. (1975) 'Women's Work and the Family in the Nineteenth Century', *Comparative Studies in Social History*, vol. 17, pp. 36–64.

Shorter, E. (1982) *A History of Women's Bodies*, New York: Basic Books.

Sigsworth, E. M. and Wyke, T. J. (1972) 'A Study of Victorian Prostitution and Venereal Disease', in M. Vicinus (ed.) *Suffer and Be Still: Women in the Victorian Age*, London: Methuen.

Smail, J. (1987) 'New Languages for Labour and Capital: The Transformation of Discourse in the Early Years of the Industrial Revolution, *Social History*, vol. 12, no. 1, pp. 49–71.

Smith, F. B. (1971) 'Ethics and Disease in the Late Nineteenth Century: The Contagious Diseases Acts', *Historical Studies* vol. 15, pp. 118–35.

Smart, C. (1976) *Women, Crime and Criminology: A Feminist Critique*, London: Routledge & Kegan Paul.

Smout, T. C. (1969) *A History of the Scottish People, 1560–1890*, London: Fontana.

Smout, T. C. (1980) 'Aspects of Sexual Behaviour in Nineteenth Century Scotland', in P. Laslett, K. Oosterveen, and R. Smith (eds) *Bastardy and its Comparative History*, London: Edward Arnold.

Smout, T. C. (1981) 'Scottish Marriage, Regular and Irregular', in R. B. Outhwaite (ed.) *Marriage and Society: Studies in the Social History of Marriage*, London: Europa.

Smout, T. C. (1986) *A Century of the Scottish People, 1830–1950*, London: Collins.

Steadman-Jones, G. (1986) 'The Threat of Outcast London', in M. Fitzgerald, G. McLennan, and J. Pawson (eds) *Crime and Society: Readings in History and Theory*, London: Routledge & Kegan Paul, pp. 173–89.

Storch, R. D. (1986) 'The Plague of Blue Locusts', in M. Fitzgerald, G. McLennan, and J. Pawson (eds) *Crime and Society: Readings in History and Theory*, London: Routledge & Kegan Paul, pp. 116–34.

Storch, R. D. (1975) 'The Policeman as Domestic Missionary', *Journal of Social History*, vol. 1, pp. 481–509.

Thomas, K. (1959) 'The Double Standard', *Journal of the History of Ideas*, vol. 20, pp. 195–216.

Treble, J. H. (1986) 'The Characteristics of the Female Unskilled Labour Market and the Formation of the Female Casual Labour Market in Glasgow, 1891–1914', *Scottish Economic and Social History*, vol. 6, pp. 33–46.

Turner, A. L. (1979) *Story of a Great Hospital, The Royal Infirmary of Edinburgh, 1729–1929*, Edinburgh: Mercat Press.

Walkowitz, J. (1980) *Prostitution and Victorian Society*, Cambridge: Cambridge University Press.

Walkowitz, J. (1982), 'Male Vice and Feminist Virtue: Feminism and the Politics of Prostitution in Nineteenth Century Britain', *History Workshop Journal*, vol. 13, pp. 80–93.

Walkowitz, J. and Walkowitz, D. (1974) ' "We are not Beasts of the Field": Prostitution and the Poor in Plymouth and Southampton under the Contagious Diseases Acts', in M. Hartman and L. Banner (eds) *Clio's Consciousness Raised*, London: Harper and Row.

Weedon, C. (1987) *Feminist Practice and Post-Structuralist Theory*, London: Basil Blackwell.

Weeks, J. (1981) *Sex, Politics, and Society: The Regulation of Sexuality since 1800*, New York: Longman.

Wilson, W. (1905) *The Origins and Development of the Glasgow Magdalene Institution*, Glasgow.

Wood, N. (1982) 'Prostitution and Feminism in Nineteenth-Century Britain', *M/F: a Feminist Journal*, vol. 7, pp. 61–77.

Wood, N. (1986) 'Foucault on the History of Sexuality: An Introduction', in V. Beechey and L. Donald (eds) *Subjectivity and Social Relations*, London: Routledge & Kegan Paul, pp. 156–74.

Wyness, F. (1972) *The Diced Cap: The Story of the Aberdeen Police*, Aberdeen: Corporation of the City of Aberdeen.

Yeo, E. (1971) 'Robert Owen and Radical Culture', in S. Pollard and J. Salt (eds) *Robert Owen: Prophet of the Poor*, London: Macmillan.

Young, J. D. (1985) *Women and Popular Struggles: A History of Scottish and English Working-Class Women, 1500–1984*, Edinburgh: Mainstream.

Index

New Lanark 65–6
New South Wales 98
North Briton 69

Owenite socialists 56, 60, 65–6, 68, 72, 86, 109, 111, 113, 156, 179n

Paisley 32, 51, 117
Parent-Duchatelets 60
Paris 44, 60, 65, 128
Parker, Leslie 6
paternalism 86, 88, 109, 157
Patterson, Alexander, Dr 71, 127–9, 144–6, 151; *see also* lock hospital
pawnbroker 110
Perth 114, 117
pimps 41, 44
Pinctor, Peter 19
Plymouth 1, 6
poorhouse 29, 38, 54–5, 78, 99, 100, 105, 111–12, 114, 116, 118, 159
power–knowledge complex 11–12; *see also* Foucault
prison 24, 29, 54–5

Queen Victoria 112

Rafter, Nicole 85, 157
Ranger's Impartial List of the Ladies of Pleasure in Edinburgh 44–5
Reformatory and Refuge Union 114
Reminiscences of Auld Ayr 41
repressive hypothesis 8; *see also* Foucault
resistance 12, 89, 101, 165, 166
reverse discourse 12, 81, 101
Roman Catholicism 55
Roman Empire 34
Ryan, Mary 170n

Scottish Women's National Association for the Repeal of the CD Acts 67
servants 22–3, 26, 58, 67, 70, 72–4, 79, 80–1, 84–7, 93–5, 102, 116, 118, 180n
shebeens 134
Smail, John 11
Smart, Carol 157
Smout, T. C. 148
Society for the Bettering of the Condition of the Poor 79

Somerville, R. N. 61, 67, 109–10, 156, 177n
Southampton 1, 6
Stirling 21
syphilis 32, 36, 77, 120, 126–8, 133, 138–41, 148, 171n, 188n; glengore, 20, 21, 25–6, 171n

Tait, William, Dr 46, 63, 65–6, 72–3, 103–5, 107–10, 177n; *Magdalenism* 61
technologies of power 1, 2, 7, 12, 17, 29, 155, 166, 167n; *see also* Foucault
Times, The 113
torture 21–5, 28; headshaving 80, 104; solitary confinement 80, 83, 89, 104
trades 70; factory 86, 94, 109; laundry 70, 86–7, 90–4, 97, 104, 109; low wages 73; millgirls 70–2, 74, 86, 116–17, 132–4; needlewomen 70, 73, 87, 109
Treble, J. H. 151

Van Diemen's Land 98

Walkowitz, J. 1, 6, 29, 41–2, 69, 102, 113, 141–2, 164n
Warbeck, Perkin 19
Wardlaw, Ralph 61, 66–8, 107–8, 110
Ware, Helen 63
Webb, Beatrice 56
Weedon, Christine 11
Weeks, Jeffery 8, 9, 168n
wet-nurse 26–7, 58n, 117n
William the Lion 131
Wilson, Henry 141; *see also* CD Acts
Wilson, Robert 66
witchcraft 22, 24, 48
Wood, Nancy 98
workhouse *see* poorhouse
working class 30, 32, 51–2, 55, 72, 97–8, 102, 120, 126, 131, 141–3, 155, 163, 168n

York 1, 5, 101, 142
Youthful Offenders Act (1854) 106, 160

Printed in Great Britain
by Amazon